Leadership

Political-economic,
Regional Business and
Socio-Community Contexts

Leadership
Political-economic, Regional Business and Socio-Community Contexts

editors

T. W. Lim
Soka University, Japan

Carol Ma
Singapore University of Social Sciences, Singapore

NEW JERSEY • LONDON • SINGAPORE • BEIJING • SHANGHAI • HONG KONG • TAIPEI • CHENNAI • TOKYO

Published by

World Scientific Publishing Co. Pte. Ltd.

5 Toh Tuck Link, Singapore 596224

USA office: 27 Warren Street, Suite 401-402, Hackensack, NJ 07601

UK office: 57 Shelton Street, Covent Garden, London WC2H 9HE

British Library Cataloguing-in-Publication Data
A catalogue record for this book is available from the British Library.

LEADERSHIP
Political-economic, Regional Business and Socio-Community Contexts

Copyright © 2020 by World Scientific Publishing Co. Pte. Ltd.

All rights reserved. This book, or parts thereof, may not be reproduced in any form or by any means, electronic or mechanical, including photocopying, recording or any information storage and retrieval system now known or to be invented, without written permission from the publisher.

For photocopying of material in this volume, please pay a copying fee through the Copyright Clearance Center, Inc., 222 Rosewood Drive, Danvers, MA 01923, USA. In this case permission to photocopy is not required from the publisher.

ISBN 978-981-121-322-9 (hardcover)
ISBN 978-981-121-323-6 (ebook for institutions)
ISBN 978-981-121-324-3 (ebook for individuals)

For any available supplementary material, please visit
https://www.worldscientific.com/worldscibooks/10.1142/11636#t=suppl

Deok Editor: Sandhya Venkatesh

Printed in Singapore

CONTENTS

About the Authors   ix

Section A   **Political Leadership**   **1**

Chapter 1   Introduction   3
T. W. Lim

Chapter 2   Introduction to Political Leadership in Northeast Asia   11
T. W. Lim

Chapter 3   The Chinese Case Study   25
T. W. Lim

Chapter 4   Leadership in East Asia   35
T. W. Lim

Chapter 5   Leadership Lessons of a Small State in Central
Asia: Kyrgyzstan, Amidst Empires   45
F. Vivien and T. W. Lim

Chapter 6   Building Emergency Management in Post-SARS China   53
Wee-Kiat Lim

Chapter 7   Toru Hashimoto's Unfinished Local Governance
Reform: A Micro Case Study of Political Leadership at
Local-Level Politics in Japan   81
Y. Godo

Chapter 8   Taiwan's Leadership Pickle   101
S. King

Chapter 9	A Case Study of Political Leadership in Taiwanese Election Campaigns: A Brief Analysis of the Han Kuo-Yu Phenomenon *T. Katherine*	111
Chapter 10	Leadership in Hong Kong: The Fragile "One Country Two Systems" and the China Factor *H. Y. Li*	121

Section B Community Leadership 133

Chapter 11	Community Leadership and Social Development in Singapore *W. Kenneth*	135
Chapter 12	Understanding Community Leadership — A Case Study of Yokohama Chinatown *W. Elim*	147
Chapter 13	Case Study of Guandi's Birthday Celebrations in Yokohama Chinatown in 2015 and 2016 *W. Elim*	169
Chapter 14	Review Chapter on Ideal Student Leadership and the Impact on Youth Development: Leadership and Psychology from a Practitioner's Perspective *D. Tan*	195
Chapter 15	Religious and Spiritual Leadership From a Devotee's Standpoint Perspective: Biopic of a Great Spiritual Leader Master Cheng Yen *W. X. Lim*	205
Chapter 16	Political/Community Leadership and Singapore's Multi-Religious Scene *J. Xue*	213
Chapter 17	Community Services, Service-Learning and Service Leadership in Hong Kong *Carol Ma*	223

Section C	**Leadership in Economic Regionalism**	**243**
Chapter 18	India in SAARC: Leader or Not?	245
	S. Shahadave	
Section D	**Concluding Section**	**253**
Chapter 19	Conclusion	255
	T. W. Lim	

Quizzes and Answer Banks — 261

ABOUT THE AUTHORS

Dr. Carol Ma is known among academics and community work practitioners as an active and passionate promoter of Service-Learning and ageing. She has dedicated herself to promote and implement Service-Learning in Hong Kong for more than 15 years. Carol was the founding member and Associate Director of the Service-Learning at Lingnan University which worked on more than 100 projects every year during her time. As a pioneer of Service-Learning in Hong Kong, she has to conduct research, community outreach and even fund raising. She has also revitalized the Service-Learning Asia Network and currently with over 50 members in the network to promote Service-Learning in the region. She believes Service-Learning can contribute a win-win situation to all stakeholders including teachers, students, community and even the Asia region. In addition, Carol has led elder learning development and age-friendly cities project (accredited by WHO) in Hong Kong. She is one of the consultants for the elderly service programme plan for the Hong Kong SAR government. From 2008 to 2016, she was appointed as a member of Active Aging Committee under the Elderly Commission in Hong Kong to advice the aging development plan. Carol has her first degree at Lingnan University and then studied at the University of California (Los Angeles), as well as a visting scholar at the National Primary Health Care Centre, University of Manchester, UK. As a young, energetic, and committed scholar, she has also published various books and articles about Service-Learning and aging, expert papers in UNESCAP publication and referee journals including *International Journal of Community Research and Engagement; Asian Journal of Gerontology and Geriatrics*; and *New Horizons in Education*. For more details, you can visit her research gate at: https://www.researchgare.net/home

Currently, Carol is Associate Professor, Head of the Master and PhD Programme in Gerontology, Head of the Graduate Certificate of Service-Learning and also Senior Fellow of Service-Learning and Community Engagement at Singapore University of Social Sciences (SUSS).

King, Sean is a senior vice president at Park Strategies, which represented Taiwan's Ministry of Foreign Affairs in the United States from 2009 to 2012. He's also a University of Notre Dame Liu Institute for Asia & Asian Affairs Affiliated Scholar.

Li, Hak Yin is an Associate Professor of International Relations at the Institute for International Strategy, Tokyo International University. He has a PhD in Politics and International Relations from the University of Nottingham, an MPhil in Government and International Studies, Hong Kong Baptist University and a BA in Government and International Studies, Hong Kong Baptist University.

Lim, Tai Wei is a Senior Lecturer at Singapore University of Social Sciences and a Senior Research Fellow adjunct at the National University of Singapore East Asian Institute (EAI).

Lim, Wee-Kiat is Associate Director, Centre for Management Practice, Singapore Management University (SMU). His research interests focus on how organisations at different stages of growth respond to disasters and technological disruption. He has written and taught cases covering Asia and issues concerning governance, innovation, and technology. He is a co-author of the book *Living Digital 2040: Future of Work, Education, and Healthcare* (World Scientific). He also co-authored a book chapter that examines the importance of being people-centric in smart cities initiatives in *Smart Cities: Innovation and Sustainability* (World Scientific). Wee-Kiat received his Ph.D. in Sociology from University of Colorado-Boulder and Bachelor of Communication Studies from Nanyang Technological University.

Lim, Wen Xin is a regular volunteer at the Tzu Chi Foundation.

Shrestha, Shahadave is an Assistant Professor at the Soka University School of Business Administration. He is also a recipient of The Grand Prize, Japanese Foreign Trade Council essay competition (2014) and the Soka University Da Vinci Award (2015 and 2018). He has also published on multiple topics.

Tan, Dean is the former President of the Singapore Institute of Management Japanese Culture & Gaming Society. His belief in human potentials and contributing to others has also spurred him to volunteer with different organizations where he engages with individuals from different age groups. Dean Tan is also a graduate from the University of London with a Bachelor of Science in Economics and Politics.

Tseng Hui-Yi, Katherine is a research associate in East Asian Institute, National University of Singapore. Tseng is studying regional legal and political issues by using an interdisciplinary approach, touching upon international law, geopolitics, history, international relations, political theory and sociology.

Wong, Kenneth, PBM, started to be involved in community service when he as young as 13 years. Inspired and motivated in serving the community in a greater capacity, Kenneth pursued his undergraduate with the National University of Singapore, majoring in Social Work. In 2016, Kenneth obtained his Master's Degree in Community Leadership and Social Development from the Singapore University of Social Sciences.

In 2006, Kenneth began to serve as a grassroots leader in the Joo Chiat constituency. Since then, he has engaged the youth meaningfully in various environmental, community and social programmes for the needy.

At the national level, Kenneth served as the Council Member for People's Association Youth Movement (PAYM) Central Youth Council and led in the organizing of PAYM Chingay Contingent since its inception in 2008. He was the Organizing Chairperson for the PAYM Chingay Contingent in 2011, 2015 and 2018.

Having assembled a strong team to take over, Kenneth relinquished his Chairmanship for the YEC and concurrently was appointed as Chairman for the Joo Chiat Community Sports Club.

Currently a lecturer with the Institute of Technical Education, Kenneth continues to engage youths meaningfully, both academically and non-academically, to contribute to the community through a service-learning programme.

In recognition for Kenneth's contributions to the community, he was conferred the National Day Award 2017 — Pingat Bakti Masyarakat (PBM) — and in May 2018, he was awarded the PAYM Excellent Youth Award in recognition for his service and contributions.

Wong, Elim studied PhD in Japanese Studies at the Chinese University of Hong Kong. Her major research interest is on overseas Chinese history in Japan, and she is also interested in East Asian popular culture and history.

Xue, Jianyue has served as a research assistant at the East Asian Institute, National University of Singapore. He has written background briefs on Chinese domestic politics, domestic regulations and bureaucracy. He also volunteers as an interfaith facilitator at Explorations into Faith.

Section A

POLITICAL LEADERSHIP

Chapter 1

INTRODUCTION

T. W. Lim

Singapore University of Social Sciences
and National University of Singapore, Singapore

This volume begins with a macro-political perspective of leadership qualities in Section A. It looks at case studies of political leadership and the factors that influence the shape and outcome of leadership styles in the region. Political leadership styles in East Asian states are shaped and influenced by a number of domestic factors. These factors include the type of political system that an East Asian state adopted from its days of independence and decolonization. There is a diverse array of political systems in the region, ranging from Western-style liberal democracies like Japan and South Korea to autocratic one-party states like North Korea. Most other East Asian countries adopt systems somewhere between these two polar ends.

Political systems themselves are dependent on ideological systems, a leftover feature from the Cold War (1947–1992) in a bipolar world when states either joined the US-led capitalist and democratic free world or stood with the Soviet Union (USSR)'s collectivized, centrally planned communist bloc. The Association of Southeast Asian Nations (ASEAN) continues to exhibit such features with its old members, which are either monarchies or democracies with a traditional affinity towards the West, and newer members, which are former communist countries but have evolved into some form of semi-capitalist market economy with socialist political systems (e.g. the CLMV countries comprising Cambodia, Laos, Myanmar and Vietnam).

Well known for its high-context culture, the symbolism behind political events, summits, negotiations and media events is reflective of the high-context culture found in Northeast Asia. Very often, in daily conversations, group dynamics and organizational cultures, inner thoughts are not articulated publicly and intentions are expressed through indirect means. Collective goals are also considered more important than individual ones. Therefore, Northeast Asian societies often practice paternalism, authoritarianism and collectivism to mould and shape individuals to fall in line with collective goals.

Sometimes, these ideas are hybridized with modern political thoughts and ideologies to create new political traditions, e.g. socialism with Chinese characteristics, the so-called "Asian Values" system, illiberal democracies, "soft" authoritarianism, "consultative democracies," and Leninist political system with market economy. By coincidence, the emergence of these hybridized political systems (which usually carry varying degrees of authoritarianism) in Northeast Asia coincided with other strongman regimes in other world regions, e.g. the rise of Trump in the US, Putin's hold on power in Russia, Modi in India, and Duterte and Hun Sen in Southeast Asia.

Besides realpolitik and hard power, in order to follow a conciliatory foreign policy with amicable contacts and interactions with other regional countries, soft power is often the neglected aspect of power and leadership in East Asia. Soft power refers to the ability to get individuals (countries in the case when the original meaning is applied) to do something for you without the need to use force and/ or coercion. Originally, the term "soft power" refers to America's global leadership in the world, but the term was appropriated for application in the cultural industries as well. Just as soft cultural power is shaped by global forces and regional traditions, Northeast Asian political systems are a hybrid of Western ideologies and Northeast Asian traditions. Many of them show pragmatic features of grafting Western ideological control over Northeast Asian traditions. The difficulties of fitting into the Western model are detailed in Chapter 3, which discusses the Chinese political system.

Chapter 4 discusses leadership issues in other East Asian states for a comparative perspective. The high-context cultural nature of leadership in East Asia is analysed in the case study of Japan in this chapter. It argues Japanese leadership style is based on consensus, much like its collectivist and groupist society. In terms of society, the Japanese had always strived for harmonious relationships between individuals. In fact, the ancient civilizational racial term for the Japanese people was the *Wa* civilization. The word *Wa* is itself the Kanji (Chinese origins) character that means "harmony." An effective leader in Japan is a person who is able to bring all different factions of the political stage together. This may require a compromise, but it ensures all are aboard when a major decision is made. This is quite different from the feature of highly centralized Chinese leadership in the previous chapter. In Japan, bringing together all factional leaders ensures strong support behind the decision, but it may also take time to make that decision. Other selected East Asian examples are also briefly discussed here.

The first three chapters of this section on political leadership focus on large powers, lay some emphases on middle powers and also look at regionalism as instruments to constrain large powers to follow international norms and behaviour. They are macro- and meso-level topics that are important and crucial in discussing big power relations, setting international norms and also detecting how domestic politics affect regional and international diplomatic behaviour. This chapter zooms in further and looks at small states instead, a micro-level analysis. Very often, small states are neglected and marginalized in international relations (IRs) literature. Chapter 5 attempts to fill in the gap for academic discussions on the role of small states in major power actions and behaviour by focusing on a single case study and examining its role in the regional/international system in relatively greater depth. In addition to interpretive work, this essay's methodology also adopts field trips and on-site observation studies as well.

Moving on from actors within geopolitical systems and macro worldviews, Chapter 6 by W. K. Lim examines and analyses how effective leadership develops institutions through the case study of a disaster management system drawn from China. Lim's case study looks at how the Chinese government exhibited leadership and developed emergency management rapidly in the wake of the 2003 SARS epidemic. W. K. Lim's research traces the remarkable genesis of the new organizational field of emergency management over a 10-year period (2002–2012). It highlights the various factors that facilitated the establishment, i.e. the network of political leadership and experts, in creating and consolidating the field, particularly the ideational origins of and manoeuvring policy conversations from management to governance.

Lim also demonstrates how the establishment, through processes of legislation and regulation, learnt and refined formal definitions and categories of emergency as threats to society that necessitated emergencies to be governed through a complex arrangement of government, private firms, and civil society. Lim discusses the theoretical and policy implications of understanding nascent field development surrounding new policy domains through the travel of ideas and trials of crises. The analytical toolkit that Lim used to analyse the rise of China's emergency management is assembled mainly from sociological neo-institutional theory and sociological literatures on disaster and risk management.

Aside from institutions, states and policy mechanisms, there is also a human face and individual political entities among the stakeholders of a political system. Chapter 7 by Y. Godo paints a political biography of Mr. Toru Hashimoto. His chapter adds a human touch and narrates an individual story to the discussion. Godo noted that the charismatic politician Toru Hashimoto is the "male Cinderella" of the Japanese political world. Unknown until the age of 33 years, Hashimoto first came to attention as a one-of-a-kind lawyer in 2003 when he appeared regularly on an Osaka-based television programme. He entered the political world by running for the gubernatorial election for Osaka Prefecture in January 2008, which he won in a landslide victory. As soon as he took up the post, he initiated a series of reforms, including the financial reconstruction of the Osaka Prefectural Government. He launched the Osaka Metropolis Plan in January 2010, which aimed to dissolve Osaka City and its neighbouring cities to form special wards and concentrate decision-making procedures for the entire area that makes up today's Osaka Prefecture in the hands of the Osaka Metropolitan Government. Hashimoto recruited politicians supporting the Osaka Metropolis Plan and formed a new political party in April 2010, which was initially known as "Initiatives from Osaka" and later renamed the Japan Innovation Party (JIP). Godo's chapter therefore is a very human story of the political rise and fall of an individual politician, a political biography within Section A.

S. King's Chapter 8 points out that Taiwan is a curious leadership case, as it's not easy to lead an entity that doesn't officially exist. He asks the thesis question: How, then, to lead Taiwan, given its unusual political predicament? In fact, Taiwan can't even be sure what to call itself. Is it simply Taiwan, as most people call it? Or, is it the Republic of China, its official name? Or, Chinese Taipei, as it's called in the Olympics? How have Taiwan's leaders fared, given such an intrinsic question of identity? Through a multidisciplinary narrative that includes Taiwan's unique history, King paints the picture of how one of the world's most dynamic economies governs itself.

Continuing with the case study of Taiwan, Chapter 9 by Katherine Tseng analyses how Han Kuo-yu, a former Nationalist Party (also known as Kuomintang, KMT) legislator and general manager of Taipei Agricultural Products Marketing Corporation, unexpectedly successfully navigated through a fiercely fought election campaign to become the Kaohsiung city mayor. Similar to Chapter 7, this chapter also tells a very human and personalized story centring it on the so-called "Han wave", where charismatic politicians are able to appeal directly to major influential demographic groups and win the election. Such charismatic leadership embodied in the "Han Wave" made a dramatic impact on the political scene and was able to raise funds and draw large crowds and quiet sympathisers from the mainstream Taiwanese society despite the lack of support from Han's own party mechanism.

Besides political personalities and a charming election campaign, Chapter 10 by H. Y. Li discusses the importance of the mechanics and institutions of the Hong Kong Special Administrative Region (HKSAR). The author argues that, though the political system is not fully a democratic one, Hong Kong people enjoyed the rule of law; free flow of people and information, academic, press and mass media freedoms; as well as rights for demonstration. However, after Hong Kong was handed over by the United Kingdom to China in 1997, there is increasing concern on the mainlandization of Hong Kong. The author discusses these important issues within the context of the executive institutions and the central government's intervention in the Special Administrative Region.

Very often, when the concept of leadership is discussed, institutionalized political leadership in the case of the government and business leadership in the case of the corporate sector are vigorously analysed in that context. However, equally important, is the idea of community leadership, which may involve local residents, civil society groups, non-profit organizations (NPOs), ethnic associations, neighbourhood groups, non-governmental organizations (NGOs), local business associations, local businesses and other stakeholders in local community well-being. The chapters in Section B examine this concept of community leadership and its impact on community well-being. Several specific case studies will be examined in depth. Unlike Section A which tends to examine political leadership from a macro theoretical and empirical perspective, Section B adopts historical-anthropological perspectives to analyse case studies. Other case studies in Section B will also examine policy formulation and implementation to look at the role of government in handling community-level issues.

The second chapter in Section B examines the concept of community leadership and studies how it is shaping society through the tripartite work of civic society organisations, government agencies and members of the public. In Chapter 11, W. Kenneth argues that the idea of leadership itself is not a fixed concept; scholars and academia have their own set of theory, belief and argument. Patterns of leadership traits, behaviours and theories vary from time to time and across different cultures and societies, and it is important within the context of social development (Bass, 1990) in a nation-state.

W. Kenneth applies the idea of national policy objectives and multiculturalism in his discussion of community leadership in Singapore. He concludes by arguing that the Singapore government is committed to forging strong social inclusion and improving the lives of its people through social investment and schemes, which are indeed reasonably successful and focus on "people-centred" development (Eade, 1997) rather than on demagogue populist approaches. W. Kenneth noted that, while the State may take the lead in strengthening and improving the social development and inclusion, nothing beats having the community taking ownership of these functions to make a difference to the community.

The second case study on community leaders in Section B is based on Yokohama Chinatown. One of the reasons for picking Yokohama Chinatown as a case study is due to its rich tapestry of ethnicities, civil society groups, local and overseas visitors and its sheer scale and size. The second largest Chinatown in the world — Yokohama Chinatown — hosts the largest population of overseas Chinese and the largest number of overseas Chinese associations among the three Chinatowns in Japan. The community is also home to two overseas Chinese schools, more than 250 Chinese restaurants and shops and two Chinese temples — the Temple of Guandi and the Temple of Mazu. These heritage sites as tourist assets enable Yokohama Chinatown to be ranked among the top three most visited sightseeing spots in Japan among domestic tourists for over 10 years. Such accomplishments in getting into high-profile national rankings by Yokohama Chinatown are partly due to the efforts of its community leaders.

Chapters 12 and 13 discuss the state of community leadership in Yokohama Chinatown. Yokohama Chinatown, according to the existing scholarly literature, is considered a model community since it is well developed and due to the self-sustainable ethnic community that brings a sense of belonging to its overseas Chinese residents. The community is led by a few overseas Chinese leaders, and one particular community leader from Yokohama Chinatown is studied as an example to investigate how a community leader contributes to the development of Yokohama Chinatown. This chapter and the next one on Yokohama Chinatown case study are divided into five parts: first of all, the definition of community and community leadership is highlighted for the readers to understand the basic elements found in a community and its mobilization by the leaders.

The second part of Chapter 12 investigates the complexities of the Yokohama Chinatown's society and how the community leaders coped with the difficulties faced by the community in the Chinatown. This is followed by a brief background of community leader Jin, whose biographical details are examined in this research. Chapter 13 examines three major contributions of Jin in developing Yokohama Chinatown with fieldwork material, including the integration of the overseas Chinese residents, introduction of Chinese folklore to the host society (referring to mainstream society in Japan), and the promotion of Tokyo/Yokohama/Japanese tourism industry using Chinese culture as an attraction. Up to the point of this writing, this is the first oral interview and fieldwork observation-based research focusing on a major Chinatown in Japan that provides new perspectives on community leadership in understanding the development of Yokohama Chinatown.

From Chapter 11's focus on community leadership at the state institutional level to community leadership in an ethnic quarter in Chapters 12 and 13, Chapter 14 tackles the idea of leadership at a micro-level (focusing on youths as well as student mobilization in a university setting) but in the ideational realm. Like Chapter 11, it is written from a practitioner's perspective and looks into the idea of leadership (especially when it is applied to the demographic group of youths). The author Dean Tan, who is a university student leader himself, writes about the theoretical aspects of leadership and contextualizes in broader idea, especially Lim Siong Guan's inspiring seminal work. Tan writes from a unique position of student leader and reflects upon his tenure through student observations, experiential learning, participation in activities and interpretive works through literature. It is a befitting chapter that contours off Section B's focus on community leadership at the state institutional, ethnic communitarian and demographic-specific micro case study.

The second review chapter (Chapter 15) in Section B is also written from the standpoint perspective of a devotee peering into the charismatic leadership of a major religious leader. It can be read as a case study of effective mobilization of people and resources, with tools such as the mass media and digital technologies. Originally hailing from Taiwan in Republican China, Master Cheng Yen is the founder of the Buddhist Compassion Relief Tzu Chi Foundation (hereafter "Tzu Chi"), the biggest non-governmental welfare organization in the Chinese-speaking world. Today, the organization has successfully established footprints in 95 countries, with more than 500 offices worldwide in 57 countries and attracting nearly 10 million supporters and followers. This chapter uncovers the reasons behind its rapid expansion. The two review chapters on specific contexts of student leadership and religious mobilization provide case studies written from a practitioner's angle into the field of community leadership.

Chapter 16 by J. Xue continues with the theme of religious leadership, but from the civil society and policy points of view. The chapter examines how, in 2002, the Inter-Racial and Religious Confidence Circles (IRCCs) set up local-level interfaith platforms across all constituencies in Singapore, aimed at promoting racial and religious harmony through interfaith and interethnic themed activities such as heritage trails, interfaith talks and various ethnic and religious celebrations.

Away from sectoral case studies like volunteer organizations, neighbourhood outfits, religious organizations, Chapter 17 written by Dr. C. Ma takes the idea of community leadership one geographical step higher to cover a major metropolitan city like Hong Kong and she adopts a longitudinal analysis to study the long-term impact of service-learning education in that city. She noted that Hong Kong stakeholders, especially those in higher education industry, use service-learning as a pedagogy to develop youth capabilities, e.g. communication skills, caring disposition, leadership skills, interpersonal skills, and serve the community. With the support of the Li & Fung Foundation together with the Hong Kong Institute of Service Leadership and Management (HKI-SLAM), service leadership was also introduced to eight UGC-funded universities in 2012 and they have been funded for 5 years to develop service leadership initiatives for the young people in Hong Kong.

The joint partnership and continuing discussion of service-leadership have inspired some stakeholders to develop a new model in both university education and post-industrial service economy. This will prepare Hong Kong's young people to not only become effective leaders but also become a caring person to the disadvantaged in an ever-changing society. Ma's chapter provides an appropriate longitudinal wrap-up of Section B's focus on community leadership.

In the last section on leadership in economic regionalism and international political economy, Dr. S. Shahadave's Chapter 18 focuses on SAARC. He makes the argument that, among all its member states, India's position within SAARC is very unique in many different aspects. India shares borders with all other South Asian nations. In terms of the size of its population, territory and GDP, it both qualifies and carries the image of an emerging economic power in the world. He opines that India's role and responsibility in the region is, without doubt, very important for the region and perhaps the world and focuses his chapter content on this regional leadership aspect.

Chapter 2

INTRODUCTION TO POLITICAL LEADERSHIP IN NORTHEAST ASIA

T. W. Lim

Singapore University of Social Sciences and
National University of Singapore, Singapore

INTRODUCTION — POLITICAL SYSTEMS

Political leadership styles in East Asian states are shaped and influenced by a number of domestic factors. These factors include the type of political system that East Asian states adopted from their days of independence and decolonization. There is a diverse array of political systems in the region, ranging from Western-style liberal democracies like Japan and South Korea to autocratic one-party states like North Korea. Most other East Asian countries adopt systems somewhere in between these two polar ends. Political systems themselves are dependent on ideological systems, a leftover feature from the Cold War (1947–1992) in a bipolar world when states either joined the US-led capitalist and democratic free world or stood with the Soviet Union (USSR)'s collectivized, centrally planned communist bloc. The Association of Southeast Asian Nations (ASEAN) continues to exhibit such features with its old members, which were either monarchies or democracies with traditional affinity towards the West, and newer members, which are former communist countries but have evolved into some form of semi-capitalist market economy with socialist political systems (e.g. the CLMV countries comprising Cambodia, Laos, Myanmar and Vietnam).

Ideology

Ideology remains an important factor that shapes the political leadership systems in East Asia. Besides Southeast Asia, in Northeast Asia, the political landscape is also divided between the capitalist free world and the hybrid socialist economies. The most distinct polar ends of ideological differences in the East Asian region range from capitalism based on market forces of demand and supply practiced by democratic countries in running their economies to command economies where resources are allocated by the state. China remains the world's largest hybrid socialist country with a free-market economy while North Korea is the last Stalinist communist state on earth. Their neighbours South Korea, Mongolia, Chinese Taipei and Japan have become functioning democracies while Russia is a strongman regime with an electoral system.

Morality

Other analysts have described East Asian states as having Confucianist ideologies with a paternalistic state in charge of affairs of East Asian populations, guiding their social relations with policies. Anti-corruption drive, for example, is sometimes cast in the image of a moral exercise. Morality in East Asia's largest state is defined by a Mencius standard in that the Son of Heaven (the Chinese Emperor) has to show benevolence to his subjects in exchange for political mandate and legitimacy. If the ruler becomes a tyrant, natural disasters, plagues and other inauspicious events will occur together with people's revolts to overthrow the tyrant. Morality is couched in the need to have a functioning sage king who showers benevolence on his people. Even East Asian economic development is also sometimes conceptualized in Confucianist terms as state-led economic developments and "miracles". There is a paternalist element in such descriptions of East Asian political systems. A disciplined workforce, paternalistic social policies, sage king leaders and anti-corruption campaigns based on political legitimacy are all reflective of such Confucianist socio-political cultures, giving rise to the popularity of strongman rule — typically characterizing semi-autocratic decision-making and policy adoption to accelerate economic development in exchange for people's support and pragmatic economic results. These ideas are accentuated in the rapid economic development in South Korea and Taiwan when they were under authoritarian rule. Weeding out corrupted officials (sometimes selectively) is equated with the mandate to rule and soft authoritarian practices as well as the maintenance of dominant parties in power.

Political Succession

Respect for the elders and those in power in Confucianism translate to complex procedures when it comes to political succession. Political succession is an issue that has to be managed gingerly in the region. The rise of core leadership centred around President Xi Jinping, the presence and factional consultative power of *genro* or elder statesmen in Japan and the choice of a 90-something-year old as the leader of the opposition bid for power in the Malaysian elections 2018 are all reflective of powerful conservative and time-tested elements in East Asian politics. To manage power transitions well, elder statesmen are often part of the process to ease any hiccups or disagreements. Respect for veteran or elder politicians springs from the Confucianist tradition of respecting seniors and the reverence for authority. In soft authoritarian and autocratic system, leadership succession is often scripted and timed carefully for execution. In the case of China, choosing the top leader is a highly secretive process that involves secret negotiations between different factions, compromises made among former top leaders, getting the top brass of the military and bureaucracy to fall into line, etc. It is a non-transparent process. Liberal democracies in East Asia like Japan and South Korea are comparatively more transparent and competitive and also involve elder statesmen in the consultative process.

Another observable tendency is for leaders to bide their time and not stand out prematurely in leadership races until they have gathered sufficient political support from the elders. Patience was also what got Chinese President Xi to his position. Xi was relatively unknown within the Chinese party hierarchy, incognito and quietly rising through the ranks without much fanfare. He was overshadowed by more flamboyant leaders like Bo Xilai who turned to stoking up Maoism in Chongqing to consolidate his power. Xi quietly consolidated power among the elders as he personally did not have credentials like Deng Xiaoping, blessings and designation, military experience or Long March experiences like his predecessors. Rallying around him, his hardcore supporters fought hard to elevate Xi to the status of "core leader" and eventually voted him to be the president without term limits (theoretically for life).

Political Retirement

Unless there are serious political struggles, retired top leaders are often treated with some form of reverence and respect and are sometimes paraded and feted in political events and anniversaries. "Face-saving" is an important ritual and unspoken rule in East Asian interactions. Even political rivals try to accommodate losers after neutralizing their power. Former Chinese presidents Jiang Zemin and Hu Jintao were featured in major Chinese Communist Party (CCP) events even after their factions were diminished in influence. Older retired top leaders also have the procedural honour of having their thoughts enshrined in the party's archives, from the "Three Represents" to "*Xiaokang Shehui* (Harmonious society)", the central ideas of Chinese top leadership are recorded and archived as policy wisdom for future party members' reference. In the case of President Xi Jinping, the decision to enshrine his thoughts was publicly initiated in the 6th Party Plenum and then concluded/officialised in the 19th Party Congress.

There are other ways of deploying retired leaders in liberal democracies. Fidel Ramos, a former Filipino president known for his firebrand ways and a well-regarded former military general, played important ambassadorial-like roles for his country even after retirement. He was considered an ASEAN elder statesman who played the role of a roving ambassador. In Japan, former prime ministers (PMs) like Yasuo Fukuda and Yukio Hatoyama continue with their active political lives in talk circuits and visits to Beijing (presumably because of their long-standing "friendship" with Chinese leaders) and the US to smoothen relations. Other retired PMs come back to political life running on no-nuclear platforms in gubernatorial/governor elections, e.g. Morihiro Hosokawa supported by Junichiro Koizumi (both were popular PMs when they were in power). In the Hong Kong Special Administrative Region, which enjoys greater political freedom relatively compared to other regions of China, former leaders CY Leung and Tung Chee Hwa were appointed as vice presidents to the Chinese national legislature, the Chinese People's Political Consultative Conference, elevating their status from the exercise of localized executive power to a national consultative role.

Confucianism and Loyalty

Confucianism demands loyalties from supporters and subjects/subordinates to the sovereign. In the same way, loyalty is an important element demanded by East Asian leaders from their supporters. Sometimes, this loyalty demand takes the form of patron–client (PC) relationships, while in other circumstances, it is loyalty shown towards an institution like the political party or the military. The military of China, People's Liberation Army, shows its loyalty to the CCP, and military power is subjugated under the political party. The selection of the chief executive (CE) of Hong Kong Special Autonomous Region (SAR) is also based on loyalty to the motherland and Hong Kong without confrontations with Beijing's rule as pre-requisites for CE candidates.

In contrast with non-confrontation with Beijing and motherland, the Chinese demand absolute loyalty to the party on the mainland itself, a much higher standard than what they impose on Hong Kong. Rallying around the leaders and demanding loyalties from subordinates in exchange for collective economic goals are all manifestations of communitarianism, thus prioritizing collective interests above self-interests. In China, the CCP transcends parochial self-interests with even the military citing their loyalties to the party instead of the state. The organization (*zhuzhi*) transcends the individual, something well understood by party members and the ordinary Chinese. Any loosening up of loyalty to the party and its central leaders may result in political purges, a process some in the West suspect is masqueraded under the cover of anti-corruption campaigns.

In Japan, politicians are also loyal to their factional leaders within the parties. There is still an *oyabun* relationship where junior politicians are protected and cultivated by senior *senpai* members in exchange for unwavering loyalty. Sometimes this loyalty trait can last through generations. For example, former Foreign Minister Shintaro Abe took former Prime Minister Junichiro Koizumi under his wings and, when Koizumi became PM, he tutored and mentored Shinzo Abe (Shintaro Abe's son). In Japan, party factional interests (*habatsu*) come before individual ambitions. These interests are then aggregated by the PM who takes into account varying factional interests and tries to arrive at the lowest common denominator to accommodate them. In South Korea, which has a liberal democratic political system with features akin to the Japanese political system, factional interests are strong. President Moon Jae-in of South Korea has personal ties and loyalty to his senior, former President Roh Tae Moo-Hyun who is rumoured to have committed suicide over an alleged corruption scandal. They were both liberal, left-leaning presidents who are friendlier to the cause of reunification and better relations with North Korean.

Loyalty Demand is Gender Neutral

The Northeast Asian form of leadership is so steeped in tradition and culture that it transcends gender categories. Before she was brought down by public outcry over her association of the military with re-election chances, Tomomi Inada (former Japanese defence minister) was a loyal follower of Prime Minister Shinzo Abe and they share similar conservative ideas about Japan's security needs. Inada was one of the most conservative politicians to assume the minister of defence portfolio and seen as a possible future PM of Japan. She stepped down when she used the Self-Defense Forces as a call for voters to support Liberal Democratic Party (LDP). The association of the military with civilian politics remains a sensitive issue with many Japanese voters in a pacifist mainstream society.

Even Stalinist authoritarian regimes have patient and loyal strong female leaders. During the Pyeongchang Winter Olympic Games in February 2018, President

Moon had meetings and conversations with Kim Yo-Jong (sister of North Korean supreme leader) and North Korean Supreme Leader Kim Jong-Un. Now widely considered the second most powerful person in North Korea, Yo-Jong controls access to her brother's schedule and access to the Supreme Leader himself. She is a fierce Kim family loyalist who has her brother's trust. Not all family members are treated in the same manner. North Korean Supreme Leader Chairman Kim had personally ordered the execution of his uncle Jang Song Taek and put his auntie into political cold storage and banished his half-brother to political wilderness before sending assassins to kill him in Kuala Lumpur. Yo-Jong conveyed her brother's wishes faithfully to South Korean president and travelled to the Winter Olympics (rumours that say allegedly during pregnancy) to execute her duties loyally to the Supreme Leader, the Kim First Family and to the regime. During the Pyeongchang Winter Olympic Games in February 2018, President Moon had meetings and conversations with Kim Yo-Jong, sister of North Korean supreme leader, and North Korean Supreme Leader Kim Jong-Un. The successful meeting resulted in summits between the North Korean Supreme Leader and his South Korean counterpart.

Even in societies that are stereotyped to be male-dominated, female leaders have risen to the forefront and taken up prominent political positions though they are also subjected to the same standard of loyalty required of their male counterparts. Former Japanese opposition leader Renho was loyal to the ideology of liberalism throughout her tenure as the opposition leader. Whether as a journalist or feminist, Renho moved to tie up with the Japan Communist Party in a united front against the conservatives. She was pragmatically consistent to the idea of a united front against the ruling party. Ironically, it was the issue of loyalty that put an end to her political career as an opposition leader. The insinuation of divided loyalty emerged during her tenure when she was questioned about her ultimate loyalty to the Japanese state due to a lingering Taiwanese nationality issue and her mixed heritage. Even with the rising trend of women joining the ranks of Northeast Asian elite leadership, it is quite likely that some of the traditional features of leadership in the region like the emphasis on loyalty will continue to persist.

Identification with the Working Class

Both moral exaltations of humility and modern ideas of political propaganda resonance with the masses highlight the importance of top leadership mingling with crowds for maximum media exposure. The elite leadership in Northeast Asia is also keen to strengthen their bonds with the working classes in their societies. Chinese President Xi, for example, has mingled with working-class people by eating buns by the side of the road. Xi is also portrayed in the official media and propaganda as an individual who once slept in the caves in Liangjiahe Village when he was sent to work in the countryside as part of Mao Zedong's program for urban youngsters to experience peasant life. Japanese Prime Minister Shinzo Abe worked in the steel industry for 3 years from 1979 to 1981 at Kobe Steel, where he gained exposure to a heavy industry and its employees. South Korean President Moon came to power by promising, among other agendas, to curtail the power of the powerful chaebol industrial groups in his country, especially after a 'nut rage' incident when the scion of the family running a major Korean airline Cho Hyun-Ah was accused of abusing her subordinate. Carrie Lam, the Hong Kong Chief Executive, also came from a humble background that endeared her to the people of the territory. At one point of her life, she had to eat and study at the same desk because there was no separate study desk for her.

All these leaders eventually climbed to the apex of political power. Xi worked as party secretary in Fujian and Zhejiang provinces, Politburo member and then as president, secretary general and chairman of the Central Military Commission in China. Abe became assistant to his father, former Prime Minister Koizumi's cabinet and then one of the longest PM in power in recent Japanese history. Moon went from a youth advocate for democracy to a defence lawyer for human rights and eventually president of South Korea. Lam got a place in the prestigious Hong Kong University and joined the elite administrative service in the government bureaucracy and rose to become CE. In all the above cases, humility, identification with the people and working-class values and identification with the common folks gave them legitimacy to pursue elite political careers. Together with personal loyalties and careful management of political succession to transition the previous leadership to retirement while acknowledging their contributions, these leaders have observed Confucian traditions of respecting one's elders/seniors, exhibiting humility for the mandate of the people, and following the wishes of the collective over individual ambitions to become the top leaders in their countries.

"Strongman" Politics

Due to the preference for Confucian moralistic authoritarian organization structures and illiberal democracies/structure predicated on collectivism/communitarianism/groupism, there is some preference for strong centralized leadership who represents the collectivist political sentiments. Northeast Asian leaders like Xi and Abe have become known as strongman leaders who carry out strongman diplomacy. Because they have strong mandates and longevity of tenures, the Northeast Asian strong leaders embodied the essence of regional diplomacy itself. Their charisma, especially larger-than-life personalities like Chinese President Xi, captured the mass media and the world's attention. Their meetings are often scrutinized and analysed. For example, President Xi is often analysed for his body language and mannerisms, especially during an earlier period in his presidency when he did not make public appearances for a short while. The scene when US President Donald Trump and Japanese Prime Minister Abe met was also ingrained in the shutters of the international media's photographers when it was analysed for personality traits found between the two strong leaders. The amount of feed given to the Japanese koi carps in Akasaka Palace was especially interesting for media analysis.

When strongman leaders get together, the gatherings become photo-ops for the mass media. Sometimes, some of these photo ops were nicknamed as "bromance" sessions. Japanese Prime Minister Abe's relatively strong and sustainable leadership is viewed positively by many in Japan as a necessary condition to lead Japan through the 2020 Olympics and also deal with a rogue state like North Korea (with its nuclear and missile testing that saw missiles flying over Hokkaido). Under Abe's strong and decisive leadership, Japan pushed through the collective self-defence arrangement, allowing it to come to the aid of its ally the US and its network of friends if they come under attack. Japanese Prime Minister Abe's strength comes from his skilful ability to aggregate interests between factions and find the denominator that tries to accommodate as much factional interests as possible.

High-context Culture

The art of staying in power is not easy in Northeast Asia, which is a region generally well known for its high-context culture. The symbolisms behind the proceedings of political events, summits, negotiations and media events are reflective of the high-context culture found in Northeast Asia. Very often, in daily conversations, group dynamics and organizational cultures, inner thoughts are not articulated publicly and intentions are expressed through indirect means. Collective goals are also considered more important than individual ones. Therefore, Northeast Asian societies often practice paternalism, authoritarianism and collectivism to mould and shape individuals to fall in line with collective goals. Sometimes, these ideas are hybridized with modern political thought and ideologies to create new political traditions, e.g. socialism with Chinese characteristics, the so-called "Asian Values" system, illiberal democracies, "soft" authoritarianism, "consultative democracies" and Leninist political system with market economy. By coincidence, the emergence of these hybridized political system (which usually carry varying degrees of authoritarianism) in Northeast Asia coincided with other strongman regimes in other world regions, e.g. the rise of Trump in the

Introduction to Political Leadership in Northeast Asia 19

US, Putin's hold on power in Russia, Modi in India, and Duterte and Hun Sen in Southeast Asia.

Sometimes, some of these strongman leaders are cited for human rights abuses, e.g. Duterte has had to bear the brunt of human rights non-government organizations' (NGOs) criticisms for his summary treatment of drug dealers in the Philippines. In the case of China, various groups either praise or criticise China's centralization of power by reducing the number of Politburo members from 9 to 7 and more recently, removed term limits on the president and vice president posts. Chinese President Xi and his right-hand man Wang Qishan (popularly known as the "anti-corruption tsar", and re-appointed as the Chinese vice president) carried out an anti-corruption campaign that removed many CCP officials from the upper ranks of the party (the so-called "Gang of Six") to the rank and file. It has cleaned up the party and enjoyed the support of the people and also faced criticisms that the entire exercise was designed to wipe out rival powerbases. Indeed, the anti-corruption campaign smashed the other elite Chinese factions like the *Jiang Pai* ("Jiang Faction"), the *Hu Pai* ("Hu Faction"), the *Shanghai Clique* ("Shanghai bang"), the so-called "Gang of Six", Princeling faction (*Taizidang*), the cadre faction, etc.

Collectivism and the so-called "Asian Values"

Strongmen are sometimes associated with the structure of collectivist societies. Sociologists/anthropologists sometimes forward the idea that agrarian societies tend to produce collective societies due to the need to work on seed-planting and harvests together. Therefore, strong centralized authoritarian structures are need for highly coordinated work. Other explanations base the differences between Eastern and Western political systems on "Asian Values" exceptionalism, in that cultures tend to have diverging value systems from each other. Cultural explanations remain under attack from scholarly critiques for their subjective views about culture and for disregarding the cross-pollination and hybridization processes associated with cultural interactions. Such explanations support the idea of a collectivist society mobilized behind a decisive leader (and in authoritarian societies, a strongman).

By sheer coincidence, East Asia is now led by a coterie of strongmen from the conservative and longest reigning Prime Minister Shinzo Abe of Japan to the "core leader" President Xi Jinping of China. Other strongmen in the region include Prime Minister Hun Sen of Cambodia, tough-talking President Rodrigo Duterte of the Philippines, Prime Minister Mahathir Mohamed of Malaysia (though he is returning as a leader of democratic reforms to Malaysia), Kim Jong Un of North Korea, etc. Sometimes when these strongmen get together, the mass media characterized it as a "bromance" meeting, given the strongman-to-strongman like-ability for each other, playing golf competitively, strolling along ranches/beaches, attending military parades, etc. Xi and Trump (also seen as an authoritarian figure by the liberals and the left in the US), for example, were seen attending Chinese operas and cloisonné workshop during Trump's visit to Beijing. These were instances of personality-based diplomacy.

Their personalized diplomatic style bore fruit for the Trump–Kim summit. Xi and Trump were able to lend their prestige and power to make the summit possible (although post-summit camaraderie swiftly broke down when the Sino–US trade war escalated). In the pre-summit days, the two leaders exchanged phone calls enthusiastically to make the summit happen. Xi even loaned Kim the use of a national carrier Air China passenger jet to fly him to Singapore to meet US President Trump. Another leader who was personally involved was South Korean President Moon Jae-in. He was also busy keeping both Tokyo and Washington informed about the progress of his communications with Chairman Kim. Strongman Trump kept up a furious pace of Asian diplomacy, along with Trump loyalist Vice President Mike Pence who gave assurance to the South Koreans that the US would protect them. At an ASEAN summit held around this date, Filipino strongman Duterte also serenaded the US president. Such events marked the rise of the age of strongman bromance.

US President Trump's leadership style in diplomacy seems to be situationally fluid, transactional and subject to emotive messages. His diplomatic conversation is not entirely scripted. He sometimes goes off the planned agendas with an element of unpredictability. This keeps his allies, partners and foes alike in anticipating his next move. This provides a degree of strategic ambiguity for foes and allies alike to work towards a compromise on bilateral and/or multilateral tough issues. Sometimes, the unconventional leadership style made US strategic competitors look reasonable (pre-Trump–Kim summit heated exchanges between President Trump and Chairman Kim of North Korea), while on other occasions, America's foes found it hard to deal with him, leaving them confused and in disarray (e.g. US trade frictions with China). US President Trump's strategic unpredictability does provide some advantage for US foreign policy because foes and partners alike find it difficult to project and predict his thoughts. Perhaps nowhere is it more unpredictable and dynamic as the trade tensions between the US and its allies than especially its main strategic competitor, China.

When Brexit occurred and US President Trump's 'America First' strategy came into prominence, there were widespread worries about the future of free trade in the world. Interestingly, Beijing and Tokyo appeared to be defenders of free trade in an age of populism, protectionism and inward-looking fortress mentality. In the case of Tokyo, it advocated fair trade as well. Beijing's credentials rested on its Belt and Road Initiative or BRI (formerly known as the One Belt One Road initiative) and its related institutions like the Asian Infrastructure Investment Bank. Together with Australia and New Zealand, Japan has championed the Comprehensive and Progressive Trans-Pacific Partnership (CPTPP). Both of them are interested to push ahead with the formation of Regional Comprehensive Economic Partnership (RCEP).

For economic cooperation to take place, the political conditions have to be favourable. Regional leadership also appears to be predicated on avoidance of conflict and face-saving diplomatic gestures to defuse tensions. Beijing and Tokyo have been playing a cat and mouse game over the East China Sea with Chinese warships entering exclusive economic zones and then leaving when Japanese coastguards arrive before entering again. Both sides show incredible wisdom and self-restraint in avoiding conflicts and deploying mostly coastguards instead of naval assets. At the time of this writing, this issue has remained quiet. In the same way, Filipino President Rodrigo Duterte's policy towards China defused tensions with Beijing and, using personal diplomacy and charm offensive, both sides have become quite effective economic partners. South Korea defused tensions with Beijing when President Moon suspended the deployment of a second Terminal High-Altitude Air Defense System in favour of better relations with Beijing and Beijing responded by standing down on boycotts against Korean supermarkets like Lotte and Korean Popular Culture.

The Application of Soft Power

In order to follow a conciliatory foreign policy with amicable contacts and interactions with other regional countries, soft power is often the neglected aspect of power and leadership in East Asia. Soft power refers to the ability to get individuals (countries in the case when the original meaning is applied) to do something for you without the need to use force and/or coercion. Originally, the term "soft power" refers to America's global leadership in the world, but the term was appropriated for application in the cultural industries as well. In the contemporary period, Japan has developed an impressive Japanese popular culture industry with its Anime, Comics and Games (ACG) products. When consumers around the world buy the ACG products, they are exposed to Japanese language and culture. Many want to learn more about Japan and so industries like tourism, language centres and traditional cultural performances benefit from this increased interest in all things Japanese.

Of course, the most universal form of popular culture is probably US Hollywood, Silicon Valley and Marvel/Disney/Fox/Lucasfilm products. Popular culture and the ideology of a democratic society attract many in the region to US global leadership. This is the reason why the US continues to set global standards for cutting-edge consumer products and technologies. It is also the reason why US has the largest and most powerful alliance network in East Asia, with South Korea, the Philippines and Thailand as its partners/allies. Japan is the foundation of the US–Japan Alliance in the region while Singapore is a strategic partner. Vietnam is increasingly warming up to the US while Indonesia, Brunei and Malaysia have traditionally cordial interactions. Only North Korea, Laos and Cambodia have somewhat closer relations with China while Myanmar is democratizing.

Major Power Leadership in East Asia — A Constructivist View

Unlike realistic zero-sum game interpretation of power in the region, constructivists conceptualize the region in terms of multilateral cooperation, deeper integration/interdependence and win–win scenarios. There are issues in which big powers can work with each other. For example, the removal of weapons of mass destruction is a common goal cherished by all major powers in the region. That explains the almost universal support that the region gave to the Trump–Kim summit. Countries of all ideological and geopolitical stripes in the region came together to support the summit. Not even Pyongyang's traditional allies China and Russia are keen to see North Korea develop nuclear weapons. The only difference in thinking among stakeholders for a denuclearized Korean Peninsula is US–Japan's united stance on Complete Verifiable Irreversible Denuclearization. South Korea mirrors US position and tries to bridge it with Pyongyang's position on staggered denuclearization with rewards inserted at every stage. While difference in positions complicates the talks, the overall support for this no-detriment regional peacemaking effort is universal and strong.

Another constructivist effort can be found in the economic realm — to intertwine economies together so intensely that they become interdependent with each other, preventing warfare and conflicts. Economic regionalism therefore is proceeding in a fast and furious manner with CPTPP, formerly led by the United States, now advocated by Japan, New Zealand and Australia. Beijing-led initiative RCEP is another example of a regionalization scheme. Both RCEP and CPTPP are slated to lead to the Free Trade Area of the Asia-Pacific. All these schemes help to forge stronger linkages between bilateral and multilateral agreements already signed into existence. Despite the Trump administration leaving the Trans-Pacific Partnership, the future does not rule out Washington D.C. considering membership or collaboration with RCEP nor Beijing and Washington D.C. joining the CPTPP. Washington D.C. has been the architect of the global post-war order. The US continues to shape the rules for regulating world trade and the global economy.

Not all constructivist schemes need to occur at the Track I level. Track II diplomacy and people-to-people exchanges are just as important for societies to understand each other at a deeper level. The US has been attracting academically strong children from well-endowed families to study in the US for decades. Some of the returnees bring important knowledge and skills back to East Asia and create the so-called "East Asian economic miracle". China's BRI is attempting to strengthen physical connectivity between countries by building transportation infrastructure, high-speed rails, highways, etc. Greater contact between individuals can lead to greater understanding, confidence-building measures and less tensions in the region and close the trust deficit. It also has the benefits of building trust for the next generation of East Asians.

Chapter 3

THE CHINESE CASE STUDY

T. W. Lim

Singapore University of Social Sciences and
National University of Singapore, Singapore

COMPARISONS BETWEEN THE EAST AND WEST — HYBRID MODELS OR DICHOTOMOUS EAST–WEST MODEL? THE CHINESE CONSTITUTION AND THE MECHANICS AND STRUCTURE OF ITS DIPLOMATIC BRANCH

Northeast Asian political systems are a hybrid of Western ideologies and Northeast Asian traditions. Many of them show pragmatic features of grafting Western ideological control over Northeast Asian traditions. The difficulties of fitting into the Western model are detailed in the section on the Chinese constitution. There are two interpretations of what the Chinese constitution stands for. One interpretation conceptualizes the Chinese constitution as something not akin to the constitution found in the West. For example, the articles within the constitution can be changed according to circumstances and the needs of the party.

The constitution was most recently changed to remove the two terms "limit on the Chinese presidency" and "vice presidency". This effectively means that the Chinese president and vice president have their terms for life theoretically. This was voted into effect during the 13th National People's Congress (one of China's "twin parliaments" or *lianghui*). The constitution was also changed to create a super-agency that would oversee disciplinary, corruption and graft matters. The move meant President Xi Jinping and Vice President Wang Qishan are able to stay in power for life theoretically and enjoy the longevity of tenure that are rare in liberal democracies. The ease in which term limit conventions on the presidency and vice presidency positions were removed would be a comparatively difficult procedure in the West. Some Western countries may even require a two-thirds majority to make any significant changes.

The other interpretation of the Chinese constitution insists that it is closer to the Western interpretation of constitutional law. The fact that the presidency and vice presidency posts have removed their term limits meant that the constitution is there to serve the needs of the party rather than as untouchable sacred items. The limits were placed in the constitution by former paramount leader Deng Xiaoping who feared the return of chaos when there is unbridled power concentrated on a single person such as Mao's time with the Great Leap Forward and the Great Proletariat Cultural Revolution. The constitutional changes to the term limits came 14 years after 2004 when the constitution was last changed to enhance the protection of human rights and private ownership of property was inserted into it.

Constitutional changes were based on political consideration of continuity of rule for Chinese President Xi Jinping so that he is able to complete the political reforms of disciplining the Chinese Communist Party (CCP). Many in the party hope he can carry on with rooting out corruption, consolidating his power by removing those in his way and completing his "China Dream" of making China a developed country and economy. Then there is the all-important priority of seeing the CCP through its 100th year anniversary in 2049 in great strides, a hope nursed by the elite party leaders. Therefore, in this sense, party priorities were important political considerations as they are in legal stipulations when it comes to the amendment of the constitution. The trinity of roles (party secretary of the CCP, Chinese president of the Chinese state and the chairman of the Central Military Commission (CMC)) combined into one makes Xi the most powerful leader since Mao. Even Mao had his political opponents. Xi had recently removed the Gang of Six (the last of whom was Sun Zhengcai, the former party secretary of Chongqing) that remained the remnants of powerful resistance to his rule. The Gang of Six consisted of former internal security tsar Zhou Yongkang, former President Hu Jintao's right-hand man Ling Jihua, one of the leading generals Xu Caihou, Sun Zhengcai and his predecessor Bo Xilai and former vice chair of CMC Guo Boxiong.

To seasoned Sinologists, the constitution is a reference document rather than the published enshrined tenets and rights of the party. The combined trinity of role means the Chinese president will inevitably have a stronger hand in China's foreign diplomacy. There could be a kind of single-mindedness to his method of leadership. It would also mean less leeway for foreign powers to play off the different factions within the CCP to extract concessions. It also signals the end to Deng-ist leadership succession style where successors were appointed successively in advance to ensure political stability, as in the case of Jiang Zemin and

Zhu Rongji as well as Hu Jintao and Wen Jiabao and the failed pair Hu Yaobang and Zhao Ziyang.

The scope for pluralism is reduced by the appointment as China firms up its foreign policy direction surgically to maximize the interests of the Chinese state and its Communist Party. In terms of foreign economic policy, the Xi administration's most important project is still the Belt and Road Initiative (BRI, formerly known as the One Belt One Road). The BRI is an ambitious economic foreign policy scheme which will require tremendous negotiations with many sovereign states. Xi has also clocked the largest number of countries visited in his presidency in addition to hosting a large number of high-profile forums like the Belt and Road Forum. These are indications of a more robust foreign policy. The centralization of elite leadership developments in China also means that the process is less transparent and will keep foreign analysts and intelligence services guessing about China's strategic ambiguities.

CASES STUDIES OF POLITICAL LEADERSHIP — THE PEOPLE'S REPUBLIC OF CHINA — THE POST-19TH PARTY CONGRESS CHINESE LEADERSHIP

There are multiple nuclei of power in the Chinese political system. Since he assumed power in 2013, Chinese President Xi Jinping has been consolidating his power, shoring up support, connecting with the people and clearing out opposition through the same anti-corruption campaigns. His administration demanded strong loyalties from subordinates and supporters. His administration is also keen to demand technocratic and bureaucratic competence from government and party officials, including performance-based key performance indicators in leadership positions at the town, city and provincial levels. Most of the existing factions in the Chinese political circles have been cleared out, leaving his administration firmly in charge. Some have commented that President Xi is the most powerful Chinese president since the Mao era.

In the days leading up to the 19th Party Congress, Chinese President Xi handpicked his most trusted allies to come into power, including those who had spent time with him since childhood, teenage years, hardship decades during the cultural revolution and his provincial tours of duties as a young and rising leader. Among his loyalists, it appears his most trusted aide was Wang Qishan, the architecture of China's anti-corruption campaign. Wang was a feared leader as the head of the party's commission for discipline inspection. For his loyalty and his pure grit in facing the wrath of Xi's enemies and foes, Wang Qishan was first made a symbolic senior leader in the legislature after stepping down from his anti-corruption tsar status at the 19th Party Congress. He was then promoted to Vice President for life.

This effectively elevated the symbolic post of Vice President to become the second most powerful position in China with a lifetime tenure.

Chinese President Xi was particularly fond of his comrades who have worked with him during his stints as a provincial party leader in the Fujian and Zhejiang provinces. This was remarked as the rise of Fujian–Zhejiang factions (Fujian–Zhejiang *pai*) in Chinese politics. Some of these loyalists were elevated and entered the Politburo, the highest echelons of state power in the Chinese political structure. Their technocratic abilities were also needed to run the world's second largest economy and the complex global presence of China in almost every field imaginable. Because power consolidation was on the top of Xi's priorities, he placed great premium on the idea of familiarity and time-honoured camaraderie (especially with his dormmates, college buddies, fellow hardship comrades, etc.). In the Chinese political realm, rising leaders who are time-tested are considered honed for higher platforms of leadership, including managing difficult and restive provinces like Xinjiang (e.g. former President Hu Jintao's testing grounds when he was a younger leader) and reform beachheads (e.g. Fujian and Zhejing for Xi Jinping as a young provincial leader and Shenzhen for his father when he fell out of favour with Deng Xiaoping at the vice premier level).

In the midst of consolidating his power, Chinese President Xi has greatly sharpened the apex of the power structure in China. The Politburo was shrunk from 9 members to 7 and the posts of president and vice president were made lifetime-tenured positions. The age of collective leadership was over, in favour of strongman leadership. Consensus among the top leaders gave way to more decisive decision-making process, something the Chinese viewed as a better way to tackle the future challenges. They are set in their goal towards becoming a moderately prosperous society by 2021, manufacture world-class products through the "Made in China 2025" initiative and fight/win wars with a strong military.

Succession

In the 6th Party Plenum and the 19th Party Congress, President Xi's thoughts were immortalized. They were officially entered into the archives of the CCP. Xi Jinping's thoughts were also elevated to the same level as the written ideologies of previous leaders like Mao Zedong, Deng Xiaoping, Jiang Zemin and Hu Jintao. Xi's thoughts are textualized in his book *Xi Jinping: The Governance of China* and translated into many different languages. The tenet of these thoughts from top Chinese leaders was meant to lay out the model of "socialism with Chinese characteristics" to chart out their own indigenous model of development.

In terms of political status, Xi Jinping was also elevated to the "Core Leader" status in the same way that Mao Zedong became the "Great Helmsman" and Deng

Xiaoping became "paramount leader". The outcome of Chinese President Xi in not picking a successor at the 19th Party Congress immediately raised eyebrows, and soon, all questions were answered when it was declared that the posts of president and vice president would become tenured for life. The element of continuity embedded in these lifelong posts indicates the desire to have political economic stability, preserving status quo with incremental adaptations to the external environment and maintaining China's prosperity with sustainable growth. Strong leadership and tenured positions are favoured in China for their qualities of handling national crises.

Legislative Institution — China's Parliament (The *Lianghuis*)

Unlike Western democracies, the parliaments or legislatures of China play an advisory role and have no real, competitive and meaningful legislative role/power. There is no concept of parliamentary sovereignty in China. The *lianghui* participants represent the diversity of races, ethnicities and occupations in China. Participants play a symbolic role in exchanging information about their communities with each other at the sittings. The National People's Congress and the Chinese People's Political Consultative Conference (CPPCC) make up the *lianghuis* or twin parliamentary sittings. The Great Hall of the People, the location of the parliamentary sittings built in 1959, can accommodate 10,000 participants.

The *lianghuis* are an interesting peak into contemporary Chinese political affairs. They provide clues for the mass media, Sinologists and other China watchers through its previews of new policies in China. Because there is a diversity of backgrounds among the participants, observers can also gauge the reactions of different communities and groups to government policies. Ultimately, however, when the vote comes about, the two bodies will rubber-stamp vote according to directions by the CCP Politburo Standing Committee alongside executive power exercised by the state and the Chinese president. In rare moments in the past, there had been dissent or symbolic votes against these CCP directions, but they are far and few in between.

Nonetheless, the *lianghuis* give Chinese local and community leaders a chance to share their views on development and concerns from their constituencies. Some of the issues raised by delegates may also be of a localized nature. This may be their only chance to air such issues at a national platform. Foreigners are also able to observe some of these processes. They may hold clues to the format and shape of leadership changes, anti-corruption campaign outcomes, economic developments, progress of the BRI and other China-centered items. This may be an important function due to the secretive and non-transparent nature of policy-making political processes in China. Sometimes, even propaganda is useful for understanding the policy mindset or external gaze of the party.

The plenums held annually are also platforms in which the CCP inks out its 5-year plans (FYPs). Plenums tend to be secretive on the details but publicly release macro-agendas (broad outlines) to the mass media. The plenums are observed carefully by experts and stakeholders with regards to Chinese economic policies. For example, due to the slowly maturing Chinese economy, the 3rd Plenum sketched out the strategy to switch from export-led economic growth to internal consumption as an engine of growth. The 3rd Plenum also laid out plans for more effective allocation of land resources. The 5th Plenum relaxed the one-child policy in favour of two-child policy due to China's rapidly aging population. Even the two-child policy looks poised to be scrapped at the point of this writing. All these are done to tackle the very complicated question of how to provide welfare and elderly care to seniors in the future. China is aware that it is facing one of the world's largest demographic challenge, perhaps unprecedented even in world history.

Economically, the 5th Plenum is keen to look at technological means of future Chinese development. This would eventually manifest itself as Industry 4.0 technologies. Regardless of plenums, *lianghui*s and FYPs, all clues related to China's views on the global order are instructive on the macro factors that shape their foreign policy. The 6th Plenum held during 24–27 October 2016 set out to impose party discipline, eliminate corruption and continue with institutionalization of corruption watchdog bodies. Such campaigns apply equally to both public and private lives of CCP members. It greatly strengthens the process of weeding out corruption measures put in place since 2003, although the critics of China's anti-corruption campaign continue to argue that it is driven by political factors rather than social and legal justice.

China and the Global Order

In the era of Brexit (British departure from European Union), America First (the Trump administration's priority in putting US interest first), Make America Great Again and populism movements, China is perceived by some to be the most important country to defend free trade. China needs global free trade as its domestic economy slows down and is now dependent on new markets for its exports and future economic growth. In response, some of the developing economies are looking to China as a possible model of development and a source of developmental funding especially for infrastructure connectivity projects. This includes less developed countries like Laos and Cambodia, Chinese allies/partners like Pakistan and large emerging economies like Kazakhstan and Indonesia.

At the same time, the BRI has also incurred the suspicions and competitive instincts of other major powers. The US, Australia, Japan and India are aligning themselves into a Quadrilateral Security Dialogue or The Quad for short. ASEAN is trying to strengthen its solidarity to manage competition with India and China. The US is raising trade tariffs and fighting a potential trade war with China. Major EU countries like France and United Kingdom (UK) are sending their warships into the South China Sea to join the US in Freedom of Navigation Operations. Australia is preventing Huawei Chinese telecom company from operating its 5th-generation telecom technologies in Australia and also sending its warships to South China Sea (April 2018). Vietnam is aligning closer to the US. Malaysia has turned away from Chinese projects to lessen dependence on Chinese investments and debts. These developments are watched carefully by Beijing.

The urgency to shore up China's global role and internal stability is partly attributed to the maturing economy with slow speeds of growth, the growing urban spaces/middle class and their demand for clean environment, lagging agricultural populations and the symbolic need to shore up the CCP's legacy on its 100th anniversary (the CCP was established in 1921). Slow but sustainable environmental economic growth appears to be a major priority for China. Thus, controlling carbon emissions is an important factor for consideration in China's near-future economic growth. These factors are crucial for maintaining China's continued relevance, legitimacy and popularity with the people.

CASE STUDY OF THE HONG KONG SPECIAL ADMINISTRATIVE REGION[1]

The previous sections discussed the parliamentary mechanism, political system, party entities, realpolitik and plenum sittings in China. They all point towards the trend of greater centralization of power to manage difficult tasks and crisis ahead for China. One such crisis appeared early in Xi's career in 2014 with the rise of the Occupy Central movement. Beyond this crisis, there remains the longer term challenge of re-integrating Hong Kong back to the mainland, especially with the young Hong Kongers' increasing aspirations towards greater autonomy and freedom and even independence (which has just been declared illegal in Hong Kong at the point of this writing). This section on the Hong Kong case study looks at the political leadership dynamics at play between Hong Kong political elites and Beijing. It will also examine how the two sides try to reach a compromise when it comes to leadership exchanges.

---

[1] This section is derived from: Lim, Tai Wei, "Hong Kong's Chief Executive Elections 2017: A Look at the Candidates" dated 9 February 2017 in IPP Review [downloaded on 9 Feb 2017], available at http://www.ippreview.net/index.php/Article/single/id/67.html.

Special Autonomous Region — Hong Kong's Designated Role

Strong leadership was meant to smoothen out China's transition from a developing economy to a mature one with slowing economic growth and to manage bilateral and geopolitical economic relations with the US. Strong stable leadership was also needed to manage the integration of Hong Kong into China's fold. Beijing had warned the organizers of the Occupy Central movement's futility. Beijing was also keen to tighten up control over the Hong Kong Special Autonomous Region (HKSAR). In the years following Occupy Central, Beijing has interpreted the Basic Law to indicate that the chief executive (CE) candidates for Hong Kong must not go against Beijing and need to have a strong sense of love for the motherland. Beijing also banned the Hong Kong independence movement, prevented its candidates from running for legislative election, expelled candidates with leanings towards the movement, etc. Beijing has also established that the new high-speed rail station in West Kowloon would come under Chinese laws. Former top Chinese leader Zhang Dejiang also met with some selected moderate pro-democracy party leaders before Chinese leader Xi Jinping's visit to the Special Administrative Region (SAR).

China's plan for Hong Kong is to turn it into the country's premium offshore *renminbi* (Chinese yuan currency) trading centre. Beijing is keen to align Hong Kong closer to its BRI, especially in the financing aspects. Hong Kong also wants to be a super-corridor to tap into the technologies and research and development opportunities afforded by the BRI. In facilitating BRI projects, Hong Kong's advantages may be in the ability to intermediate in English language, familiarity with Western law (especially British common law in contract law, property law, tort, shipping law, etc.) as well as traditional relationships with Southeast Asia, Japan and the West. Hong Kong also has a strong reputation and history in finance and banking activities which can be of benefit to BRI funding activities. Hong Kong is likely to coordinate such activities closely with Shanghai, Shenzhen and Qianhai, as they compete with other East Asian first-tier cities like Singapore, Seoul, Tokyo, Osaka, Taipei and Kuala Lumpur in the financial, logistics, banking and insurance industries.

At a macro-level, Beijing is also keen to align Hong Kong closer to China's sovereignty and overall masterplan of development. Patriotism, national interests and political systems have to converge gradually, in accordance with Beijing's thinking. A number of prominent individuals and organizations have emerged to support Beijing's priorities and causes. They include pro-Beijing groups in the unions, trade associations, political parties, etc. They also include pro-Beijing politicians or those who toe the line like C.Y. Leung, Regina Yip and Carrie Lam.

Older politicians like Tung Chee Hwa and C.Y. Leung were elevated to elder statesmen status and now participate in China's mainly rubber-stamp but still indirectly influential parliaments (the *lianghui*).

In the business sector, the so-called red chip or mainland companies are also gradually moving into Hong Kong and using the SAR as a platform to launch their businesses, trade and exports overseas. They are displacing some of the multinationals' presence as well as the British-era tycoons in the SAR. HKSAR's best hope for state policy lobbying and also gathering informational scoops from top leaders is probably at the CPPCC level where they have some representation by former CEs (i.e. CY Leung and Tung Chee Hwa). CY Leung, the retired CE at the point of this writing, was appointed one of the vice chairs of CPPCC. He can now participate in politics at the national level and try to look out for Hong Kongers' interests. Even though some of his Hong Kong political foes tried to block the appointment, Beijing granted him the appointment, reflecting their tacit approval of his work when he was the CE of HKSAR.

In the post CY Leung era, several candidates vied to succeed him. Among them, Carrie Lam obtained Beijing's strongest support. Carrie Lam Cheng Yuet-ngor, the former Chief Secretary of Hong Kong under the CY Leung administration, was also popular with the public and among women. She made history when she became the first female to assume the Hong Kong's highest political appointment. Despite being less savvy with social media, making a few faux pas during campaigning and not Facebooking her campaign earlier in the CE elections, Carrie Lam won the election. Her working-class roots appealed to Hong Kongers, and her abilities were demonstrated through entering Hong Kong University (HKU), and rising up in Hong Kong's elite administrative service. In the civil service, Lam was known to be a caring and affable superior, almost like a likeable nanny. To the mass media, Lam was no nonsense and professional with an iron-lady touch. Initially reluctant to run for CE, Lam was persuaded by her husband to do so and decided to serve the general public. Finally, Lam was well-loved by the womenfolk as housewives gathered round her to take photos during the campaigning season.

Another elite female political figure is Regina Ip. Born to a HKSAR-based business family, Ip has experienced her share of downturns when her family's business ran into economic challenges. Thus, she had a taste of humbler living conditions at a time. Politically, at this moment, Ip is known as a pro-Beijing figure and was a former head of the internal security apparatus in Hong Kong. As the HKSAR's first Secretary of Security, Ip was also known as the iron lady. Like Lam, Ip was no-nonsense in the public realm. Schooled in Stanford University, Ip was in favour of Article 23, a strengthening of internal security procedures in Hong Kong. She also founded a think tank, ran for legislative elections and participated in the Article 23 debate.

The previous HKSAR CE Tung Chee Hwa had attempted to introduce it into the legislations but failed. After the Occupy Central movement, Beijing is redoubling its effort to introduce this piece of law. Like Lam who graduated from HKU, Ip is also a HKU graduate but in the field of literature. Like Lam, she also rose up in the bureaucracy to become the Director of Immigration in the 1990s. A straight-talker, Ip is not afraid to critique other prominent figures in HKSAR. She has also made housing provision and social equity her CE candidature platforms in the past. Gender rights appear to be high on Ip's agenda. Other issues included removing discrimination against same-sex marriage/unions. Ip has fought for women's rights too and has a reputation for not giving up on her advocacy.

Remarks

The Chinese case study appears to indicate a growing trend towards centralization of power, including Politburo membership reduction, making presidential and vice presidential posts tenured for life, extending stronger control over special autonomous regions and strengthening a strongman regime. These measures are put into place due to perceptions of threats from the external changing environment and the accent on maintaining internal political stability. The Chinese government has many transitions to manage. Its economy is switching gears from Chinese exports to meet external demand to internal consumption as an engine of growth. Hong Kong is transiting from a British colonial outpost to an autonomous region with a high degree of self-rule to re-integrating to become a part of China. The CCP is also trying to stay relevant as questions of its legitimacy, legacy and relevance are raised. China is also coping with rapid urbanization as its rural populations shrink below 50% and the rise of the middle class which is vocal about its environmental expectations and lifestyle choices. The challenges that China has to surmount are enormous. Though leadership systemic changes are put in place to manage, only time can tell the level of success attainable. The next chapter will go on to discuss leadership issues in other East Asian states for a comparative perspective.

Chapter 4

LEADERSHIP IN EAST ASIA

T. W. Lim

Singapore University of Social Sciences and
National University of Singapore, Singapore

THE CASE STUDY OF JAPAN

Japanese leadership style is based on consensus, much like its collectivist and groupist society. In terms of society, the Japanese had always strived for harmonious relationships between individuals. In fact, the ancient civilizational racial term for the Japanese people was the *Wa* civilization. The word *Wa* is itself the Kanji (Chinese origins) character that means "harmony". An effective leader in Japan is a person who is able to bring different factions of the political stage together. This may require a compromise, but it ensures all are aboard when a major decision is made. This is quite different from the feature of highly centralized Chinese leadership in the previous chapter. In Japan, bringing together all factional leaders ensures strong support behind the decision, but it may also take time to make that decision.

The Japanese ruling and opposition parties are led by senior factional leaders and *genro* party elders, and their opinions are crucial in policy-making. Seniority, prestige and pedigree count in the seniority systems within each political faction. It is a form of *oyabun* system where a compassionate factional boss takes care of his subordinates in exchange for their loyalties. Past attempts by former Japanese Prime Minister Junichiro Koizumi to destroy party factions have only be partially successful. The *habatsu* (faction) system remains today, although in a somewhat weakened form but is nevertheless influential. At the very top of the political structure, Japan has a symbolic monarchy that assumes the role of the head of state.

CONSTITUTIONAL MONARCHY IN JAPAN

The Japanese imperial family system is considered the world's oldest monarchy by some observers/historians. This view is not universally accepted. While some intellectual works noted that it has been a continuous line for 2000 straight years since Emperor Jimmu, other scholarly work noted the mythical nature of the pre-historic eras. Throughout much of Japan's history, the Japanese emperor was a weak figure who listened to the leader of the samurai class (the Shogun) and/or received protection from him. The emperor was at the peak of his military and executive powers during the militarization period of the 1930s as he became the central figure in deciding the deployment of troops for war.

The current carnation of the Japanese emperor system follows US postwar reforms that converted the status of the emperor from a god-like figure and leader of the state religion of Shinto to a pacifist symbolic emperor who embodied values of the Japanese nation. He was also recast as a mortal and gave up his executive/legislative power to the Japanese bicameral parliamentary system. At the time of this writing, the Heisei emperor who assumed power in 1989 has decided to step down in favour of his eldest son due to reasons of ill-health. This is a rare abdication event that has not happened for about 200 years. The last emperor who abdicated was Emperor Kokaku in 1817. The Heisei emperor sought consultation with the Japanese government under the constitution and he was procedurally cleared to step down. The constitutional monarchy is governed by Article Four of the Japanese constitution. It is a political system where executive powers are delegated to the parliament and cabinet.

The affairs of the Imperial family are also governed by the Imperial Household Law. The public is mostly supportive of his abdication, sympathetic to health reasons. The government expert panel was also supportive. Japan is careful to reach consensus on all issues before proceeding with major decisions, whether in the political realm or the corporate sector. As for the future, the Crown Prince is likely to be succeeded by his younger brother Prince Akishino or his son Prince Hisahito. The young prince reminds some Japanese people of his grandfather, because both Prince Hisahito and Emperor Hirohito (the Showa emperor) have an interest in rice planting. Rice has both symbolic and practical meanings in Japanese culture, as a staple food for the people and also an important component of the agricultural industry.

Emperor Akihito was schooled by a Philadelphia-born Quaker female teacher and kids' book writer, Elizabeth Gray Vining. Quakers are pacifists, so she must have had a lasting liberal and pacifist influence on the Heisei emperor. The young Emperor Akihito was raised separately from the parents by the state under the influence of Vining who prescribed publications by Gandhi (who came up with non-violent passive resistance) for the prince's reading list. Vining herself was part of the resistance against the US-led Vietnam War and had been arrested by the authorities. She passed away in 1999. Vining's pacifism influenced the Japanese emperor who preached peace during the duration of his appointment as emperor. Prince Akihito married his wife Princess Michiko in an unprecedented marriage due to the commoner status of Michiko. Although she was not royalty, Michiko came from a powerful business conglomerate family. In these ways, he was very much a people's emperor.

JAPANESE FEMALE POLITICAL LEADERS

While Empress Michiko played the symbolic and meticulously performed role of an Empress, Japanese women were imprinting their leadership marks on the political system consistently. A pioneering (probably the first) Japanese female leader in contemporary Japan and the former head of the Social Democratic Party of Japan, Doi Takako led her party to credible results in the February 1990 elections in Japan and garnered ~25% of the ballots. Like her, all female candidates running under Doi's party secured a seat in the parliament (known as the "Diet" in Japan). This was a milestone for opposition leadership and for women's rights. Doi herself was a constitutional law professor, a no-nonsense politician and more pragmatic. She was a pragmatist who preferred to take her ideas mainstream rather than identifying dogmatically with a particular political ideology. A reformist, Doi did battle with ideological purists within her own political party who were not agreeable to reform the party's image to make it more palatable to mainstream voters. In terms of economic influence, companies and agricultural units that found it hard to compete against foreign competitors and cope with globalization supported the social democrats.

Opposition parties continued to attract crops of women to their causes. The most recent entrant was Renho (full name Renho Murata, a half-Japanese, half-Taiwanese politician). Renho not only broke the gender barriers (although the first), she broke racial barrier as a mixed-race candidate. Her Taiwanese ancestry was used against her during election campaigns and leadership races. Renho became a poster child for both racial diversity causes as well as feminism as the leader of the Democratic Party of Japan (DPJ or Minshinto in Japanese). In the 16 September 2016 edition of *TIME* magazine, an article noted that Renho may even have a shot at female prime ministership. Renho's appointment ended in a leadership tussle between her colleagues Yukio Edano and Seiji Maehara (the winner).

Despite this, her achievement may open the way for other women to follow suit. The opposition parties are not the only entities to have attracted capable female political leaders. Makiko Tanaka, daughter of charismatic and powerful heavyweight politician Kakuei Tanaka, became Japan's first female foreign minister in the Koizumi administration. Tanaka was outspoken, pragmatic on foreign affairs and carried the legacy of her famous father Kakuei Tanaka, a person instrumental in leading Japan to normalize relations with China and was seen as an old friend of China, even after he was brought down by a scandal. Tanaka was a popular politician, especially with women but sometimes ruffled the feathers of conservatives within her own party.

Liberal Democratic Party's (LDP) long-standing ruling party also oversaw the rise of two female defence ministers — Yuriko Koike and Tomomi Inada. Yuriko Koike spoke fluent Arab and was a well-known TV journalist. Under the patronage of former Japanese Prime Minister Morihiro Hosokawa, Koike was introduced into politics. She eventually joined the LDP. Known for her conservative views, she rose through the rank and file and took over the portfolio of defence minister. Exposing her ambitions of prime ministership, she ran against Taro Aso to become the prime minister of Japan. She eventually fell out of favour with the party leadership in the Abe administration and left the party to run for the Governor of Tokyo. LDP did not support her bid. She won and became Tokyo's first female Governor. Koike now handles the challenging task of organizing Tokyo Olympics 2020 and appears to be effective in managing the difficult task, including the politically sensitive issue of relocating the Tsukiji fish market (world's largest) from Tsukiji to a new site in Toyosu (that was discovered to be benzene-tainted but has since been comprehensively cleared up). She also formed her own party to run in the national elections but was soundly defeated. Koike is now concentrating her energies on managing Tokyo's day-to-day pulse effectively.

Tomomi Inada is Japan's second female defence minister after Yuriko Koike. A conservative, Inada has been compared to her counterpart in the US, Sarah Palin of the Conservative Tea Party within the Republican Party. Graduating from the prestigious Waseda University's Faculty of Law, she entered politics and advocated for the policies that can help Japan prepare for the knowledge-based enterprises in the future. Inada eventually had to step down for associating her party with the Self Defence Forces to canvas for votes. Regardless of their political outcomes, Inada and Koike both blazed the way for future women in politics to take up ministerial posts, governorships and leaders in the corridors of power in Japan.

JAPAN'S REGIONAL ECONOMIC ROLE

Like China, Australia, New Zealand and Canada in the Asia Pacific, Japan is also advocating the maintenance of free trade in the region. Unlike China, Japan and the other Western countries in the Asia Pacific also want fair trade. Japan plays a crucial role in aggregating all the regional trade pacts together as it lends support to Beijing-led Regional Comprehensive Economic Partnership (RCEP) and to the formerly US-inclusive Trans-Pacific Partnership (TPP). For the latter, the TPP is now led by Japan and Australia in the newly minted Comprehensive and Progressive Trans-Pacific Partnership (CPTPP). Japanese leadership in advocating regional free trade is lauded by all who want to rollback populism and protectionist sentiments in the developed economies. CPTPP remains open for the US to rejoin in the future when it is ready.

Japan is also keenly considering to join the Asian Infrastructure Investment Bank (AIIB), an item the country mentioned during the One Belt One Road Forum (now known as Belt and Road Initiative or BRI) in 2017 where 29 world leaders and delegations participated. At that point of time, old China hand, Toshihiko Nikai, General Secretary of the ruling LDP (re-appointed in his post by Prime Minister Abe after Abe won the right to stay as a leader in his own party for the third term), galvanized sentiments of Japanese people who wished to join China's regional body.

Japan is also open to the idea of working with China in RCEP and BRI. RCEP is a low-lying fruit for free-trade advocates in Japan. RCEP has lower standards for free trade (compared to the golden standards for TPP in terms of labour rights, human rights, intellectual property rights, etc.) and therefore Japan and other RCEP-interested countries may be able to agree and sign the agreement relatively easily compared to TPP.

JAPAN'S SOFT POWER

Besides tangible economic power, Japan is said to have considerable soft cultural power. Originally, the term "soft power" was meant to refer to US global leadership qualities. The term originated from Prof Joseph Nye, former dean of the Harvard University's Kennedy School of Government and a one-time senior diplomat. Soft power is the ability to get something done by allies/partners/friends without using force. Some popular cultural scholars have appropriated the term to refer to popular cultural consumption. A good example of a Japanese product that has gone global is Pokemon with its "Gotta catch em all" battle cry.

Pokemon first became popular with children in Japan as a card game and TV show before its sales penetrated the lucrative US market and became a global sensation. It is considered cultural soft power because many consumers bought the products willingly and, through the products, children and fans all over the world wanted to find more about Japanese language and traditional culture and were interested to travel to Japan for tourism. This can be a great boost to Japanese Track II diplomacy. The following section will highlight some comparative leadership styles in the context of East Asia. It does not pretend to be comprehensive.

INDIVIDUAL CASE STUDY: THE KOREAN PENINSULA

Next to Japan, the Korean Peninsula is undergoing an important change. After former conservative President Park Geun Hye ended her presidency in disgrace and was jailed for improper exercise of influence through a close confidante (Choi Soon-sil who extorted money from Korean conglomerates for political favours), South Koreans voted a liberal/left-leaning leader President Moon Jae-in (64 years old) into power. Park's presidency saw her administration upgrading relations with China. In fact, Park and Russian President Vladimir Putin were the two major world leaders who attended 70th anniversary of the end of Second World War and the war against fascism in Beijing.

Other world leaders from the West questioned the validity of the event based on Nationalists (Kuomintang) and Taiwanese accounts of the Pacific War history. Park also lobbied hard to join the TPP, before the TPP was torn up by US President Donald Trump who succeeded the pro-TPP Obama administration. In an unexpected twist, Park reconciled with Japan over the comfort women issue. Under Park's watch, South Korea became a much-aspired middle power in the East Asian region.

The successor President Moon once served in the South Korean Special Forces. Popular with the working-class/middle-class folks, Moon came from humble roots as the son of a Korean War refugee from North Korea who became a hardworking employee in South Korea. Moon grew up in Geoje and was a student activist who demonstrated against South Korean dictator General Park Chung Hee (former President Park Geun Hye's father). Moon worked his way through constitutional legal studies and had former liberal President Roh Tae Moo-Hyun as his political patron. (Roh is suspected to have committed suicide after he was involved in a scandal). Moon's liberal rule followed the conservative administrations of presidents Lee Myung Bak and Park Geun Hye. Due to the problems Park had with the country's family-owned *chaebol* conglomerates (i.e. her confidante's undue influence over them), there were public expectations for Moon to tackle the *chaebol*s by promoting transparency, accountability, corporate governance and equal opportunities for promotions and appointments. These conglomerates were the industrial foundations for South Korean global manufacturing prowess.

Moon's appointment was opportune at a time when the Korean Peninsula tensions were red hot. North Korea under the third generation of the Kim dynasty (Kim Jong Un) tested nuclear devices and missiles repeatedly. It provoked strong reactions from the US and its allies, including the deployment of USS Carl Vinson fleet to the waters surrounding the Korean Peninsula. US destroyers armed with Tomahawk cruise missiles were also deployed to the waters off the Korean

Peninsula. They were joined by South Korean, Japanese and even French forces at times. Pyongyang's belligerent behaviour also triggered Beijing to deploy troops and long-range bombers. South Korea was spooked enough to deploy the Terminal High-Altitude Area Defense missiles to intercept North Korean missiles. It was a decision that was criticized by Beijing and resulted in almost 1 year of trade/business/tourism embargo from China on South Korea. The tensions however died when President Moon worked overtime to help bring about the Trump–Kim summit in Singapore, with the support from Beijing and Washington. He constantly updated Tokyo about the latest developments. The Trump–Kim summit to bring about Complete Verifiable Irreversible Denuclearization was almost universally welcomed by the East Asian region.

While South Korea was managing challenges from a nuclear-armed Pyongyang and trying to stave off a hot war between Pyongyang and Washington, North Korea was undergoing a carefully managed leadership transition with the death of Kim Jong Il and the rise of Kim Jong Un. North Korea is ideal for the study of dynastic autocratic leadership succession. The Kim dynasty in Pyongyang was founded by the patriarch Kim Il Sung (grandfather of the current North Korean Supreme Leader). During the Cold War, the North Korean state enjoyed support from the Soviet Union (USSR) and the People's Republic of China (PRC). In fact, the USSR provided equipment for the North Koreans while the PRC supplied "volunteers" to support Pyongyang in the Korean War (1950–1953). This was the first hot war of the Cold War era and the only one that remains unresolved till today.

According to family seniority and family hierarchy, the heir apparent was supposed to be Kim Jong Nam (Kim Jong Il's eldest son, alias Kim Chul) but he displeased his father with erratic behaviour like going to Disneyland on a fake Dominican Republic passport with his helper and son. He was repatriated back to Pyongyang via Beijing but the deed was done. Jong Nam was disgraced and never regained legitimacy to be the heir apparent to rule North Korea thereafter. Jong Nam was born in 1971 and his mother Song Hye Rim was former Supreme Leader Kim Jong Il's favourite lady companion and wife. (In contrast, current North Korean leader Kim Jong Un's mother Ko Yong Hui was an ambitious lady who pushed her son hard to become the next North Korean Leader.) In exile, Jong Nam married one of his all-female group of bodyguards and bought properties in Malaysia, Singapore, Hong Kong, Macau and China. He apparently surrounded himself with some female friends in all these places.

Jong Nam was eventually assassinated in Kuala Lumpur by a Vietnamese woman (supposedly a former contestant in an American Idol-like talent show in Vietnam) and an Indonesian lady (said to be a former helper who was abused by her lover) who allegedly thought they were part of a gag on TV. With Jong Nam out of the way, Jong Un's regime faced no succession rivals and the regime focused their energies on developing weapons of mass destruction. Pyongyang saw these weapons as their best insurance for regime survival. Pyongyang accelerated their missile and nuclear programs, especially the Inter Continental Ballistic Missiles (ICBMs) with the longest ranges that can reach continental mainland USA.

Even without the confirmed development of nuclear weapons, Pyongyang already has sarin-tipped missile warheads that are mountable onto former Cold War-vintage Soviet Scud-inspired missile systems, alongside some atomic weapon devices, potentially deliverable using a bomber (antiquated Soviet-era bombers in the case of North Korea) and maybe even a Sinpo class (Cold War-vintage, Soviet era) submarine (Sinpo is apparently named after a North Korean submarine base constructed in mid-20th century). The vintage sub is modified to launch cruise missiles. It may be possible that, in the future, the cruise missiles may be fitted with some kind of nuclear and/or chemical weapons warhead. North Korea still has not shown that it is capable of miniaturizing atomic/nuclear warheads to fit on top of long-range missiles (especially ICBMs) or possess the radar systems that can navigate such complicated weapons.

CONCLUDING REMARKS

Perhaps, one of the most significant event at the point of this writing between 2013 and 2018 is Sino-Japanese rapprochement. With the outbreak of the North Korean missile crisis, Japan and China, at odds with each other since 2010, suddenly found common strategic issues to rally around. When the Japanese political opposition DPJ was voted into power, their leaders lacked experience in dealing with China and caused Sino-Japanese relations to spiral out of control. (Placing into context, the ruling LDP was a dominant party for more than half a century and had briefly lost power only twice in the early 1990s and 2010–2013. It was always able to form a coalition with minor parties like the Buddhist-rooted Komeito Party to return to power.) The bilateral relations took a further hit with the confrontation over Senkaku/Diaoyu islands (Senkaku are administered by the Japanese government, the Chinese government calls them Diaoyu while the Taiwanese authorities name them Diaoyutai). It took all the way till November 2014 for two strongmen, Chinese President Xi Jinping and Japanese Prime Minister Shinzo Abe to reach some form of rapprochement reinforced through further meetings in Bandung and other regional events before both sides became comfortable with bilateral meetings on a regular basis. One of the things they agreed on was to set up a maritime hotline to prevent accidents at sea, especially around the Senkaku/Diaoyu areas.

Due to the efforts of many stakeholders including the experienced old China hands in Japan (politicians and government officials) and hardworking state councillors in Beijing, the bilateral relations got back on track again. Icy relations between the two thawed gradually and incrementally. At the point of this writing, Beijing was extremely keen to repair relations with Tokyo, due to its ongoing trade conflict with the US. Beijing needed Tokyo's support in the RCEP agreement. Tokyo wanted to have more regional free-trade agreements to stave off the onset of populist movements and anti-globalization sentiments unleashed around the world, especially the West. Beijing is also keen to invite Japan to join the AIIB and contribute to the BRI. Beijing is facing a tough time in a trade conflict with the US, a tit-for-tat trade sanctions application. Japan is cautious about membership due to its strong alliance with the US. When Prime Minister Abe was voted for the third term as LDP's party leader in late September 2018, one of his major pledges was to put Sino-Japanese relations on a more stable footing henceforth.

In the growing contestation between China and the US, Beijing is trying to reach out to all friends, competitors and partners alike for solidarity in maintaining free trade. Thailand and China are bound together in "comprehensive strategic cooperative partnership", although skilful Thai diplomacy is hedging against Beijing's growing regional power and influence by tapping into its traditional friendship with the US (especially through military exchanges, e.g. Exercise Cobra Gold). The Thai royalty have had both positive and challenging exchanges in the past with the Chinese, justifying the approach of engaging all major powers simultaneously. The Islamic Republic of Pakistan is an ironclad brother (*tiegermen*) for Beijing, while North Korea is propped up by Beijing's material help. Perhaps the most important aspect of Sino-Thai relations is the personal ties between the Thai royal family with the Chinese leadership since both established official ties in 1975.

Bilateral visits were quite regular and common. The late Thai King Bhumibol welcomed former Chinese President Jiang Zemin to the Bangkok airport in 1999 while Princess Maha Chakri Sirindhorn visits China regularly. In fact, historically, paramount leader Deng visited Thailand to witness the Crown Prince's ordination ceremony and even presented him with a robe as a gift. For a long time, skilful Thai diplomacy and leadership skills have historically positioned Thailand as a buffer state between great powers. Initially, Thailand was able to play the French against the British and vice versa during the age of imperialism (in fact Thailand and Japan were the only two East Asian states that were not colonized), and now the Thais have preserved a good relationship with both the Chinese and the Americans. Regionally, China's diplomatic skills in Indo-China appear to be somewhat more successful than in the maritime Southeast Asian sector.

Perhaps, this is due to the fact that Indo-China is much more proximate to China's borders than maritime Southeast Asia. Currently, Cambodia and Laos are the strongest partners/allies to China in Southeast Asia. In the case of Cambodia, the close relationship had been around since the days of Prince Sihanouk's exile and Chinese support for the hard-line Khmer Rouge regime. Landlocked Laos is now integrated into the Chinese BRI (critics say it has gotten too close and chalked up excessive debt, i.e. overdependence on China) while Beijing maintains a close relationship with Myanmar's former military junta rulers. The latter relationship was affected by the democratization of Myanmar under Aung San Suu Kyi but has since recovered in favour of the Chinese due to Beijing's vote of support against discussing the Rohingya crisis at the United Nations (UN) level. In the Indo-China area, the only exception is Vietnam which has historical animosities against the Chinese (most recently in Qing dynasty and was a Chinese vassal state for more than 1,000 years) and also wants to stand as an independent pole against Beijing's interests in the region.

Chapter 5

LEADERSHIP LESSONS OF A SMALL STATE IN CENTRAL ASIA: KYRGYZSTAN, AMIDST EMPIRES

F. Vivien* and T. W. Lim[†]

*Asie21 and IÉSEG Business School, France
[†]Singapore University of Social Sciences and
National University of Singapore, Singapore

INTRODUCTION

The first three chapters of this section on political leadership have focused on large powers, laid some emphases on middle powers and also looked at regionalism as an instrument to constrain large powers to follow international norms and behaviour. They are macro- and meso-level topics that are important and crucial in discussing big power relations, setting international norms and also detecting how domestic politics affect regional and international diplomatic behaviour. This chapter zooms in further and looks at small states instead, a micro-level analysis. Very often, small states are neglected and marginalized in literature on international relations (IRs). This chapter attempts to fill in the gap for academic discussions on the role of small states in major power actions and behaviour by focusing on a single case study and examining its role in the regional/international system in relatively greater depth. In addition to interpretive work, this essay's methodology also adopts field trips and on-site observation studies as well.

SMALL STATES: A LITERATURE REVIEW OF THE SUBJECT MATTER

Small states are often associated with vulnerability in international affairs. The idea of smallness is often associated either with their comparatively small land areas (e.g. Pacific Island nations) or with their relatively smaller populations (e.g. the Sultanate of Brunei). Small states are sometimes defined as countries having population between 10 and 15 million people or less.[1] Consequently, they evolve different strategies to cope with these vulnerabilities. Some jumped on the bandwagon with other major powers to ensure their survival in the international system. Bandwagoning extends to even middle powers like South Korea and Japan that are engaged in formal alliances with the United States and its security umbrella. Others join regional organizations for economy of scale in negotiating with other big powers. Association of Southeast Asian Nations (ASEAN) and European Union (EU) are examples of such regional organizations that have become important vehicles for collective self-defence and/or economic cooperation and integration.

While some countries see size as a disadvantage, some small states have turned their sizes into an advantage by demonstrating global and/or regional leadership in some niche areas. Iceland, for example, is a global benchmark for gender equality in pay. It therefore exudes some form of moral leadership in international social affairs. Singapore is often regarded as an exemplary example of statecraft and the intellectual 'brain of the regional organization of ASEAN' and is respected for its pragmatism in international economic affairs like the promotion of free trade agreements (FTAs). Hong Kong, a Special Autonomous Region (SAR) of China, is a leading financial centre in the world with rule of law. Brunei has exceptional fossil fuel wealth and is one of the richest countries in the world per capita. In fact, some scholars argue that the only way for small states to survive is to demonstrate leadership in regional and international affairs. For example, Baldur Thorhallsson argues: "Moreover, to become active and successful, small states need to demonstrate strong leadership, excellent coalition-building skills and an ability to prioritize heavy workloads."[2]

This writing focuses on a less prominent entity like Kyrgyzstan that has neither exceptional wealth per capita, nor a role as a leading financial centre of the world, nor widely recognized moral leadership (at least not according to traditional Western definition) nor widely known statecraft (at least in textbook

---

[1] Thorhallsson, Baldur, "Small States in the UN Security Council: Means of Influence?," *The Hague Journal of Diplomacy* 7 (2012), p. 136, available at http://uni.hi.is/baldurt/files/2012/08/Small-States-UN-Security-Council-by-Thorhallsson.pdf [downloaded on 1 January 2018].

[2] *Ibid.*, p. 140.

example). It contributes to existing literature on small-state diplomacy by looking at the practical difficulties faced by small states with limited resources and yet are being courted by the world's major powers. In the case of Kyrgyzstan, it is being courted by Beijing, Moscow and Washington among other major powers.

Its main potential for leadership and strategic value is its central geographical position that lies in the middle of larger regional entities. Providing access for major powers then becomes a major bargaining chip for Kyrgyzstan to extract more economic and strategic benefits for its economic well-being and security interests. Its restive population with proud nomadic roots combined with a relatively democratic system ensures the country is not beholden to any single great power as any major power's lobby group has to contend with a restive population that is ever ready to assert its rights. In other words, it is not an easy country to subjugate.

The fact that it has shifted itself into a pivotal position among the regional and major powers lends credibility to Kyrgyzstan's role as an intermediating platform between these major powers. The residual influence of Moscow is present in its media and political groups, which is counterbalanced by a robust American diplomatic presence in the country, which in turn is pivoted by rising Chinese economic power in the country and the region. In other world regions, countries in Kyrgyzstan's position have ended up playing important global roles as the intermediator of regional interests, including major power interests in those regions. In Europe, neutral Switzerland and strategic Austria have been able to contribute to peacemaking in the region by aggregating the various regional interests of those powers and reaching a point of compromise or equilibrium amidst those varying interests.

In the case of Southeast Asia, Singapore has played an important role as a traditional friend of US and Japan while serving as an economic model for the economic development of the People's Republic of China (PRC) and a contributor to regional trade and development within ASEAN. If Kyrgyzstan positions its own national interests well, it can move itself into such an intermediating platform in the Central Asian region as an entity small enough not to pose a threat to regional and global powers yet strategic enough to offer tangible benefits to regional countries. Its leadership lies in skilful statecraft to navigate the interests of these countries.

INTRODUCTION TO THE CASE STUDY OF KYRGYZSTAN

Kyrgyzstan, a small Central Asian republic, is the target of Chinese economic appetite. While the local population and political elites are torn between historical ties with the Russians and the Chinese future prospects, Beijing is using its financial weight to increase the extent of its economic influence. However, between the rise of radical Islam among the Uighurs, Russian resistance and a fierce and proud indigenous nationalistic population, China faces many challenges in extending its influence into Kyrgyzstan and the region. Stuck between the Kazak and Uzbek giants, less than 200 km from North Pakistan and Afghanistan, and separated from China by the so-called "Celestial Mountains" (a literal translation of the mountain known as *Tian Shan* in Chinese Hanyu Pinyin Romanisation), Kyrgyzstan is the Gordian knot of Central Asia.

The only real democracy in the region, the country is also the only country to adopt a flexible attitude towards the acceptance of different religions and religious practices. But the country is also one of the hubs of drug trafficking and the arrival point for Chinese products, including a large majority of legal products, as well as counterfeiting and smuggling products. The United States also makes a strategic point with an embassy staffed by more than 300 members, against two for the French Embassy in the same locale. For Nargiza Muratalieva, a researcher of Central Asian Bureau for Analytical Reporting think tank, "…the sanctions against Russia since 2014 have accelerated the phenomenon of financial disengagement from Moscow in the area."[3]

In the need for developing its infrastructures, the country has looked for other opportunities. Turkey was seen as a potential support given the cultural and political ties, but the funds offered by Turkey were too low and the recent tensions between President Atambayev and Erdogan about the Gulen weight in Kyrgyzstan have not improved the situation. China, on the contrary, has proposed the construction of infrastructures under very favourable conditions with the Belt and Road Initiative (BRI). Kyrgyzstan, by way of its central position in the region, is one of the points of interest to convey the Chinese products to not only Uzbekistan and Turkmenistan but also Afghanistan and Iran. How can one truly blame the leaders of one of the poorest countries in the world, a GDP just above Somalia and lower than Niger, for accepting the Chinese offer? On top of that, European and American funds are virtually absent.

POPULAR PROTEST

What is clearly a politically coherent decision, however, raises important contentions. The two recurrent complaints concern the lack of economic benefits (especially spin-off benefits for the local community) from infrastructure projects financed and built by Chinese companies (especially the large state-owned enterprises, SOEs, often involved in infrastructural development), as well as environmental damages

---

[3] Quotation supplied by Vivien Fortat.

arising from the mega projects. The financing of infrastructure projects, generally granted under the Chinese BRI project, is essentially developmental work carried out by Chinese companies (usually SOEs), employing Chinese workers. The Kyrgyz population believes that these projects, requiring low-skilled labour, could reduce employment in areas affected by poverty.

Nevertheless, Chinese companies explain that they had tried to hire local people but their productivity was too low, and their social requirements always increased. On top of that, "…Some nationalist groups have also exploited rumors such as the theft of donkeys by Chinese workers or the fact that workers who died during the works were buried under recently built roads,"[4] argued Gulnara Ibraeva, a Kyrgyz media specialist. The Kyrgyz, historically a nomadic people, have a special relationship with nature. The "Switzerland of Central Asia", as some have nicknamed Kyrgyzstan, is well known for its lakes, including the famous Issyk-Kul, the second largest saline lake in the world, and its rolling mountains and clean air. The country can count on an indigenous population with a strong desire to defend its natural resources.

Indeed, popular revolt is a very established social phenomenon in the Kyrgyz culture when it comes to asserting individual rights. It leads the authorities to be extremely cautious about large projects. Several Chinese mining projects had to be cancelled or heavily amended after the facilities were attacked by the local population following rumours of health impacts arising from the projects. According to Begayim Esenkulova, researcher at the American University of Central Asia,

> … *mining remains a polluting activity, but no significant health impact was observed on the places where incidents with the population took place.*"[5]

(Some are accusing the local populations of raising the auctions with companies conducting projects.)

These difficulties also encouraged China to turn to other countries in the region for economic opportunities, such as Tajikistan which is considered more politically stable. Even if such incidents remain limited and contained, they could become potentially explosive if not dealt with properly by the authorities and bottled over the long term. The development of mixed marriages and the appearance of theories of a "Great replacement"[6] may cause serious incidents in the future. The recurrent difficulties of the Kyrgyzstan authorities in controlling large

---

[4] Quotation supplied by Vivien Fortat.
[5] Quotation supplied by Vivien Fortat.
[6] Theory of demographic evolution leading to a situation where the native population is being demographically replaced by a foreign population from another country.

movements of popular protests make the identification of the trigger point by the Chinese authorities critical for their projects to work. The latter, aware of the danger, have also slowed down several projects and limited their desire for cultural influence.

BEIJING AND MOSCOW IN COOPETITION

Even if Russia has strongly disengaged itself economically from the region, it still has all its grip on the politics, military and media of the region. But Beijing, now having a significant economic weight in the region, has seen its political influence grow, causing some to grind teeth in Moscow. "For the Russians, the railway is historically the perfect vehicle for moving military troops. Some of the Russian authorities therefore see the proposed railway network currently being deployed by the Chinese people with a very bad eye,"[7] says Alexander Wolters, Director of the OSCE Academy. The project has been the subject of several attacks by Atambayev, former Kyrgyz President, on the basis that the economic benefits would not be sufficient for his country to outweigh the strategic detriments. However, according to regional observers, manoeuvring from Moscow to disrupt the Chinese plan is visible behind these statements.

According to a security source, China is not trying to increase its political influence so much as it is trying to seize business opportunities. The Russian financial disengagement since the end of the Cold War has strongly affected the local think tanks, allowing China to poach many highly qualified experts to decipher the local political environment for its economic strategies. This allows Beijing to get, upstream of large projects, special attention from future decisionmakers. The potential defence or telecom ministers of the main candidates for the Kyrgyzstan presidential election have, for example, been the subject of special interests.

Yet, both powers know that they need each other. This coopetition, cooperation between competitors, is observed in particular in the political and economic fields. Beijing has an interest in maintaining good relations with Moscow to ensure that there is only one strategic front, open presumably against the United States, the superpower of the world with a strong presence in the region. There is also the necessity that the railroad carrying Chinese goods to Europe continues to be able to cross Russia. Moscow, on the contrary, no longer has the means to economically support a region comprising several of the poorest countries in the world and where radical Islam flourishes. Therefore, it needs a financial partner.

---

[7] Quotation supplied by Vivien Fortat.

CHINA, NEW REGIONAL SECURITY ACTOR

Beijing is aware of not being, historically, a regional power in Central Asia in the modern era. Despite the presence of common borders between China and several countries of Central Asia, western China has always been at the margins of the Chinese dynastic empires. The "Middle of Kingdoms",[8] as Michel Jan and René Cagnat called it in an eponymous book from the mid-1980s, has only recently been of interest to the Chinese authorities. Beyond the needs of economic development, it is the unstable nature of the region and the associated security threat that preoccupy China. In August 2016, the Chinese Embassy in Bishkek was the target of the first major attack on Chinese interests abroad. Although the investigation findings and the official conclusions have not yet been made public, preliminary disclosure of information seems to favour the interpretation of the involvement of Uighurs and their brand of radicalism. This ethnic group from Xinjiang, China has a large diaspora present in Kyrgyzstan. Although the number and means of the radicals remain very limited, their potential for harm in the small Central Asian republic remains significant given the weakness of the local security services. Beijing's fear is that, unable to commit attacks in China, radical Uighurs have turned against Chinese interests abroad.

Faced with this challenge and beyond the actions of security cooperation, the question of an increased Chinese military presence in the area is becoming more relevant. Between 2014 and 2015, recurring rumours emerged in the form of plans to establish a Chinese military base in southern Kyrgyzstan. If the settlement of such a base did not materialize and if, according to Alexander Wolters, it "was perhaps a bluff of influential politicians in the south in internal political conflicts in the country," it would probably be a *casus belli* for Russians. They already have four military installations on site and a fifth largest location is under consideration. Russian President Vladimir Putin himself recalled in an interview in September 2017 the importance of Kyrgyzstan's strategic position for the Russian armed forces, particularly in view of the growing instability in Tajikistan and Afghanistan.

---

[8] Cagnat, Jan, "Le milieu des empires — Entre URSS, Chine et Islam, le destin de l'Asie centrale," Ed. Robert Laffont, 1990.

Chapter 6

BUILDING EMERGENCY MANAGEMENT IN POST-SARS CHINA*

Wee-Kiat Lim

Centre for Management Practice, Singapore Management University

INTRODUCTION

How did the Chinese government develop emergency management so quickly in the wake of the 2003 Severe Acute Respiratory Syndrome (SARS) epidemic? My research traces the remarkable genesis of the new organizational field of emergency management over a 10-year period (2002–2012). It highlights the various factors that facilitated the establishment, i.e. the network of political leadership and experts, in creating and consolidating the field, particularly the ideational origins of and manoeuvring policy conversations from management to governance.

I also demonstrate how the establishment, through processes of legislation and regulation, learnt and refined formal definitions and categories of emergency as threats to society that necessitated emergencies to be governed through a complex arrangement of government, private firms and civil society. I discuss the theoretical and policy implications of understanding nascent field development surrounding new policy domains through the travel of ideas and trials of crises. The analytical toolkit that I used to analyse the rise of China's emergency management is assembled mainly from sociological neo-institutional theory and sociological literatures on disaster and risk management.

---

*A version of this chapter was presented as a conference paper at *From the Management of Crisis to the Governance of Risk: Time for a Paradigm Shift?* Haikou, China, 9 January 2017.

As a country that is constantly afflicted by natural extreme events, it was never apparent that China did not have a single, centralized authority to govern emergency response until March 2018 when the government established the ministry of emergency management.[1] However, it would be a mistake to assume that the Chinese state did not invest considerable resources into building emergency management capability. In fact, in the wake of the SARS outbreak in 2002–2003 until 2012, it has assiduously harnessed disasters to create and curate its national emergency management design. One result of such persistent administrative attention was the formation of "modern" emergency management in China. The account of its swift development over that decade is the topic of this research study.

My discussion proceeds as follows. First, I introduce my theoretical toolkit assembled mainly from sociological neo-institutional theory and related concepts in sociological literature on risk and disasters. Following that, I provide an overview of China's then-nascent organizational field of emergency management in the post-SARS era. Next, I elaborate on the three prominent administrative and legislative landmarks of the fledgling emergency management field that suggest a discernible approach towards managing and responding to risks that has been institutionalized. The three landmarks are the 2003 Administrative Regulation on Public Health Emergencies, the 2005 State Master Plan for Emergency Response, and finally the 2007 National Emergency Response Law. Specifically, I highlight the idea of curation to explain the emergence of categories, severity grades, emergency management phases and several other components across the three landmarks.

ASSEMBLING MY THEORETICAL TOOLKIT

This section assembles the four key concepts in my theoretical toolkit. First, I begin with neo-institutional theory, focusing on the concept of organizational field and the role of institutional vocabulary and theorization in field creation. Next, I highlight the social constructionist roots that connect neo-institutional theory and sociological literature on disaster and risk. This allows me to introduce the third concept, the idea of establishment.

Neo-institutional Theory

Neo-institutional theory is one of the most significant research programmes in contemporary sociology, especially in organizational studies.[2] It began as a project

---

[1] Hou, L. (2018). "New Authority Focuses on Emergency Response." *China Daily*.
[2] Jepperson, R. L. (2002). "The Development and Application of Sociological Neoinstitutionalism." In Berger, J. and Lanham, M. Z. Jr. (eds.), *New Directions in Contemporary Sociological Theory*. MD: Rowman & Littlefield Publishers, Inc., pp. 229–266.

that deliberately shifted away from the atomistic and realist philosophical commitments that were entrenched in the intellectual culture of American sociology in past decades. This intellectual movement recognizes that collective action is not simply the sum of individual actions and inter-relationships among social collectivities, and thus reinstates society as a distinct and meaningful level of analysis.[3] Furthermore, it adopts a more social constructionist view of society.[4] Coming from this vantage point, actors — individuals, organizations and nations — are no longer conceived as purposive, well-bounded and independent entities. Instead, actors are conceived as entities embedded in their cultural environments.[5,6] Consequently, their conduct is organized by the scripts and schemas that are available to them within those environments.

This realization also emphasizes the shared knowledge and meanings that emerge through social interactions.[7] It takes social collectivities — communities, organizations and nations alike — seriously as interpretive systems,[8] noting how they purposefully tap into wider worlds of meaning and leverage their power.[9–11] It emphasizes the cultural-cognitive elements of the institutional order, the most deeply rooted conceptions of social reality that have become taken for granted.[12–14] In other words, cultural-cognitive elements formulate the meaning, rationality and

---

[3] Friedland, R. and Alford, R. R. (1991). "Bringing Society Back In: Symbols, Practices, and Institutional Contradictions." In Powell, W. W. and DiMaggio, D. J. (eds.), *The New Institutionalism in Organizational Analysis*. Chicago, IL: The University of Chicago Press, pp. 232–263.

[4] Jepperson, R. L. (2002). *Op cit.*

[5] Meyer, J. W. (2008). "Reflections on Institutional Theories of Organizations." In Greenwood, R., Oliver, C., Sahlin, K. and Suddaby, R. (eds.), *The Sage Handbook of Organizational Institutionalism*. Thousand Oaks, CA: Sage, pp. 790–812.

[6] Powell, W. W. and DiMaggio, P. J. (eds.) (1991). *The New Institutionalism in Organizational Analysis*. Chicago, IL: University of Chicago Press.

[7] Berger, P. L. and Luckmann, T. [1966] (1991). *The Social Construction of Reality: A Treatise in the Sociology of Knowledge*. New York: Penguin Books.

[8] Daft, R. L. and Weick, K. E. (1984). "Toward a Model of Organizations as Interpretation Systems." *Academy of Management Review* 9(2), 284–295.

[9] Mohr, J. W. and Friedland, R. (2008). "Theorizing the Institution: Foundation, Duality, and Data." *Theory and Society* 37, 421–426.

[10] Oliver, C. (1991). "Strategic Responses to Institutional Processes." *Academy of Management Review* 16(1), 145–179.

[11] Scott, W. R. (1991). "Unpacking Institutional Arrangements." In Powell, W. W. and DiMaggio, P. J. (eds.), *The New Institutionalism in Organizational Analysis*. Chicago, IL: University of Chicago Press, pp. 164–182.

[12] Scott, W. R. (2001). *Institutions and Organizations*. Thousand Oaks, CA: Sage Publications.

[13] Scott, W. R. (2008a). *Institutions and Organizations: Ideas and Interests*. Thousand Oaks, CA: Sage Publications.

[14] Scott, W. R. (2008b). "Approaching Adulthood: The Maturing of Institutional Theory." *Theory and Society* 37, 427–442.

the categories and classification systems of the scripts and schemas available in the institutional environments. Scott (1991)[15] provides a lucid description of how organized actors import and improvise such scripts and schemas from their environments, rather than reinvent the wheel from within: "All of us to some degree design or tailor our worlds, but we never do this from raw cloth; indeed, for the most part we get our worlds ready to wear" (p.170).

It is this "ready-to-wear" quality in organized action that I find useful as a first principle in assembling my conceptual toolkit. Organized actors strive to configure their structures and practices and to develop products that demonstrate alignment with the goals espoused and values expected of them within their institutional environment, such as the need to be efficient or productive in their performance.[16,17] Consequently, actors who appropriately adapt to these expectations gain acceptance from other actors sharing the same institutional environment.[18]

Organizational Field

An organizational field can be defined as a collection of "sets of institutions and networks of organizations that together constitute a recognizable area of life".[19] In terms of properties or characteristics, an organizational field manifests itself when it demonstrates an increase in the interaction and information load among a set of organizations to the extent that "interorganizational structures of domination and patterns of coalition" become obvious and "mutual awareness of a common enterprise" emerges among participants in that organization set.[20]

An organizational field can also be established *a priori*, with different conceptualizations mobilized according to espoused research agendas and desired theoretical payoffs, such as in terms of administrative categories (e.g. Standard Industrial Classification codes), recognizable organization populations (e.g. banks), well-defined geopolitical boundaries (e.g. regions, nation-states) or functional attributes.

---

[15] Scott, W. R. (1991). *Op cit.*

[16] DiMaggio, P. J. and Powell, W. W. (1983). "The Iron Cage Revisited: Institutional Isomorphism and Collective Rationality in Organizational Fields." *American Sociological Review* 48(2), 147–160.

[17] Meyer, J. W. and Rowan, B. (1977). "Institutionalized Organizations: Formal Structure as Myth and Ceremony." *American Journal of Sociology* 83(2), 340–363.

[18] Tolbert, P. S. and Zucker, L. G. (1983). "Institutional Sources of Change in the Formal Structure of Organizations: The Diffusion of Civil Service Reform, 1880–1935." *Administrative Science Quarterly* 28(1), 22–39.

[19] DiMaggio, P. J. and Powell, W. W. (1983). *Op cit.*, p. 148.

[20] *Ibid.*

With respect to the last example, Lægreid and Serigstad (2006)[21] identify homeland security as the organizing function in corralling governmental organizations in Norway, such as the Ministry of Defence and Ministry of Justice, as well as a hybrid organization, the National Security Authority that reports to both ministries, into the newly created field.

Here, I treat the Chinese emergency management as an issue-based organizational field. This departs from the more common organizing categories such as "settled markets, technologies, and policy domains"[22] that I highlighted above and moves closer to issues and interests. This manoeuvre not only builds on and emphasizes the "common enterprise" undertaken by entities in the same field, as in earlier foundational definitions[23] but also introduces a more deliberative and dynamic quality to what an organizational field entails and engenders, particularly in institutional terms: the persistent quest for social acceptance. An issue-centred organizational field also offers a more sophisticated reading of the varying degrees of influence each constituent exerts and a more dynamic view of field membership.[24] Treating Chinese emergency management as an issue-based organizational field also becomes more salient when I relate it to the concept of "establishment" in the disaster literature later. Briefly, an establishment is a network of organized actors motivated to frame an issue as a putative threat or problem.[25] This treatment also highlights the "relational space" in which organized actors, through the process of referencing one another, bring a field into existence.[26]

Institutional Vocabulary and Theorization

The literature has highlighted how ideas in their travels are used by organized actors in institutional settings to enact change,[27] a notion that is well anchored in the social constructionist tradition. Such attempts by organized actors involve

---

[21] Lægreid, P. and Serigstad, S. (2006). "Framing the Field of Homeland Security: The Case of Norway." *Journal of Management Studies* 43(6), 1397–1413.

[22] Scott, W. R. (2008b). *Op cit.*

[23] DiMaggio, P. J. and Powell, W. W. (1983). *Op cit.*

[24] Wooten, M. and Hoffman, A. J. (2008). "Organizational Fields: Past, Present and Future." In Greenwood, R., Oliver, C., Sahlin, K. and Suddaby, R. (eds.), *The Sage Handbook of Organizational Institutionalism*. Thousand Oaks, CA: Sage, pp. 130–147.

[25] Stallings, R. A. (1995). *Promoting Risk: Constructing the Earthquake Threat*. New York: Aldine de Gruyter.

[26] Wooten, M. and Hoffman, A. J. (2008). *Op cit.*

[27] Czarniawska, B. and Joerges, B. (1996). "Travels of Ideas." In Czarniawska, B. and Sevón, G. (eds.), *Translating Organizational Change*. Berlin; New York: Walter de Gruyter, pp. 13–48.

mobilizing institutional vocabularies, which are "clusters of repetitive words, attributes, and referential texts linked to distinct conceptions" associated with specific ideas, for instance, articulating the archetypical qualities of professionalism.[28] Occasionally, they survive succeeding waves of change and condense into institutions in the form of public administrative reforms, developmental models and best practices. Seen this way, ideas are also visible in more tangible and material forms, from artefacts that are conceptual and provisional such as designs and prototypes to those that offer concrete, itemized checklists and prescriptions, such as standards and guidelines, and then finally to those that have become more ideal-typical, obdurate and taken for granted, such as archetypes and templates.[29-33]

However, mobilizing institutional vocabularies alone is not sufficient. "Theorizing" change is also an integral part of the ensemble of tools that organized actors deploy to enact change.[34-36] By theorizing, I refer to purposeful actions and accounts that assemble, develop and specify abstract categories and articulate their patterned relationships; for example, in the forms of cause-and-effect where activity A leads to activity B, which in turn brings about outcome C.[37-39]

---

[28] Suddaby, R. and Greenwood, R. (2005). "Rhetorical Strategies of Legitimacy." *Administrative Science Quarterly* 50, 35–67.

[29] Czarniawska, B. and Joerges, B. (1996). *Op cit.*

[30] Greenwood, R. and Hinings, C. R. (1993). "Understanding Strategic Change: The Contribution of Archetypes." *Academy of Management Journal* 36(5), 1052–1081.

[31] Greenwood, R. and Hinings, C. R. (1996). "Understanding Radical Organizational Change: Bringing Together the Old and the New Institutionalism." *Academy of Management Journal* 21(4), 1022–1054.

[32] Purdy, J. M. and Gray, B. (2009). "Conflicting Logics, Mechanisms of Diffusion, and Multilevel Dynamics in Emerging Institutional Fields." *Academy of Management Journal* 52(2), 355–380.

[33] Sahlin, K. and Wedlin, L. (2008). "Circulating Ideas: Imitation, Translation and Editing." In Greenwood, R., Oliver, C., Sahlin, K. and Suddaby, R. (eds.), *The Sage Handbook of Organizational Institutionalism*. Thousand Oaks, CA: Sage Publications, pp. 218–242.

[34] Greenwood, R., Suddaby, R. and Hinings, C. R. (2002). "Theorizing Change: The Role of Professional Associations in the Transformation of Institutionalized Fields." *Academy of Management Journal* 45(1), 58–80.

[35] Strang, D. and Meyer, J. W. (1993). "Institutional Conditions for Diffusion." *Theory and Society* 22(4), 487–511.

[36] Suddaby, R. and Greenwood, R. (2001). "Colonizing Knowledge: Commodification as a Dynamic of Jurisdictional Expansion in Professional Service Firms." *Human Relations* 54(7), 933–953.

[37] Greenwood, R., Suddaby, R. and Hinings, C. R. (2002). *Op cit.*

[38] Strang, D. and Meyer, J. W. (1993). *Op cit.*

[39] Zilber, T. B. (2008). "The Work of Meanings in Institutional Processes and Thinking." In Greenwood, R., Oliver, C., Sahlin, K. and Suddaby, R. (eds.), *The Sage Handbook of Organizational Institutionalism*. Thousand Oaks, CA: Sage Publications, pp. 151–169.

Theorizations are also typically conducted and promoted vigorously by communities of "culturally legitimated theorists", who occupy prestigious and influential positions within their institutional environments.[40] These intellectual communities, including scientists, policy analysts, and professionals, are considered "the bona fide producers" of specialized knowledge.[41]

Other organized actors in organizational fields are also implicated in how ideas travel in organizational space, even though relative to intellectual communities they are usually not the originators of ideas or models. Instead, they contribute by reproducing the shared meanings and understanding within the field.[42] This is especially true for regulatory agencies, which also adjudicate and push for negotiations among competing claims. Regulatory agencies include nation-states and government bodies but are not limited to them. Non-governmental organizations such as professional bodies also serve similar purposes.

Introducing Sociological Disaster Research

Disaster research has been moving away from a functionalist conception of natural disasters as purely obdurate, physical events that are "out there," disrupting society. This is because, researchers realize social constructionism can be a productive lens to understand how organized actors — individuals, organizations and other social collectivities — are implicated in manufacturing and managing disasters.[43,44] Disaster researchers also recognize that a social constructionist approach does not claim that disasters are non-existent.[45,46] Rather, this brand of social constructionism in disaster research emphasizes the social aetiology of disasters,[47] by showing that "social agents create and use boundaries to

---

[40] Strang, D. and Meyer, J. W. (1993). *Op cit.*

[41] Ainsworth, S. and Cynthia, H. (2012). "Subjects of Inquiry: Statistics, Stories, and the Production of Knowledge." *Organization Studies* 33(12), 1693–714. doi: 10.1177/0170840612457616.

[42] Ruef, M. and Scott, W. R. (1998). "A Multidimensional Model of Organizational Legitimacy: Hospital Survival in Changing Institutional Enginronments." *Administrative Science Quarterly* 43(4), 877–904.

[43] Fritz, C. E. (1961). "Disaster." In Merton, R. K. and Nisbet, R. (eds.), *Contemporary Social Problems.* NY: Harcourt, Brace & World, pp. 651–694.

[44] Tierney, K. J. (2007). "From the Margins to the Mainstream? Disaster Research at the Crossroads.". *Annual Review of Sociology* 33, 503–525.

[45] Best, J. (2008). "Historical Development and Defining Issues of Constructionist Inquiry." In Holstein, J. A. and Gubrium, J. F. (eds.), *Handbook of Constructionist Research.* NY: The Guilford Press, pp. 41–84.

[46] Stallings, R. A. 1997. "Sociological Theories and Disaster Studies." University of Delaware Disaster Research Center Preliminary Paper 249.

[47] Turner, B. A. (1979). "The Social Aetiology of Disasters." *Disasters* 3(1), 53–59.

demarcate that which is dangerous".[48] In other words, social groups come together to define and attach meanings to what are risky and constitute disasters.[49,50] For example, within the US earthquake establishment, past experiences, knowledge differentials, vested interests and value differences shaped the way engineers, scientists and policy analysts put forth claims and established their views on disasters as a threat to societal order.[51]

The social constructionist tradition in disaster research asserts that extreme events — despite their resultant human injuries and deaths, as well as economic costs — are not disasters in and of themselves; extreme events accomplish that status only when refracted through social interpretation and action. For example, heat waves are usually not treated as disasters, even though they kill more people than floods and hurricanes combined in the US in some years.[52] Whether an event constitutes a disaster is associated with social perceptions of and public reaction to its occurrence.[53]

Neo-institutional Connections to Disaster Research

The state and organizations are legitimate actors in society that select and define what counts as risks and disasters and what does not.[54,55] Whether the reading of those events is "distorted" through the prism of cognitive biases or mental heuristics becomes moot because the broader institutional arrangements have already "decided" what should constitute disaster risks for the public and which parties should bear them. In other words, these actors are the "true assessors for society" in terms of disasters and risks.[56]

Both sets of literature agree on the significance and impact of events that are perceived as exogenous and catalysts for transformational change, which is

---

[48] Clarke, L. and Short, J. F. Jr. (1993). "Social Organization and Risk: Some Current Controversies." *Annual Review of Sociology* 19(1), 375–399.

[49] Douglas, M. and Wildavsky, A. (1982). *Risk and Culture*. Berkeley and Los Angeles: University of California Press.

[50] Tierney, K. J. (1999). "Towards a Critical Sociology of Risk." *Sociological Forum* 14(2), 215–242.

[51] Stallings, R. A. (1995). *Op cit.*

[52] Klinenberg, E. (2002). *Heat Wave: A Social Autopsy of Disaster in Chicago*. Chicago, IL: University of Chicago Press.

[53] Abbott, P., Claire, W. and Matthias, B. (2006). "Chernobyl: Living with Risk and Uncertainty." *Health, Risk & Society* 8(2), 105–21.

[54] Clarke, L. (1988). "Explaining Choices among Technological Risks." *Social Problems* 35(1), 22–35.

[55] Stallings, R. A. (1995). *Op cit.*

[56] Clarke, L. (1988). *Op cit.,* p. 30.

evidenced by the plethora of terms in their vocabulary: "jolts",[57] "shocks",[58,59] "focusing events",[60,61] "critical junctures",[62,63] "field events"[64,65] and "punctuated events".[66] In addition, both recognize that the selection and presentation of organizational problems and their solutions are not independent of the specialized knowledge that organized actors, particularly experts, bring to bear on the issues.[67]

The affinity between neo-institutional theory and disaster research allows me to use the social constructionist stream of work on disasters as a theoretical resource. Here, I return to the term "establishment" that emerged from the social constructionist literature on disasters.

Coining the term "establishment," disaster sociologist Stallings (1995)[68] calls attention to a loose but stable network of US technocrats and bureaucrats who profess and promote the threat of earthquake as a problem to be managed, particularly with government support. Just as important, the movement is restricted to the establishment because its members are the ones who are deemed to possess the requisite research, managerial and policy know-how to address the putative problem. These members are connected through interlocking webs of elite and specialized knowledge production entities and social facts, such as universities, research programmes, government policies and mission-oriented operational agencies.

---

[57] Meyer, A. D. (1982). "Adapting to Environmental Jolts." *Administrative Science Quarterly* 27(4), 515–537.

[58] Fligstein, N. (1990). *The Transformation of Corporate Control.* Cambridge, MA: Harvard University Press.

[59] Fligstein, N. and McAdam, D. (2012). *A Theory of Fields.* NY: Oxford University Press.

[60] Birkland, T. A. (1997). *After Disaster: Agenda Setting, Public Policy, and Focusing Events.* Washington, D.C.: Georgetown University Press.

[61] Birkland, T. A. (2007). *Lessons of Disaster: Policy Change after Catastrophic Events.* Washington, D.C.: Georgetown University Press.

[62] Collier, R. B. and Collier, D. (1991). *Shaping the Political Arena: Critical Junctures, the Labor Movement, and Regime Dynamics in Latin America.* Princeton, New Jersey: Princeton University Press.

[63] Olson, R. S. and Gawbronski, V. T. (2003). "Disasters as Critical Junctures? Managua, Nicaragua 1972 and Mexico City 1985." *International Journal of Mass Emergencies and Disasters* 21(1), 5–36.

[64] Edelman, L. (1992). "Legal Ambiguity and Symbolic Structures: Organizational Mediation of Civil Rights Law." *American Journal of Sociology* 97(6), 1531–1576.

[65] Schneiberg, M. and Clemens, E. S. (2006). "The Typical Tools for the Job: Research Strategies in Institutional Analysis." *Sociological Theory* 24(3), 195–227.

[66] Tilcsik, A. and Marquis, C. (2013). "Punctuated Generosity: How Mega-Events and Natural Disasters Affect Corporate Philanthropy in U.S. Communities." *Administrative Science Quarterly* 58(1), 111–148.

[67] Knowles, S. G. (2011). *The Disaster Experts: Monitoring Risk in Modern America.* Philadelphia, PA: University of Pennsylvania Press.

[68] Stallings, R. A. (1995). *Op cit.*

The network that formed from these webs receives and accumulates resources that allow them to finance projects and training and build technical standards. In addition, earthquakes offer "teachable moments"[69,70] that can also be capitalized not only for public awareness but also to garner funds and political influence. Through this concerted effort by organized actors in problem selection and their subsequent definitions and solutions, the governing and expert class and their espoused ideas made inroads into policies and policy-making.[71] This general insight of establishment influence is well documented in disaster literature, albeit limited to single disaster triggers or events and seldom applied at the organizational field level to natural disasters in general, which in this case refers to the creation of the Chinese emergency management field.

FIELDWORK AND DATA COLLECTION

I conducted fieldwork in Beijing from July to December 2012. My data collection strategy during fieldwork comprised three components: document review, interviews with academic experts on emergency management and observation of conferences and seminars. My focus was primarily document review, supplemented by interviews and observation of conferences and seminars. My proficiency in Mandarin/Chinese allowed me to analyse documents, explain study procedures and conduct interviews. My multi-method approach encourages using triangulation to reveal consensus and contradictions across events, issues and themes.[72] Triangulation further adds "richness, rigor and breadth and depth" to my inquiry.[73] In reviewing documents (e.g. laws and annual reports) and observing participants (e.g. conferences and seminars), I also respond to the call in disaster research to consider less obtrusive methods, in addition to the current "toolkit" of surveys and interviews.[74]

Documents that I collected were mainly from publicly available sources (e.g. scholarly journal databases, commercially available publication). Most materials

---

[69] Stallings, R. A. (1986). "Reaching the Ethnic Minorities: Earthquake Public Education in the Aftermath of Foreign Disasters." *Spectra* 2(4), 695–702.

[70] Stallings, R. A. (1995). *Op cit.*

[71] *Ibid.*

[72] Small, M. L. (2011). "How to Conduct a Mixed Methods Study: Recent Trends in a Rapidly Growing Literature." *Annual Review of Sociology* 37, 57–86.

[73] Denzin, N. K. and Lincoln, Y. S. (2008). "The Discipline and Practice of Qualitative Research." In Denzin, N. K. and Lincoln, Y. S. (eds.), *The Landscape of Qualitative Research*. Thousand Oaks, CA. Sage Publications, pp. 1–43.

[74] Phillips, B. (2002). "Qualitative Methods and Disaster Research." In Stallings, R. A. (ed.), *Methods of Disaster Research*. Philadelphia, PA: Xlibris Corporation, pp. 194–211.

were in Chinese. They included but were not limited to: (1) formal and public proclamation related to emergency management released by the Chinese government at the national level, such as laws, regulations, guidance and white papers; (2) non-government publications related to Chinese emergency management released for public consumption, such as a UNESCO report on the 2008 Wenchuan Earthquake; and (3) academic publications, focusing on China-based emergency management-related journals. These documents, especially academic journals, were sites for "establishment intellectuals"[75] in emergency management to present their ideas and arguments. They familiarized me to the appropriate professional and cultural jargon that China's emergency management "natives" would be proficient in. Displaying such "selective competence"[76] enhanced my credibility with my gatekeepers and informants as a junior researcher gaining mastery in Chinese disaster research.

Interviews helped me understand the extent to which academic experts were involved in the laws, regulations, policies and practice of emergency management in China, focusing on how and the extent to which their production of knowledge was assimilated into the establishment's thinking. On several occasions, I followed Gold's[77] "guerrilla interviewing," which are "unchaperoned, spontaneous but structured participant observation and interviews as opportunities present themselves" (p. 180). These usually took place at conferences and seminars where I "waylaid" prospective informants with requests for interview. In total, I conducted 23 interviews with 21 individuals. All names of informants mentioned are pseudonyms. Each interview on average took about 76 minutes. All informants had extensive dealings with officials in emergency management. Some were members of the communist party on record. Several were also either former or current government officials holding dual appointments at their academic institutions and governmental emergency management offices.

In Beijing, I observed four conferences, four seminars (e.g. brown bag sessions) and two informal meetings (among academics). The observation notes provided insights beyond what were available in formal documents and even interviews. I complemented my Beijing fieldwork with a panel on China's emergency management policy domain that I organized at a US disaster management conference. Specific to interviews and participant observation, I adopted the stance of the

---

[75] Hamrin, C. L. and Cheek, T. (eds.) (1986). *China's Establishment Intellectuals*. Armonk, NY: M. E. Sharpe.

[76] Lofland, J. and Lofland, L. H. (1995). *Analyzing Social Settings: A Guide to Qualitative Observation and Analysis*. Bermont, CA: Wadsworth Publishing Company.

[77] Gold, T. B. (1989). "Guerilla Interviewing among the *Getihu*." In Link, P., Madsen, R. and Pickowicz, P. G. (eds.), *Unofficial China: Popular Culture and Thought in the People's Republic*. Boulder, Colorado: Westview Press, pp. 175–192.

"known" investigator.[78] Informants knew then that I was a foreign-born albeit ethnically Chinese researcher seeking to understand their contribution to China's emergency management. I deployed a "portfolio" of roles and identities that was contingent on the context of the interviews. Using the "teach-me approach"[79] served me well, especially with senior academic experts. This approach typically encouraged them to be more engaging and flesh out their arguments.

Coding and Analysis

I used both inductive and deductive methods simultaneously. Similar to how Hoffman and Ocasio (2001)[80] examined the influence of media coverage on the responses of the US chemical industry to environmental issues, I began my analysis based on literature and my data to form my working hypotheses and theoretical model.[81] This is especially clear when I use neo-institutional theory as a lens to understand emergency management as an organizational field. It guides me *where* and *what* to look for (e.g. new organizational forms, practices, rules, regulations, methods), but it cannot tell me *how* manifestations of institutionalization in the Chinese emergency management context are going to look like in precise terms. The design and definition of China's emergency management ultimately had to emerge from data.

To recount the development of emergency management in post-SARS China, I adapted heavily the analysis strategy from my previous collaborative work on the social construction of risks in complex IT projects.[82] I used a process approach to analyse how the organizational field was socially constructed. I paid attention to the "the sequences of interactions and activities that unfold over the duration of the entity being studied in context".[83] I also followed Langley's (1999)[84] suggestion of using a narrative strategy for my analysis. Narrative strategy essentially

---

[78] Lofland, J. and Lofland, L. H. (1995). *Op cit.*

[79] See Wildavsky (1989, p. 69) cited in O'Brien, K. J. (2006). "Discovery, Research (Re)Design, and Theory Building." In Heimer, M. and Thøgersen, S. (eds.), *Doing Fieldwork in China*. Honolulu, HI: University of Hawai'i Press, pp. 27–41.

[80] Hoffman, A. J. and Ocasio, W. (2001). "Not All Events Are Attended Equally: Toward a Middle-Range Theory of Industry Attention to External Events." *Organization Science* 12(4), 414–434.

[81] By working hypotheses, I do not mean that I adopted a purely positivist approach towards research. I simply mean data verification.

[82] Lim, W-K., Sia, S. K. and Yeow, A. (2011). "Managing Risk in a Failing It Project: A Social Constructionist View." *Journal of the Association for Information Systems* 12(6), 414–440.

[83] Van de Ven, A. H. (2007). *Engaged Scholarship: A Guide for Organizational and Social Research*, edited by A. H. Van de Ven. New York. Oxford University Press, p. 197.

[84] Langley, A. (1999). "Strategies for Theorizing from Process Data." *Academy of Management Review* 24(4), 691–710.

involves the construction of a detailed story from data. Accordingly, I crafted an in-depth and chronological narrative of the entire field formation. The narrative formed the base document to summarize the vast amount of information available in my archival and interview data. I focused on the ideas and achievements that built the organizational field of emergency management in China legislatively, administratively and organizationally and more importantly forged a common identity that inhabitants of and new entrants to the field could recognize as "emergency management".[85]

EMERGENCY MANAGEMENT IN CHINA: A FIELD COBBLED THROUGH CRISES

The 2003 SARS crisis was China's turning point in emergency management. By revealing significant weaknesses in existing crisis management policy, this focusing event[86] mobilized both mass and elite attention to consider ways the nation-state could improve its response to public health threats and other hazards. China seized the opportunity to review comprehensively its established organizational model and practices and move towards "a risk-based, all-hazards integrated national system".[87] The government launched initiatives to centralize and standardize planning and operations and strengthen interagency coordination, calling the newly consolidated organizational field, the "National System for Emergency Management 2.0".[88] Some analysts even assert that China's "modern" emergency management began only after the SARS crisis.[89]

Why was the SARS epidemic such a catalysing event? Based on any objective criteria of losses, the SARS crisis did not kill or injure nearly as many people as the 1976 Tangshan earthquake and other disasters in China. While significant, its economic impact was also in no way comparable to the Great Yangtze Flood of 1998. That said, SARS was also different from natural disasters, industrial accidents or demonstrations: categories of emergencies that are intelligible to the

---

[85] DiMaggio, P. J. and Powell, W. W. (1983). *Op cit.*

[86] Birkland, T. A. (2007). *Op cit.*

[87] Xue, L. and Zhong, K. (2010). "Turning Danger (危) to Opportunities (机): Reconstructing China's National System for Emergency Management after 2003." In Kunreuther, H. and Useem, M. (eds.), *Learning from Catastrophes: Strategies for Reactions and Response.* Upper Saddle River, NJ: Pearson Education/Prentice Hall, pp. 190–210.

[88] *Ibid.*

[89] Bai, V. (2009). "Emergency Management in China." *Comparative Emergency Management: Understanding Disaster Policies, Organizations, and Initiatives from Around the World,* http://training. fema.gov/EMIWeb/edu/Comparative%20EM%20Book%20-%20Chapter%20-%20Emergency%20 Management%20in%20China.doc.

government to administer control. Unlike natural disasters, SARS did not announce its arrival with sudden death and mayhem. Unlike industrial accidents, no sophisticated technologies and heroic efforts could be mounted, for example, to access collapsed coal mines. Unlike demonstrations, or officially known as "public security emergencies," there were no physical sites where the government could direct its security forces. SARS came silently and invisibly in late 2002, still unintelligible as a virus when it claimed its first victims in China.

The new Hu Jintao-Wen Jiabao administration that just assumed political leadership in late 2002–early 2003 learned quickly to frame SARS not merely as an epidemic but also as a revelation of the risks that confront a society in transition. To illustrate, one of the "misalignments" cited as a source of SARS was the dissolution of the traditionally more collective and static society to a more individualistic and mobile one that was urbanizing at an amazing pace. The scale and speed at which internal migration was occurring lied beyond the complete grip of party-government control. As pointed out by Zhuang, a policy researcher[90]:

SARS is a societal phenomenon. It's about transmission between individuals. Because of that, even if we had mobilized the masses (to deal with the crisis), and tried to resolutely defend ourselves (from the epidemic), I realized that without (putting in place) a system, without a way to organize everyone based on some strategy, we basically cannot resist it... It's a reality of China at that point in time, our *danwei* societal system (单位制) had collapsed, and we had not formed new mechanisms to defend and prevent (such crises).[91]

By striking the capital Beijing during February–April 2003,[92] SARS abruptly shifted the world's attention away from China's once-in-a-decade political leadership transition to itself. It directed intense domestic attention on issues concerning accountability that were also spawning adverse international publicity. The confluence of both domestic and international scrutiny drove intense institutional

---

[90] Interview with Zhuang, December 2012. Zhuang is a pseudonym.

[91] *Danwei* can be translated as a work unit. Each *danwei* was responsible for almost all basic services and infrastructure for its members, from housing, childcare and schools to clinics and post offices. The influence of work units on society was substantial. Chinese required permission from their work units to, for example, travel and marry. However, with economic reform and subsequent restructuring of *danwei vis-à-vis* the rise and expansion of private enterprises, as well as rural-to-urban migration, work units gradually lost their influence. For more information on *danwei*, see also Chapter Nine, especially pp. 246–247, in Saich, Tony (2011). *Governance and Politics of China.* NY: Palgrave Macmillan.

[92] Wu, G. (2014). *Sociological Research on Disaster Relief: A Comparative Study on Indonesia, China and Japan (Zaihai Jiuzhu De Shehuixue Yanjiu: Yinni, Zhongguo, Riben Anli Bijiao).* Beijing, China: Peking University Press (Beijing Daxue Chuban She).

transformation.[93] But by the end of 2012, there were no significant changes to the legislative, administrative and organizational components in the organizational field of emergency management.

The umbrella National Emergency Response Law had been passed for 5 years and was considered by the establishment to be due for revision. Existing laws, regulations and plans related to emergency management were being updated and new ones were being created, all using the National Emergency Response Law as their reference. This produced a homogenizing effect, standardizing the fundamental principles, categories of emergencies and types and phases of activities that constitute emergency management. By 2012, the Emergency Management Office at the State Council[94] had been operational for almost 6 years with similar offices established at provincial and municipal seats of government.

In addition to emerging markets focusing on emergency management, there were also expert committees, training centres and a specialized journal as well as national and provincial quasi-professional organizations designed to create and consolidate a body of knowledge on emergency management. The research and training centres not only infused new and old members with "value beyond the technical requirements of the task at hand"[95] they were also the sites of theorizing for borrowing, creating and disseminating ideas that would further entrench the field. There was hence a plethora of organizational types, from suppliers and regulatory bodies to consultants and schools, coming together to define "a recognizable area of life" as an organizational field called emergency management.[96,97]

CURATING A FIELD: FROM ADMINISTRATIVE REGULATION TO NATIONAL LAW

I discuss the administrative and legislative landmarks that appeared in the field chronologically, highlighting components of curation that I identified inductively from my data. The components include definitions that claimed emergencies as problems that required government intervention, principles of organization, emergency management categories, stages of emergency management and methods of risk management.

---

[93] Hoffman, A. J. and Ocasio, W. (2001). *Op cit.*

[94] The State Council is China's *de facto* Cabinet. It is helmed by the Premier.

[95] Selznick, P. (1996). "Institutionalism: 'Old' and 'New'." *Administrative Science Quarterly* 41(2), 270–277.

[96] DiMaggio, P. J. and Powell, W. W. (1983). *Op cit.*

[97] Scott, W. R. (2008a). *Op cit.*

2003 Administrative Regulation on Public Health Emergencies

By April 2003, when China was still grasping the extent of the SARS epidemic, there were already murmurs within the State Council about formalizing emergency management as a governmental function.[98] In a month, the State Council approved a new administrative regulation on public health emergencies (*tufa gonggong weisheng shijian yingji tiaoli* 突发公共卫生事件应急条例). This regulation incorporated the prototyping of a definition for emergency, organizing principles for the practice of emergency management, as well as the early signs of risk management, and the involvement of academic experts.

Article 2 of the regulation is the centrepiece of the document. It provided the definition of a public health emergency and the motivation for government intervention: a sudden, unexpected incident that is causing or potentially could cause harm to public health. Such an incident could arise because of (but not limited to) a known or yet-to-be identified epidemic, an incident of severe food poisoning or a case of industrial contamination. Given that the document could not realistically cover every root cause of a public health emergency, the most important feature of the article is therefore the consequences of such an emergency. This is to say, what the document emphasized is that the occurrence was harming or a potential danger to public health, and thereby necessitated state intervention. This definition continued to be refined by the emergency management establishment in subsequent regulations and laws.

In retrospect, the regulation already contained some of the principles that would organize the field in the future. Specifically, it referenced the State Council as the highest authority to provide unified command for crisis response during public health emergencies. It also stated the principle of a tiered approach, suggesting each level of government would be responsible for public health emergencies in its region. The regulation indicated that each level of government needed to conduct emergency response planning that covered the emergency management cycle from pre-emergency to post-emergency phases. To elaborate further, it identified the three stages of prevention and preparedness (*yufang and zhunbei* 预防与准备), monitoring and early warning (*jiance yu yujing* 检测与预警) and emergency response (*yingjichuli* 应急处理). Furthermore, the regulation stipulated that emergency response plans for public health emergencies must be created and

---

[98] State Council executive meeting chaired by Premier Wen held on April 14, 2003. See Xue, Lan, Qiang Zhang and Kaibin Zhong (2003). *Weiji Guanli: Zhuangxingqi Zhongguo Mianlin De Tiaozhan (Crisis Management in China: The Challenge of Transition)*. Beijing, China: Qinghua Daxue Chuban She, p. 6. The State Council is the *de facto* Cabinet of the Chinese government.

contain components on the building and training of dedicated emergency management staff. Though not explicitly mentioned in this regulation, risks were alluded to as "hidden dangers" (*yinhuan* 隐患) that needed to be identified, analysed and reported. The insertion of identification of "hidden dangers" and their analysis and monitoring paved the way for formal risk management to be included in future administration and legislative components of the field. Last but not least, the regulation also highlighted the specific role academic experts should assume in emergency management: to assess the impact of public health emergencies.

2005 State Master Plan for Emergency Response Plans

In January 2005, almost a year after a working group and an expert advisory team were established in the State Council for emergency planning, the State Council approved the State Master Plan for Emergency Response Plans (*Guojia Tufa Gonggong Shijian Zongti Yu'an* 国家突发公共事件总体预案). As the State Master Plan, it was the authoritative document that directed all levels of government and administrative departments to create emergency response plans.

The purpose of the master plan was stated upfront in the document: to strengthen the government's ability to protect public safety and security and deal with emergencies so as to promote comprehensive economic and societal development in a coordinated and sustainable manner.[99] What is most salient in the statement of purpose was the deliberate reference to the scientific outlook on development, the political ideology that was endorsed by the political leadership. A balanced and sustainable development in the Chinese economy and society was a prominent feature of Hu's signature ideology on "scientific view on development".

The State Master Plan also contained several components that would be further elevated in the subsequent emergency response law. In the next few paragraphs, I touch on the components: the continued reworking of the definition of an emergency and its categories; the emergence of risk assessment as a key governmental responsibility; the principles of organizing emergency management; the roles and responsibilities of academic experts; and the four grades of emergency severity.

Similar to how a public health emergency was defined in the 2003 regulation, the definition of an emergency also gestured towards the negative consequence of the event. It is an unexpected and sudden event that causes or could cause death and serious levels of injury, property damage and loss, environmental degradation and societal harm and threatens public safety and security. The definition in the

---

[99] See Article 1.1 in State Master Plan.

master plan also retained the characteristics of unexpectedness and suddenness from that of a public health emergency, but expanded the coverage to emergencies in general. It also stipulated the emergencies that were under its administrative coverage: natural disasters, accident-disasters, public health emergencies and public security emergencies, which are the four official categories of emergencies. In addition, the definition specified the potential harm emanating in these emergencies: death and injury, property loss and damage, environmental degradation (particularly for accident-disasters which covered industrial accidents such as oil spills) and threats to public safety and security (from protests and riots).

No longer couched in opaque language, such as "hidden dangers" in the regulation on public health emergencies, risk assessment was highlighted explicitly as an activity to be performed by the government. The organizing principles of unified command and a tiered responsibility approach were also present in the document. The involvement of academic experts went up a notch; no longer just confined to post-event impact assessment, experts were expected to be involved in emergency management as policy advisors. The state master plan stipulated that a database of experts on various specialized emergency situations should be created.

There was a new component not found in the 2003 regulation on public health emergencies. The four categories of emergency severity made their debut in the State Master Plan and were subsequently elevated into law. The emergency categories did not emerge *de novo*. They were suggested during the planning stage for national science and technology development which began in 2003.[100] Emergency management was an area to be developed under the domain of public safety and security.[101]

Because of the difficulties and complexities involved, I was expecting that another new component — grading of emergency severity — might turn into a point of contention during field formation. While emergency severity was prominent during field development, what I did not anticipate was the espoused consensus between academic experts and the rest of the establishment on the grading

---

[100] Refer to the record dated April 13, 2004, p. 120 in Shan, Chun Chang, Lan Xue, Xiu Lan Zhang and Hui Ding (eds.) (2012). *Zhongguo Yingji Guanli Dashi Ji (2003–2007) (Memorabilia of China's Emergency Management)*. Beijing, China: Shehui Wenxian Kexue Chuban She.

[101] The National Program for Long- and Medium Term Science and Technological Development, 2006–2020 (*Guojia Zhongchangqi Kexue he Jishu Fazhan Guihua* 国家中长期科学和技术发展规划) subsumed capability- and capacity-building for emergency management under public safety and security, a newly coined domain that was listed among the 20 domains to be developed at the national level from 2006 to 2020. The year 2020 has political significance too. China announced that it intended to quadruple its GDP per capita from US$800 in 2000 to about US$3,000 by 2020. See also Saich (2011).

system. What finally made it into State Master Plan and later the emergency response law was the agreement that the criterion of severity would be based on the general idea that the severity of a calamity depended on the extent to which it had exceeded the coping ability of the affected region. Yang, a scholar in the field of disaster prevention, highlighted this to me when he recounted the development of the field:

> It's determined by the scope of the impact from the extreme and sudden event. … [W]e realized different geographical regions did not have the same capability to manage the same disaster situation, and so [we decided] it would be the scope of impact and not the disaster situation.[102]

As the quote demonstrates, disaster severity was not based on definitive figures related to the physical attributes of the natural disaster (e.g. seismic strength) and losses (e.g. economic cost, death toll). This was a departure from the research trajectory of the natural disaster research community. Researchers over time had produced several models to assess severity, typically measuring the impact of extreme events in terms of economic costs and human losses.[103] Instead, the academic experts in China agreed with government officials to endorse a different idea of what counted as sufficiently severe for the state to intervene in emergencies, which was to base severity on the coping capacities of governments, a practice-based concept to the officials.[104]

Most of the components were either worked into or elaborated in the 2005 State Master Plan. I will next discuss the 2007 National Emergency Response Law, the legislative document in which we see the various components fully elaborated.

Enter the "Dragon": 2007 National Emergency Response Law

Hailed as the "dragon head" (*long tou* 龙头) and *de facto* constitutional document for emergency management, the 2007 National Emergency Response Law was the long-awaited umbrella legislation that closed the legislative gap in the field. The

---

[102] Interview with Yang, November 2012.

[103] See, for example, the 10 grades of severity in Xu, Feiqiong (1997). "Zaiji jiqi shiyi (Disaster grades and their interpretation)." *Zaihai Xue (Journal of Catastrophology)* 12(1), 16–18 and Feng's four-grade system based on Zhongjin Ma's established three-grade system in Feng, Lihua (2000). "Zaihai dengji yanjiu jinzhan (Development of research on disaster grades)." *Zaihai Xue (Journal of Catastrophology)* 15(3), 72–76.

[104] Interview with Yang, November 2012.

new law provided the overarching legal basis for the establishment to be involved across the entire spectrum of emergency management, from preparatory work before an emergency to response and containment as the emergency unfolds and to recovery after the emergency has subsided.[105]

To be clear, the Chinese government had long been involved in dealing with emergencies, especially natural disasters, such as floods and earthquakes. For those emergencies that were known to the Chinese since imperial times, the state had accumulated experience and established practices, as well as established organizational arrangements to manage them. However, before November 2007 when the emergency response law came into effect, the Chinese state not only had weaker legal power to govern emergencies, existing laws and administrative regulations were also fragmented and piecemeal. They either catered to specific singular events (e.g. earthquakes or floods) or covered only specific phases of emergency management (e.g. the response or recovery stage). In turn, the 2007 law encompassed all the necessary components. Among these components, the definition of an emergency seemed to receive the most curatorial efforts prior to its inclusion in the emergency response law. The definition now not only neatly weaved in the four categories of emergencies but also stated explicitly that their negative consequences necessitated state intervention:

> An emergency as mentioned in this Law shall refer to a natural disaster, accident-disaster, public health emergency or public security emergency, which takes place suddenly and unexpectedly, has caused or might cause serious societal damage and needs the adoption of emergency response measures.[106]

Unlike how it was presented in the State Master Plan, this definition customized the law's scope to fuse with the emergency categories, to the extent that it did not need to describe the negative consequences anymore because the impact was implicit in the categories it encompassed. The establishment seemed to be learning

---

[105] See, for example, Zhong, Kaibin (2009). "Huigu yu qianzhan: Zhongguo yingji tixi jianshe (Constructing China's emergency management system: A review and its prospects)." *Zhengzhi Xue Yanjiu (CASS Journal of Political Science)* (1):78–88; Shan, Chun Chang and Lan Xue (eds.) (2012). *Yingji Guanli Gailun: Lilun Yu Shijian (an Introduction to Emergency Management: Theory and Practice)*. Beijing, China: Gaodeng Jiaoyu Chubanshe; It has also been given other accolades, such as the "silver bullet" for managing the crises of tomorrow (*shangfang baojian* 尚方宝剑; literally imperial sword and a symbol of *carte blanche* power bestowed by an emperor on officials, granting them complete discretion when discharging their duties, especially to execute criminals immediately). See *People's Daily Online*. "Jujiao Tufa Shijian Yingdui Fa (Focusing on the National Emergency Response Law)" Retrieved January 15, 2014 (http://politics.people.com.cn/GB/8198/106624/index.html).

[106] See Article 3 in the National Emergency Response Law. I have amended the English translation of the law from www.lawinfochina.com.

from the successive enactments of the public health regulation and the master state plan (State Master Plan) to perfect the definition of emergency. The resultant effect is that the definition was not only more condensed but also made clear when an emergency was assessed as consequential enough to warrant governmental intervention. The definition now contained its causes, effects and solutions.

The new law covered not one but four broad classes of sudden and extreme events and provided a universal four-level severity-grading system. These two components were already present in the 2005 State Master Plan and remained more or less unchanged. However, the organizing principles for emergency management evolved into five principles: unified command (*tongyi lingdao* 统一领导), a comprehensive and integrated approach (*zonghe xietiao* 综合协调), responses to be pegged to the emergency category (*fenlei guanli* 分类管理), tiered responsibilities (*fenji fuze* 分级负责) and that emergency operations should be driven by local governments (*shudi guanli* 属地管理).[107]

The stages of emergency management were another component elaborated. Previously missing activities specific to preparedness and prevention were explicitly mentioned in the emergency response law. The new law also covered all phases of emergency management, subscribing to an "all-hazards" and comprehensive model that academic experts had advocated that the establishment adopt in the organizational field. Disaster and risk governance as a guiding concept could not have been more obvious: besides highlighting risk management and establishing a national catastrophe insurance system, it touched on multiple stakeholders, including academic experts, the military, businesses and citizens.

My analysis demonstrates that at the time when the emergency response law was enacted, a particular set of thinking, processes and organizational arrangements had come together. The law represented *curatorial* efforts engendered by the establishment to govern emergencies, especially with the view of treating emergencies as risks that could be measured and managed by government officials. Table 1 juxtaposes the three legislative products of the emergency management field. It demonstrates a progressive articulation and emergence of prominent components, including the principles of operation, the treatment of risk and its methods, inserting planning and academics into the process, various categories of emergencies to be subject to governance and clear definitions of the stages of emergency.

My account of how the various components were coming together shows that the organizational field of emergency management was forming in specific ways that were envisioned by the establishment and followed prominent ideas produced by the academic experts. The academic experts managed to develop and embed their ideas gradually, first in regulations and plans produced by the State Council, and then in

---

[107] See Article 4 in the National Emergency Response Law.

Table 1. Comparing the development of the components across time.

Components	Administrative regulation on public health emergency (2003)	State master plan on emergency response plans (2005)	National emergency response law (2007)
Definition of emergency	A sudden and unexpected incident that is causing or potentially causes harm to public health. An incident could be due to, but not limited to, an epidemic, known or yet to be identified, a case of severe food poisoning, or industrial contamination.	A sudden and unexpected event that is causing or potentially causes serious levels of death and injury, property damage and loss, environmental degradation and societal harm and endangerment to public safety and security.	A natural disaster, accident-disaster, public health emergency or public security emergency, which takes place suddenly and unexpectedly, is causing or potentially causes serious societal damage and needs the adoption of emergency response measures.
Principles of Organization	(1) Unified command (*tongyi lingdao* 统一领导) (2) Tiered responsibilities (*fenji fuze* 分级负责)	(1) People-centred (*yi ren wei ben*), reduce danger, harm and loss. (2) Be mindful of danger (*ju'an si wei*), focus on prevention (3) Unified command, tiered responsibilities (4) Act according to law, strengthen management (5) Rapid and coordinated response (6) Relying on technology, improving emergency management quality*	(1) Unified command (2) Comprehensive and integrated approach (*zonghe xietiao* 综合协调) (3) Responses to be pegged to the emergency category (*fenlei guanli* 分类管理) (4) Tiered responsibilities (5) Operations driven by local governments (*shudi guanli* 属地管理)
Emergency categories	NA**	Yes, all four categories	Yes, same four categories

Risk management	Alluded to as "hidden dangers" (*yinhuan* 隐患) that needed to be identified, analysed, and reported, but not explicitly as risks.***	No, but it specifies that emergency response plans need to be drilled and exercised.	Yes, conducting risk assessment under Prevention and Preparedness stage Various levels of governments shall take out personal accidental injury insurance for emergency responders and provide them with protective gear The state shall develop the insurance industry and a catastrophe insurance system
Prevention and Preparedness	Yes	Yes	Yes
Monitoring and Early Warning	Yes	Yes	Yes
Emergency Response and Rescue	Yes, but not in exact same terms.	Yes	Yes
Recovery and Reconstruction	No	Yes	Yes
Role of academic experts	Should be consulted *after the onset of emergency* to assess and advice on emergency response.	Specifies the creation of an expert database, the involvement of experts as policy advisors *prior* to the onset of emergencies and to involve them in response if necessary.	Specifies that experts should be involved *prior* to the onset of emergencies, particularly in assessing the risk of emergencies (expressed as the possibility and consequence of the events in the law) and its likely severity grade *after its onset.*

Note: *See Article 1.5 of the State Master Plan. **As the regulation only pertained to public health, it would not highlight other types of emergencies. ***See articles 15 and 24 of the Administrative Regulation on Public Health Emergencies.

legislative documents that enjoyed far more legal power than the administrative documents. Specifically, recognizable components such as emergency categories, risk assessment, severity grades and emergency management phases were gradually introduced, became better defined as they moved from the Administrative Regulation on Public Health Emergencies to the State Master Plan for Emergency Response, and finally enacted in the all-encompassing National Emergency Response Law.

DISCUSSION

The 2003 SARS crisis accentuated the various shifts that were changing and continued to configure Chinese society, especially the crumpling of *danwei* as a social institution coupled with rapid urbanization that facilitated virus contagion. It generated a sense of crisis within the governing elites, prompting them to modify their thinking, especially their conceptualization of risk and disasters, on the scenarios that could unsettle them and destabilize China. The SARS epidemic also became the focusing event[108] because of the historical and accidental interplay between the time and place of its occurrence: the virus struck the capital at the height of decadal political leadership transition.[109]

The emerging or formative phase of the Chinese emergency management organizational field from 2002 to 2012 provides an occasion to generate insights on the dynamics of early field formation, a knowledge gap that has been recently acknowledged and highlighted.[110] The hiatus between the realization of the knowledge gap and DiMaggio's (1991)[111] in-depth study on the formation of US museums was a long one. Until a few years ago, most institutional analyses focused on organizational fields that were already established or mature.[112] My study thus adds to a growing number of studies that examine early field formation or emerging fields.[113–115]

---

[108] Birkland, T. A. (1997). *Op cit.*

[109] Wu, G. (2014). *Op cit.*

[110] Wooten, M. and Hoffman, A. J. (2008). *Op cit.*

[111] DiMaggio, P. J. (1991). "Constructing an Organizational Field as a Professional Project: U.S. Art Museums, 1920–1940." In Powell, W. W. and DiMaggio, P. J. (eds.), *The New Institutionalism in Organizational Analysis*. Chicago, IL: University of Chicago Press, pp. 267–292.

[112] Greenwood, R. and Suddaby, R. (2006). "Institutional Entrepreneurship in Mature Fields: The Big Five Accounting Firms." *Academy of Management Journal* 49(1), 27–48.

[113] Lawrence, T. B. and Phillips, N. (2004). "From Moby Dick to Free Willy: Macro-Cultural Discourse and Institutional Entrepreneurship in Emerging Institutional Fields." *Organization* 11(5), 689–711.

[114] Maguire, S., Hardy, C. and Lawrence, T. B. (2004). "Institutional Entrepreneurship in Emerging Fields: Hiv/Aids Treatment Advocacy in Canada." *Academy of Management Journal* 47(5), 657–679.

[115] Purdy, J. M. and Gray, B. (2009). *Op cit.*

Chinese emergency management as an emerging organizational field has already established clear hierarchical and administrative structures and also assumed identifiable patterns of interaction, such as relationships of domination and subordination,[116] among its constituents fairly quickly. The uncharacteristically swift consolidation within the Chinese context is owed partly to the fact that existent existing entities were strategically incorporated into emergency management. To give a brief illustration, the State Committee on Disaster Reduction, the highest level of committee on emergency management for natural disasters, was under the purview of the State Council, and the latter entity preceded the appearance of this new organizational field by more than a decade.

Next I highlight the notion of curation. The notion of curation emphasizes careful positioning, piecing together and taking away ideas, be they expressed in discursive (e.g. regulations and laws) or embodied forms (e.g. new organizational unit, practices). The notion of careful calibration of such scripts and schemas is not unique to or absent from neo-institutional theory. Notions of building and mobilizing "institutional vocabularies" in order to articulate specific qualities, such as professionalism,[117] are also present in the Chinese emergency management case.

Curation includes attempts at theorization,[118–120] in which purposeful (re) assembly of ideas and practices specifies the relationships and claims among them, especially by "culturally legitimated theorists," i.e. the emergency management establishment who occupy prestigious and influential positions within their institutional environments.[121] Acts of curation are not constrained to only removing ideas that do not fit. They assume a more nuanced quality towards ideas that might not be central but are still germane to the gatekeepers who perform the curation.[122] As in the practice of curation in museums, a select number of artefacts take centre stage, whereas others are positioned in ways that complement or contrast with them.

The definition of emergencies concerned categories of events that disrupt or threaten to disrupt the societal stability with death, injury, property damage and loss. As a result, these emergencies were a danger to continued economic growth and societal status quo and thus warranted state intervention. This

---

[116] DiMaggio, P. J. and Powell, W. W. (1983). *Op cit.*

[117] Suddaby, R. and Greenwood, R. (2005). *Op cit.*, p. 43.

[118] Greenwood, R., Suddaby, R. and Hinings, C. R. (2002). *Op cit.*

[119] Strang, D. and Meyer, J. W. (1993). *Op cit.*

[120] Zilber, T. B. (2008). *Op cit.*

[121] Strang, D. and Meyer, J. W. (1993). *Op cit.*

[122] Khaire, M. (2014). "Fashioning an Industry: Socio-Cognitive Processes in the Construction of Worth of a New Industry." *Organization Studies* 35(1), 41–74.

understanding of emergency as dangerous converges and aligns with Stallings's analysis of putative threat that the US earthquake establishment was constructing, in which earthquakes were cast as problems that could be solved by policy and scientific experts familiar with that natural hazard. This parallels sociologist Dombrowsky's (1995)[123] observation of the tautological relationship between a definition and its definers (i.e. organized actors) of disasters from the case of the German government, in how the self-referential claim is enshrined into legislation:

> The German law … defines "disaster" … by saying it involves "such severe interference of the public order and safety that an intervention of the centralized, coordinated disaster protection units is necessary"[124] … Even more tautological is the definition by law: A disaster is what the intervention of disaster relief units make necessary…For the state, the breakdown of public order and safety is the key, not the phenomena [i.e. storm, flood etc.] (p. 242).

CONCLUSION

In this chapter, I demonstrated the depth and extent of effort the establishment, i.e. the Chinese political leadership and experts, invested in building the nascent organizational field from 2002/2003 to 2012 as its *de facto* "laboratory" to experiment with and refine its ideas around emergency management practices — particularly ideas about risk and governance — as it designed its policies and organizations. In reconfiguring its ensemble of laws, regulations and organizational processes on disaster management, we saw curation at work: the emergence and evolution of an ensemble of components that were inscribed into the field. The institutional vocabularies, i.e. the ideational components, were most obvious in legislative and administrative landmarks, such as the regulations and laws that were approved and enacted, especially during the intensive institutionalized period of field formation.

ACKNOWLEDGMENTS

I am grateful for the financial support from the following bodies to conduct my research: Sociology Department (Graduate Student Research Awards, 2012 and

---

[123] Dombrowsky, W. R. (1995). "Again and Again: Is a Disaster What We Call a "Disaster"? Some Conceptual Notes on Conceptualizing the Object of Disaster Sociology." *International Journal of Mass Emergencies and Disasters* 13(3), 241–254.

[124] Seeck, E. (1980). *Gesetz uber den Katastrophenschutz in Schleswig-Holstein (LkatSG) vom 9 Dezember 1974*. Wiesbaden: Kommunal und Schul-Verlag A. Heinig.

2013) and the Graduate School (Center to Advance Research and Teaching in the Social Sciences [CARTSS] Graduate Fellowship, 2012; Summer Graduate Fellowship, 2013) at University of Colorado-Boulder, and Ministry of Science and Technology, People's Republic of China (Grant Nos. 2012CB955404 and 2012DFG20710).

Chapter 7

TORU HASHIMOTO'S UNFINISHED LOCAL GOVERNANCE REFORM: A MICRO CASE STUDY OF POLITICAL LEADERSHIP AT LOCAL-LEVEL POLITICS IN JAPAN

Y. Godo

Department of Economics, Meiji Gakuin University, Minato City, Tokyo 108-0071, Japan

DISCUSSION FRAMEWORK AND THESIS STATEMENT

The charismatic politician Toru Hashimoto is the "male Cinderella" of the Japanese political world. Unknown until the age of 33 years, Hashimoto first came to attention as a one-of-a-kind lawyer in 2003 when he appeared regularly on an Osaka-based television programme. He entered the political world by running for the gubernatorial election for Osaka Prefecture in January 2008, which he won in a landslide victory. As soon as he took up the post, he initiated a series of reforms, including the financial reconstruction of the Osaka Prefectural Government. He launched the Osaka Metropolis Plan in January 2010, which aimed to dissolve Osaka City and its neighbouring cities to form special wards and concentrate decision-making procedures for the entire area that makes up today's Osaka Prefecture in the hands of the Osaka Metropolitan Government. Hashimoto recruited politicians supporting the Osaka Metropolis Plan and formed a new political party in April 2010, which was initially known as "Initiatives from Osaka" and later renamed the Japan Innovation Party (JIP).

Using the Osaka Metropolis Plan as an election platform, Hashimoto and his sworn friend Ichiro Matsui won the mayoral and gubernatorial elections, respectively, in November 2011. These victories pressured members of the national Diet to pass the Act Allowing Establishing Special Wards in Metropolitan Areas Outside in August 2012, which enabled any city to be dissolved to form special wards after an affirming referendum in the city. However, as the governments of Osaka City's neighbouring cities objected to the Osaka Metropolis Plan, Hashimoto and JIP members prepared a new plan to introduce the special ward system only to Osaka City. The referendum for the new plan took place in Osaka City in May 2015.

The outcome of the vote was the rejection of the Osaka Metropolis Plan by a narrow margin. This did not necessarily mean that Hashimoto had to relinquish the mayoralty. Indeed, Hashimoto's popularity was maintained even after the referendum. However, he considered that the defeat in the referendum provided the right time for him to retire from the political world. In spite of repeated requests from Hashimoto's supporters, he has never run for an election for public office since the referendum. Moreover, Hashimoto has seceded from JIP. While he is still popular in the mass media as a TV personality, he no longer occupies any official position in political circles. This study investigates the factors that brought Hashimoto to sudden prominence and sudden disappearance. Why did he disappear as abruptly as he appeared? Would the Osaka Metropolis Plan have achieved the revitalization of Osaka's economy? Seeking answers to these questions, this study seeks to understand the implications of Hashimoto's unfinished reform attempts.

INTRODUCTION

Toru Hashimoto had a meteoric rise from obscurity to fame in the Japanese political world.[1] He produced a good (but not excellent) performance in sports and academics at school, but his star grew bright only after the age of 33 years when he became a household name in Osaka as a one-of-a-kind lawyer after regularly appearing on an Osaka-based TV programme in 2003. By adopting an unusual modern fashion and presenting sharp (sometimes blunt and coarse) comments about current events as a regular member in the TV programme, he became a charismatic opinion leader in Osaka and expectations began to increase about his entrance into politics among

---

[1] "Hashimoto" is a popular family name in Japan and there are many famous people whose family name is Hashimoto. For example, Ryutaro Hashimoto served as the 82nd and 83rd Prime Minister of Japan from 11 January 1996 to 30 July 1998. Seiko Hashimoto has the most Olympic appearances of any Japanese athlete. However, readers should be careful not to assume that Toru Hashimoto is related to other famous people named Hashimoto.

the citizens of Osaka. In these circumstances, Hashimoto ran for the Osaka gubernatorial election in January 2008 and won with a landslide victory. As the governor of Osaka Prefecture, he launched various reform plans and enjoyed a high approval rate in public opinion polls. However, instead of running for a second consecutive term as governor, he ran for the mayoral election of Osaka City in November 2011, and again won with a landslide victory.

During his terms as governor of Osaka Prefecture and mayor of Osaka City, Hashimoto was also active in party politics. By establishing a new political party and becoming its leader, he participated in state affairs in addition to Osaka's local affairs. Hashimoto's fresh ideas and bold power of political action and reform calls excited public attention and were popularly called Hashimoto-ism. Hashimoto-ism received both applause and resentment nationwide. Some groups supported Hashimoto as a long-awaited reformer. Others criticized Hashimoto-ism as a "dangerous drug" that would sacrifice socially disadvantaged people.

The centrepiece of Hashimoto-ism was a radical policy proposal, called the "Osaka Metropolis Plan", which attracted the general public's attention on the nation stage because it included an overall reform for Japan's long-instituted local governance system. Hashimoto asserted that the Osaka Metropolis Plan was a last-ditch effort to revive Osaka's economy, which had been stagnant for more than two decades. However, some groups opposed the Osaka Metropolis Plan as a figment of Hashimoto's imagination, which, if implemented, would worsen local problems, not solve them, as Hashimoto argued. Arguments for and against the Osaka Metropolis Plan heated up. In order to settle the debate, Hashimoto held a referendum on the Osaka Metropolis Plan in May 2015. He lost by a narrow margin, as the number of people voting against the Osaka Metropolis Plan surpassed those in favour of it.

In response to the referendum result, Hashimoto abandoned the Osaka Metropolis Plan and decided to retire entirely from politics. In spite of burning requests from his supporters, Hashimoto has never since run for any election for public office. While he remains popular in the mass media as a TV personality, he no longer holds any official position in political circles. Why did such a previously obscure personality rise to fame so suddenly? What was Hashimoto-ism? Why did Hashimoto retire from politics? What should we learn from Hashimoto's challenges? This study aims to answer these questions. The rest of this paper is structured as follows. The following section reviews Osaka's poor performance, which frustrated Osaka citizens and was a fertile ground for the emergence of a radical reformist, such as Hashimoto. Thereafter, we outline Japan's local governance system, which Hashimoto's reform challenged. Section "Hashimoto's Challenges in Reforming Osaka" discusses the details of the Osaka Metropolis Plan. The final section considers the lessons that should be taken from Hashimoto's challenges.

THE OSAKA PROBLEM

Historical Background

Tokyo is Japan's leading metropolis. The national government's offices, leading research institutes, popular theatres and museums, headquarters of famous companies, and major entertainment facilities cluster in Tokyo — a nucleus of cultural and economic activities within Japan. However, this has not always been the case. Japanese society used to be more diversified. In particular, Osaka was a formidable rival for Tokyo. Osaka, located 400 km from Tokyo, developed as a commercial and port city. Osaka's nickname is *Tenka No Daidokoro,* which means the "Unrivalled Kitchen of the Nation," in reference to the storage area of a common household kitchen. Throughout the Tokugana Shogunate period (1608–1868), Osaka was more advanced in economic and cultural activities than Edo — which was renamed Tokyo during the Meiji Restoration of 1868. Japan's top-level merchants lived in Osaka and fostered their own culture. In fact, Tokyo was not Japan's capital city, until only after the Meiji Restoration of 1868. From 794 to 1867, Kyoto, located only 40 km from Osaka, was the capital of Japan and housed the residence of the Imperial Family.[2] Kyoto is an inland city, connected to Osaka by the Yodo River, one of the largest rivers in Japan.[3] Thus, Osaka also functioned as the gateway to Kyoto.

Even after the capital moved to Tokyo in 1868, Osakans were proud of Osaka's economic power. They proclaimed that Osaka should be regarded as the centre of the economy while Tokyo should be the centre of politics. This was not an exaggeration in terms of industrial history. When Japan started its heavy industrialization period after the First World War, Osaka was referred to as "Great Osaka" because new modern businesses, such as steel, developed faster in Osaka than in any other regions in Japan. Osaka has various advantages as a factory site for heavy industries. First, Osaka is endowed with a rich water supply from Yodo River. In the process of producing heavy industry commodities, factories need large volumes of water. Second, Osaka is suitable for shipping heavy industry commodities, for which water transport is necessary. Third, Osaka has easy access to low-wage manual workers because it has a long history of fostering communities of migrant workers from less developed areas in Japan.

In the 1920s, Osaka surpassed Tokyo in population and flourished as the sixth largest city in the world.[4] However, Osaka underwent an ordeal when Japan introduced a rationing system for industrial materials and fuels in 1938 as part of

---

[2] The capital city temporarily changed from Kyoto in Japan's mediaeval era when civil war took place, but these were only very short periods.

[3] There are 965 tributaries of the Yodo River system (the largest in Japan).

[4] In contrast to Osaka's stellar economic performance in the 1920s, Tokyo's economy suffered huge damage from the Great Tokyo Earthquake of 1923.

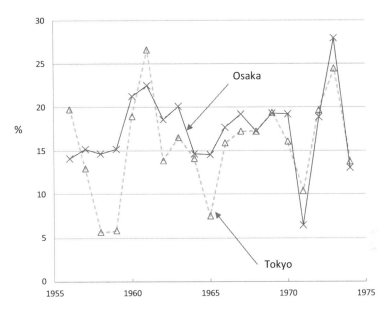

Figure 1. Comparison of GDP annual growth rate between Osaka and Tokyo.
Source: Report on Prefectural Accounts produced by the Cabinet Office.

militarization.[5] To prepare for war, the Japanese government pressed for production resources in Tokyo. This policy placed Osaka at a disadvantage relative to Tokyo. In addition, repeated bombing by the US Air Force in the Pacific War severely damaged Osaka. In the 1950s, when Japan restarted heavy industrialization, economic vitality returned to Osaka. As shown in Figure 1, Osaka's economy grew faster than Tokyo's. Osaka's per capita income was the highest among all 46 prefectures throughout the 1950s, 1960s and 1970s. The oil crisis in the 1970s marked the turning point.[6] Because of political instability among Middle East oil-producing countries, the oil price soared to nearly 10 times the level it was during the pre-oil crisis period. Japan's self-sufficiency in oil is less than 1% and Japan relies heavily on oil imports from the Middle East. Thus, the oil crisis seriously undermined the international competitive power of Japanese manufacturing companies. As a result, Japan's leading sector changed from manufacturing to services, signalling the arrival of the Japanese economy at the post-industrialization stage.[7]

---

[5] The Japanese government employed a rationing system for industrial materials and fuels through the National Mobilization Law in 1938.
[6] The oil crisis took place twice in the 1970s, the first happened in 1973 and the second in 1979.
[7] According to the Japanese population census, the secondary sector (light and heavy industry companies make up the majority of the secondary sector) accounted for a peak of 34.1% of the labour force in 1975 and has kept declining since then (the Japanese population census takes place every 5 years).

Table 1. Tokyo and Osaka's GDP as percentages of Japan's GDP.

	Tokyo				Osaka			
Year	2015 standard	2005 standard	1990 standard	1980 standard	2015 standard	2005 standard	1990 standard	1980 standard
2014	18.5				7.4			
2001	18.2	16.9			7.8	7.7		
1990		17.0	16.9			8.5	8.0	
1975			16.8				9.0	
1970				17.1				10.2
1955				16.9				7.4

Source: Report on Prefectural Accounts produced by the Cabinet Office.

After the oil crisis, in contrast to Japan, its neighbouring countries, such as Korea, Taiwan and Thailand, sped up heavy industrialization. These newly industrialized countries in Asia started eroding Japan's international market share. This severely damaged Osaka, whose heavy industries led the high-speed economic growth in the nation before the oil crisis. As shown in Table 1, Osaka's share of national GDP continued to decline over three decades. In addition, as Figure 2 shows, Osaka's per capita income, at one stage the highest among the 46 prefectures, became lower than the national average in 2002 (and remains so even now). Osaka's social statistics are just as bad as its economic statistics. Among the 46 prefectures, Osaka has the highest unemployment rate, crimes per capita, child abuse per capita, homeless people per capita and number of welfare recipients per capita, while it has the lowest scholastic ability of middle school students.[8] Osaka's poor performance on these indicators has been termed the "Osaka Problem".

Importantly, it is possible that Osaka could have performed better even in the post-industrialization stage. Indeed, Kanagawa and Fukuoka, which, together with Osaka, led Japan's heavy industrialization until the oil crisis, performed better than Osaka after the oil crisis. For example, in these 10 years, Osaka's per capita income kept declining while that of Fukuoka and Kanagawa remained almost constant.[9] What is the reason for Osaka's poor performance? There are many

---

[8] More statistical information on Osaka's performance is provided in Sakaiya, Taichi, Shin-ichi Ueyama and Eiji Hara (2012), *Osaka Ishin towa Nanika* (Initiatives from Osaka). Tokyo: Togensha.
[9] According to the Report on Prefectural Accounts produced by the Cabinet Office, the per capita income in Fukuoka, Kanagawa and Osaka in 2006 was 3,098, 2,654 and 3,303 yen, respectively. In 2015, these were 2,986, 2,724 and 3,127 yen, respectively.

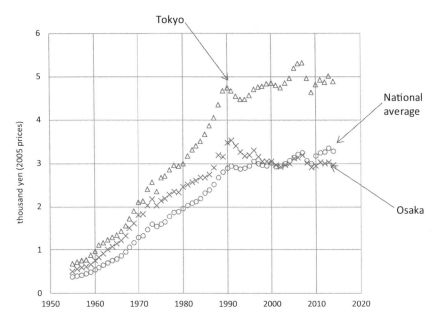

Figure 2. Comparison of per-capita income.

Source: Report on Prefectural Accounts produced by the Cabinet Office.

possible answers to this question. As shown in section "Hashimoto's Challenges in Reforming Osaka", Hashimoto regarded the inefficiency of Osaka's local governance system as one of the biggest problems. First, it would be useful to provide an overview on the relationship between Japan's national and local governments.

JAPAN'S LOCAL GOVERNANCE SYSTEM

The Local Governance Act stipulates the legal framework of Japan's local governance system. Tokyo's local governance system is different from other areas. This study first reviews Japan's local governance system for areas outside Tokyo.

Two Layers of Local Government

There are two layers of local government in Japan. The administrative system of the first layer of governance is known as the "municipality" and is the basic unit of local governance. Japanese citizens living within the boundaries of these administrative units must register as residents of that area with the municipal government and must provide details of their residence to their registry. Municipal governments are responsible for providing basic public services, such as operating public elementary schools and granting pension payouts/allowances to the elderly. The administrative unit of the second administrative layer is called a "prefecture". The prefectural government supports the municipal governmental units within its jurisdiction by providing public services that require specialized knowledge or additional resources and/or that cover a broader scope than a municipality. For example, the prefectural government is responsible for constructing main roads, granting approval for and providing guidance to public nursing-care organizations and constructing and operating wide-area sewerage facilities.

A municipality can be classified into three categories (village, town and city) according to its population size. If the population of a municipality is less than a certain number (usually designated as ~8,000 in most municipal units) stipulated by a prefectural order, then the municipality is termed a "village." The municipality is a "city" if the population exceeds 50,000. A municipality whose population ranges between these two figures is designated as a "town." If the population of a city exceeds 500,000 and the Prime Minister's Office recognizes the city office as having a high level of administrative ability, the city qualifies to become an "ordinance-designated city". By this definition, there were 181 villages, 739 towns and 768 cities (20 ordinance-designated cities and 748 ordinary cities) in Japan's 46 prefectures in June 2018.

Administratively, towns and villages are treated equally by the Local Governance Act.[10]

However, when a "town" becomes a "city," it acquires greater autonomy for the municipal unit. For example, in providing social benefits, city municipal governments can decide which groups in their jurisdiction are needy, whereas in towns and villages, this decision rests with the prefectural government instead of the municipal government. An ordinance-designated city government has far greater autonomy than an ordinary city government. For example, while an ordinary city government needs the approval of the prefectural government to design a city development plan, an ordinance-designated city government can make its own decisions. With an increase in population, effective communication between the municipal government and citizens becomes more difficult. To overcome this, ordinance-designated cities have a unique administrative system called the "ward" system. The area of an ordinance-designated city is divided into wards, each with its own office, which provides basic services to the residents in the

---

[10] As the word "village" suggests, villages comprise agriculture-oriented, traditional societies. A "village" becomes a "town" after it has undergone modernization symbolically and in real terms, although there is no actual change in the role of the municipal government when the former becomes the latter's unit.

ward. Every citizen of an ordinance-designated city comes under the purview of the ward. For example, paperwork for residential registration, marriage registration, and a seal certification service are provided at the ward office of the applicant's residential area.

Each municipal or prefectural government has its own head and assembly. The heads of a municipal government and a prefectural government are called the "mayor" and "governor", respectively. Residents older than 18 years have voting rights in the elections of the municipal mayor, the prefectural governor and members of the municipal assembly and prefectural assembly, each of whom is elected for a term of 4 years. In the municipal assembly elections of villages, towns and ordinary cities, the boundaries of a single constituency (i.e. whole area of a municipality) are drawn up and an elector votes for a single entry, even though there is more than one assembly member. For the prefectural assembly election, the prefecture is divided into plural constituencies. The total number of assembly members varies according to the constituencies: some are single while others are plural. Whichever is the case, an elector may vote for only a single entry.

As in the case of an ordinary city, an ordinance-designated city has a single mayor and a single assembly. However, unlike the case of an ordinary city, the assembly member's election in ordinance-designated cities takes place in plural constituencies that use each ward as a constituency. The number of assembly members for a ward is determined by the city ordinance. The basic unit of local governance is not a ward but an ordinance-designated city. The head of each ward is appointed by the mayor of the ordinance-designated city (not by election). This is because the head of a ward is responsible for administrative matters only, and not for making political decisions.

Tokyo's Unique Local Governance System

Similar to the 46 prefectures, Tokyo's local governance system also comprises two layers of administration. However, the upper layer is called a "metropolis" instead of a "prefecture." There are eight villages, five towns, and 26 cities (all of which are ordinary cities) in Tokyo Metropolis, which also has another type of municipal unit (in the lower layer of administration) called the "special ward." Unlike the wards in ordinance-determinant cities, a special ward is recognized as the basic unit of local governance in Tokyo. The head of each special ward is elected by residents who are 18 years and older, and each special ward has its own assembly, with members who are elected by voting procedure in a single-constituency system. A term of the head and assembly members of the special ward is 4 years.

There are 23 special wards in Tokyo. The administrative activities/powers of a special ward government are limited compared to the other municipality types (i.e. village, town and city). The Tokyo Metropolitan Government oversees some of the activities/powers that are often conducted by ward-level municipal governments in other municipality types.[11] For example, while the public bus system is usually operated by the municipal government in Japan, it is operated by the Tokyo Metropolitan Government in the 23 special wards of Tokyo. The taxation powers of special ward governments are also limited. Whereas the imposition and collection of asset taxes in the 23 special wards is within the purview of the Tokyo Metropolitan Government, in the rest of Japan, it is usually undertaken by the municipal governments. A portion of the asset taxes imposed on special wards collected by the Tokyo Metropolitan Government is transferred to the 23 special ward governments. Every year, the Tokyo Metropolitan Government and the 23 special ward governments negotiate on the allocation of duties to provide basic services to residents and to divide the tax revenues. As for prefectures, the Tokyo Metropolitan Government has its own assembly, whose head is the "governor". Residents aged 18 years and older have voting rights in the elections for the Tokyo Metropolitan Governor and the Tokyo Metropolitan Assembly. The election for the Tokyo Metropolitan Assembly takes place within the 42 constituencies. The term of the Tokyo Metropolitan Governor and the Tokyo Metropolitan Assembly members is each 4 years. In 12 of the relatively large cities and in 23 special wards, the municipality forms a constituency for election to the Tokyo Metropolitan Assembly. The other 14 cities, five towns and eight villages are grouped into seven constituencies. The total number of assembly members from a constituency varies among constituencies: some have only one and others have more. In either case, a voter casts a vote for a single entry alone.

Figures 3 and 4 depict the two types of local governance systems. In Figure 3, the area of the ordinance-designated city government overlaps with that of the prefectural government, indicating that the ordinance-designated city government is qualified to perform more functions than are other types of municipal governments. In Figure 4, the Tokyo Metropolitan Government enters the administrative purview of special ward governments. This reflects the fact that budgets and activities of special wards are dependent on the Tokyo Metropolitan Government.

---

[11] Up until 1 July 1943, Tokyo City existed as the basic unit of local government in the area where the headquarters of national ministries were located. Expecting that the US Air Force would carry out large-scale bombing at Tokyo, the national government hastily attempted to build air defence facilities to protect high-ranking officials. To save time doing so, the national government permitted the Tokyo City Government to skip the process of administrative procedures. For this reason, Tokyo City was dissolved and transformed into the prototype of today's special ward system.

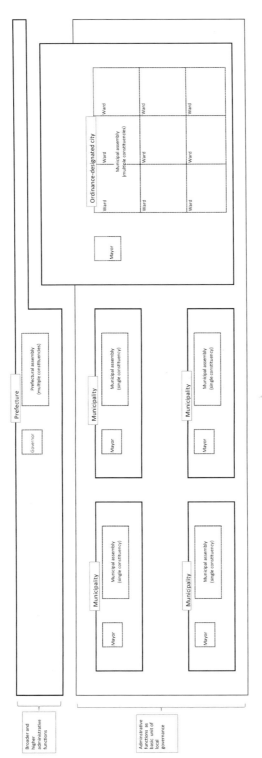

Figure 3. Local governance in 46 prefectures.

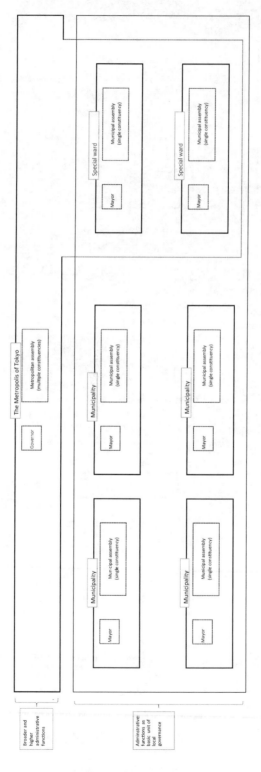

Figure 4. Local governance in Tokyo.

Local Governance Problems in Osaka

Osaka Prefecture has one village, nine towns, and 33 cities. Osaka City and Sakai City are ordinance-designated cities and have 24 and 7 wards, respectively. Osaka City contributes 70% of the GDP of Osaka Prefecture. In the pre-Pacific War period, Osaka City constituted 70% of Osaka Prefecture's total population. However, based on the development of the public transportation system in the post-Pacific War period, the population of individuals who live outside Osaka City and commute to Osaka City for work has increased; in particular, an increasing number of high-income families moved to luxurious residential areas that sprouted during the post-Pacific War period. This has led to various problems. A typical example is the Osaka Metro, which is owned by the Osaka City Government.[12] A limitation of the Osaka Metro is that it operates only within the jurisdiction of Osaka City, while 60% of passengers using the Osaka Metro live outside Osaka City. The Osaka City Government has constructed new subway lines based on its own city development plan. However, the plan might not be suitable for neighbouring municipalities. As a result, the overall layout of the railway network in Osaka Prefecture has turned out to be inefficient.

Duplicate investments by the Osaka City Government and the Osaka Prefectural Government present another significant local governance problem. Each invests in its own libraries, sport facilities and schools without coordination. Duplicate investments in water supply between Osaka Prefecture and Osaka City are one of the most serious problems.[13] The Osaka City Water Works Bureau (OCWWB), a bureau of the Osaka City Government, handles the water utility services for citizens in Osaka City. In the other 42 municipalities in Osaka Prefecture, water utility services are provided by a special local public entity called the Osaka Water Supply Authority (OWSA), jointly founded by the Osaka Prefectural Government and all 42 municipal governments in the prefecture.

---

[12] Up until 1 April 2018, the Osaka Metropolitan Subway, instead of Osaka Metro, was in charge of operating the subway system in Osaka City. The Osaka Metropolitan Subway was directly operated by the Osaka City Government and was known as the biggest subway system operated by a local government in Japan. Researchers often complained that Osaka Metropolitan Subway was too big as a municipal enterprise to have efficient management (e.g. see Shin-ichi Ueyama (2012), *Kokyo Keiei no Saikochiku* (Public Enterprise Reform). Tokyo: Nikkei BP). Osaka Metro was founded on 1 June 2017 as a publicly financed private enterprise. All the shares of the Osaka Metro were (and still are) owned by the Osaka City Government. On 1 April 2018, the operation of Osaka Metropolitan Subway was transferred to Osaka Metro. Even after this transformation, all the ownership of fixed assets for the subway system has been vested in the Osaka City Government.

[13] For more details, see Yoshihisa Godo (2016), "Osaka's Attempt at Restructuring its Public Water Utility Services," *FFTC Agricultural Policy Articles.*

The OCWWB and OWSA have constructed independent water pipelines. The lack of coordination has led to pipeline layouts becoming complicated and inefficient. For example, some areas in Osaka City were better served when water was supplied via the OWSA than via the OCWWB. There is potential for substantial improvement in the water utility service system of Osaka Prefecture. Experts on local governance assert that the water utility service in Osaka would be more efficient if the OCWWB merged with the OWSA. However, for fear of losing their jobs after the merger, public servants of the OCWWB, who form a powerful section of the labour union of public servants of the Osaka City Government, raised their opposition.

HASHIMOTO'S CHALLENGES IN REFORMING OSAKA

Hashimoto's Debut as a Politician

Toru Hashimoto has a unique background. He was born in 1969 in Tokyo, the son of a family of the discriminated class known as *burakumin*. Hashimoto's father passed away during his childhood and he moved to Osaka with his mother. He was multitalented from his youth. In his high school days, he was nominated as a candidate for Japan's national high school rugby team. He graduated from Waseda University, one of the top universities in Japan. He passed the bar examination immediately after and started his career as a lawyer in Osaka. He was not an orthodox lawyer. While the majority of Japanese lawyers behave and dress as custom dictates, Hashimoto loves to veer off the beaten track. His impudence has given him both good and bad reputations among the people who were close to him.

Picking up on this reputation, an Osaka-based broadcasting company hired Hashimoto as a one-of-a-kind commentator in 2005. His showy looks and frank discussion style attracted the audiences, especially as Osaka has a culture of resisting government authority. He quickly became one of the most popular TV personalities in Osaka. Political issues were Hashimoto's most favourite issue to tackle as a TV personality. His daring policy reform proposals excited audiences. As a result, Osakans' expectations grew that Hashimoto would become a politician instead of a TV commentator. Such local support prompted Hashimoto to run for the gubernatorial election of Osaka Prefecture in January 2008. His electoral rivals were two candidates who were supported by Japan's major national parties.

Despite his inexperience in the political world and his lack of a strong political base, Hashimoto won in an overwhelming victory with 1.83 million votes — more than half of the total votes. This victory was reported extensively in mass media nationwide. A majority of political commentators, however, took a sceptical view about Hashimoto's abilities as the governor. Indeed, there had been instances in the 1990s and 2000s of personal misconduct and/or poor political performance by TV personalities who had become governors.[14] Thus, it was natural to consider that the same thing could happen to Hashimoto.

Contrary to expectations, Hashimoto demonstrated high ability in politics as soon as he took office. He actively launched a series of reforms in the administrative system of the Osaka Prefectural Government. For example, under Hashimoto's leadership, the management of the two international airports in Osaka Prefecture, namely, Osaka International Airport and Kansai International Airport, were unified and privatized. Hashimoto urged the national government to reduce the local governments' share (and increase the national government's share) of the expenses in public construction projects in Osaka Prefecture. He also succeeded in financially reconstructing the Osaka Prefectural Government by revision of the prefectural government's management system of public-sector accounting, wage cutting for public servants and relinquishment of business ventures jointly financed by the prefectural government and private sector.

Hashimoto was active in party politics, too. In April 2010, by recruiting like-minded people, Hashimoto established a political party, Osaka Restoration Association (ORA). The ORA won a majority in the Osaka Prefectural Assembly in the local election in April 2011. To extend the field of party activities from the local level to the national level, the ORA was transformed into the Japan Restoration Association (JRA) in September 2012. With the participation of interested members of the national Diet, the JRA formed a faction within the national Diet in October 2012. The JRA was renamed the Japan Innovation Party (JIP) in September 2014[15] and has played a key position with its proportion of votes in the national Diet. As the party's leader, Hashimoto participated in state affairs as well as in Osaka's local affairs.

---

[14] Isamu Yamada, who had been the governor of Osaka Prefecture from 1991 to 1995, can be regarded as a typical example of a hugely popular TV personality but incompetent politician. Before Yamada entered the political world, he was one of the most widely sought-after comic dialogists. He ran for the gubernatorial election of Osaka Prefecture twice consecutively: first in 1995 and then in 1999. He won landslide victories in both elections. However, he committed an indecent assault during his second election campaign and stepped down from the post of the governor immediately after the second term of his governorship started.

[15] From September 2015 to September 2016, there were several realignments of national parties. The JIP absorbed other parties and then split into several parties. Each time, the party name changed. Eventually, founding members who joined the JIP got together in September 2016 and restarted the JIP. This study ignores the difference in the party names in these 13 months as long as the majority of the party members were in the mainstream of today's JIP.

Hashimoto's Osaka Metropolis Plan

Hashimoto's attempts to reform Osaka reform were called Hashimoto-ism and drew both appreciation and resentment. Some groups regarded Hashimoto-ism as a desirable model of local governance reform. For them, Hashimoto was a long-awaited leader in Japanese political circles. Others criticized Hashimoto-ism as a "dangerous drug" that would sacrifice socially disadvantaged people. For them, Hashimoto was a harmful advocator of populism and/or market fundamentalism. One of the strongest blocs of resistance to Hashimoto's reforms was politicians and public-sector labour unions in Osaka Prefecture. For example, Kunio Hiramatsu, the mayor of Osaka City, warned that Hashimoto's approach would simply sacrifice the weak without improving administrative efficiency.

Hiramatsu considered Hashimoto to be a showy performer for the mass media and to have no real reform intentions in mind. However, on the flipside, critics of Hiramatsu regarded him as trapped in the mindset of the old guard, as were a majority of Osaka City Assembly members and labour union members. Hiramatsu's political opinions (and resistance) were brushed aside by Hashimoto. However, as Osaka City is the biggest municipality in Osaka Prefecture, to proceed with Hashimoto's reform plans, such as merging the OCWWB and OWSA, Hashimoto needed to overcome Hiramatsu's opposition.

In January 2010, Hashimoto launched the Osaka Metropolis Plan to change the framework of local governance. The Osaka Metropolis Plan aims to convert Osaka Prefecture to Osaka Metropolis, convert Osaka City and its neighbouring nine cities to 20 special wards. It modelled the Osaka Metropolitan Government and the governments of the 20 special wards on that of the Tokyo Metropolitan Government and the governments of the 23 special wards in Tokyo. Hashimoto believed that concentrating the decision-making procedures of the entire area that makes up today's Osaka Prefecture in the hands of the Osaka Metropolitan Government would make planning more consistent and innovative. He also considered that by re-zoning today's Osaka City and its neighbouring cities into a more reasonable layout for resource allocation and introducing elections for the heads of special wards, the relationship between citizens and the local government would become closer and more accountable.

One of the biggest problems for Hashimoto's Osaka Metropolis Plan was the lack of a legal framework. To launch his plan, he needed the support of the public.

Arguments exist both for and against the Osaka Metropolis Plan. On the one hand, some experts, such as Taichi Sakaiya, Shin-ichi Ueyama and Eiji Hara, supported Hashimoto's view.[16] On the other hand, one of the most compelling counterarguments was that the Osaka Metropolis Plan might invite serious conflicts

---

[16] Taichi Sakaiya, Shin-ichi Ueyama, and Eiji Hara (2012), *Osaka Ishin Towa Nanika* (Guidebook for Osaka Innovation). Tokyo: Gentosha.

between special ward governments and the Osaka Metropolitan Government.[17] In Tokyo, the Tokyo Metropolitan Government and the 23 special ward governments often cannot agree on the allocation of budgets and administrative power/tasks, making discussions fruitless and time-consuming. As such, special ward governments in Tokyo occasionally advance the idea of converting special wards to cities. There is also fear that the introduction of the special ward system would reduce the tax transfer from the national government to local governments in Osaka.[18]

Hiramatsu was one of the most vociferous critics of the Osaka Metropolis Plan. In July 2010, Hiramatsu presented the Declaration of Regional Sovereignty, a policy proposal that maintains the framework of the ordinance-designated city while advocating the transfer of more power from the national government to ordinary designated city governments. The confrontation between Hashimoto and Hiramatsu became more heated with the presentation of two competing manifestos. When Hiramatsu's term of office was about to expire, a mayoral election was scheduled for November 2012. Hiramatsu decided to run for re-election. Hashimoto decided to take on Hiramatsu to prevent his re-election. He resigned as the governor of Osaka Prefecture and ran for the mayoral election. In the vacuum left by Hashimoto's resignation, Ichiro Matsui, a sworn friend of Hashimoto, ran for the gubernatorial election.

---

[17] Osaka Jichitai Mondai Kenkyusho (2011), *Osaka Ishin Kaikaku wo Tou* (Problems on Osaka Metropolitan Plan). Osaka: Seseragi Shuppan.

[18] Japan has a unique money transfer system between the national government and local governments (prefectural and municipal governments) based on the Tax Allocation to Local Governments Act (TALGA). This is called the Local Government Block Grant (LGBG). The LGBG was meant to support local governments to supply the minimum level of services to citizens by making up a part of the financial shortage of local governments. The Ministry of Internal Affairs and Communications (MIC) of the national government is in charge of the implementation of TALGA. To determine how much the national government should pay as the LGBG to each local government, the MIC calculates the Financial Capability Index (FCI) for each local government. The equations for the FCI are complicated but basically, it is obtained by dividing the local government's "standard financial revenues" (estimated from the population and social conditions of the prefecture or the municipality, and calculated from various types of local tax revenues) by the local government's "amount of basic fiscal demand" (minimum expenditure for the local government to provide reasonable services to its citizens). Local governments whose FCI exceeds 1.0 do not receive the LGBG. The others receive the LGBG from the national government, which fills the gap between "amount of basic fiscal demand" and "standard financial revenues". A majority of local governments receive the LGBG. On average, the LGBG accounts for nearly 20% of the total revenue of municipal governments. The TALGA stipulates that the LGBG is applicable to cities, towns, villages, 46 prefectures and Tokyo Metropolis. Special wards are not on the list. However, this does not affect their financial condition because the FCI of the 23 special wards exceeds 1.0 (owing to Tokyo's economic prosperity). In Osaka Prefecture, except for Tajiri town, a small town where Kansai International Airport is located, all the municipalities receive the LGBG. This means that if the special ward system were introduced in Osaka, the tax transfer from the national government to municipal governments would be reduced. This is one of the disadvantages of the Osaka Metropolis Plan and the JIP draft.

In November 2011, Hashimoto and Matsui won the mayoral and gubernatorial elections, respectively. These victories showed the strong support for the Osaka Metropolis Plan among voters in Osaka City and Osaka Prefecture. Thus, national Diet members were pressured to establish a legal framework for converting an ordinance-designated city to special wards. The national Diet passed the Act Allowing Establishing Special Wards in Areas Outside of Metropolitan (Special Ward Act, hereafter) in August 2011. The Special Ward Act stipulates the adoption of two steps to dissolve a city into special wards.

Step 1: The city government and the prefectural government should jointly prepare a plan to dissolve the city into special wards.

Step 2: The plan should be approved by a citywide referendum.

The Special Ward Act does not allow any prefecture to rename itself as a "metropolis." Other than that stipulation, the contents of the Special Ward Act largely satisfied Hashimoto's political thinking, giving him and the JIP the green light to experiment with special ward introduction.

Hashimoto's Retirement from the Political World

After winning the mayoral election in November 2011, Hashimoto succeeded in pushing Hiramatsu out from the Osaka City Government. However, he faced resistance to the Osaka Metropolis Plan from another source: the neighbouring municipalities of the governments of Osaka City. One of the major objections was the weakened discretionary power of special ward governments relative to that of city governments. Thus, Hashimoto decided to revise the Osaka Metropolis Plan with the following three changes:

 (i) give up renaming Osaka Prefecture as the Osaka Metropolis;
 (ii) introduce the special ward system only in Osaka City;
(iii) make the relationship between the Osaka Prefectural Government and the governments of special wards analogous to that between the Tokyo Metropolitan Government and the 23 special wards in Tokyo.

Based on the Special Ward Act, the Council for Converting Osaka City into Special Wards (CCOCS) was established. The CCOCS consists of the governor of Osaka Prefecture, mayor of Osaka City, nine members of the assembly of Osaka City (three from the JIP and six from outside the JIP) and nine members of the assembly of Osaka Prefecture (five from the JIP and four from outside the JIP). The 20 CCOCS members discussed the outstanding matters, such as the number of special wards, zoning of special wards and administrative assignments and budget allocation between the Osaka Prefectural Government and special wards. However, during this discussion, JIP and non-JIP members could not see eye-to-eye on many issues. JIP members' proposed draft, which included the plan for dissolving Osaka City into five special wards, as proposed by the CCOCS, met with objection from non-JIP members, leading to an impasse.

Frustrated with these developments, Hashimoto took a drastic decision and resigned as the mayor in February 2014. He ran for mayoral election again in March 2014 on the JIP draft platform. During the election campaign, Hashimoto urged those who supported the JIP draft to vote for him as the mayor for another term. Politicians who opposed the JIP draft did not take kindly to Hashimoto's strategy, as this re-election would pose a huge financial and personnel burden on the Osaka City Government. To express their displeasure to the citizens of Osaka City, they did not nominate any candidate for the re-election. Only minor candidates ran for the election. As a result, Hashimoto won nearly 90% of votes, with a voting rate of only 23.6%, the lowest record in the history of mayoral elections of Osaka City.

After the re-election, Hashimoto and JIP members took further aggressive measures. By pushing out non-JIP members from the CCOCS, they had the JIP draft approved. Thereafter, according to the Special Ward Act, a referendum for the JIP draft took place. Eligible voters were citizens aged 20 years or over who had residential registration records with the Osaka City Government. An announcement was made on 27 April 2015 that the referendum would be held on 17 May 2015. Throughout the 3-week campaign period to win support for the JIP draft, Hashimoto repeatedly promised that he would retire from the political world if the JIP draft was rejected. In theory, it was not necessary for him to risk his political life in the referendum. However, by doing so, he presented his determination to the public.

The JIP draft was opposed by the majority of members of the Osaka City Assembly and many scholars for three main reasons. First, they said that the aggressive measures of Hashimoto and the JIP were unfair. Second, the replacement of the original Osaka Metropolis Plan with the JIP draft appeared opportunistic. If Hashimoto and JIP members really believed that the Osaka Metropolis Plan was necessary for revitalizing Osaka economy, they should first convince politicians and citizens living in the neighbouring cities of its merits. Not doing so implied that Hashimoto and JIP members lacked confidence. Third, from some perspectives, the introduction of the special ward system might not improve the situation of Osaka City, as discussed earlier.

The number of votes in favour of the referendum, 694,844 or 49.6% of the total votes, was marginally lower than the number against, 705,585 or 50.4% of the total votes. Although the rejected margin was narrow, the JIP draft had been rejected. Accepting defeat, Hashimoto decided to retire from the political world. When his term as mayor of Osaka City ended in November in 2015, he did not run for re-election.[19] In addition, Hashimoto seceded from the JIP in August 2015. While he is still popular in the mass media as a TV personality, he no longer holds any official position in political circles.

Hashimoto's appearance in Osaka's political world in 2008 was sudden and brief. During the 8 years he spent in office as the governor of Osaka Prefecture and the mayor of Osaka City, he made various attempts to implement his reform plans. The Osaka Metropolis Plan failed to materialize, and it is unclear whether it would have achieved the revitalization of Osaka's economy if implemented. Indeed, the Osaka Problem persists even today.

CONCLUDING REMARKS

Toru Hashimoto occupied a central position of the political world during his terms as governor of Osaka Prefecture and mayor of Osaka City. He can be regarded as a new type of political leader in Japan. His behaviour and family background are totally different from those of ordinary politicians. His bold and provocative behaviour, which the general public did not expect from an ordinary type of politician, attracted public attention. In addition, he is not reluctant to reveal that he was born into an ostracized community, the *burakumin*, which is unusual in the Japanese political world.

There are various views among political scientists on how to evaluate Hashimoto-ism. Among them, Manabu Miyazaki presents an excellent review on Hashimoto-ism.[20] Miyazaki recognizes Hashimoto as a distinguished politician in the sense that he possesses a brilliant ability to adjust his behaviour according to the circumstances. Miyazaki also points out that Hashimoto does not have any particular political ideology. This affords him flexibility to cope with any public issue. This is how he attracted voters. Miyazaki's review ends in 2013. However, applying Miyazaki's ideas to the period after 2013, it seems natural that Hashimoto would retire from the political world without the slightest backward glance when his Osaka Metropolis Plan was rejected in the 2015 referendum. However, given that the Japanese society is beset by a sense of helplessness with recession ongoing since the early 1990s, a new political ideology is needed to have a breakthrough. In that sense, Japan's current situation is one in which politicians and citizens are passively waiting for a knight in a shining armour to rescue them. However, even a charismatic personality like Hashimoto failed to present a new political ideology.

---

[19] Heads of local governments can serve only for the remainder of their original terms even if they step down mid-term and win subsequent elections.

[20] Manabu Miyazaki (2013), *Hashimoto Ishin no Chosen to An Shan Rejiimu* (Hashimoto-ism and Ancient Regime). Tokyo: Ningenshuppan.

Chapter 8

TAIWAN'S LEADERSHIP PICKLE

S. King*
Park Strategies, LLC, USA

INTRODUCTION

Taiwan is a curious leadership case, as it's not easy to lead a *country* (or, whatever one wants to call it) that, for many the world over, doesn't officially exist. How, then, to lead Taiwan, given its unusual political predicament? In fact, Taiwan can't even be sure what to call itself. Is it simply *Taiwan*, as most people call it? Or, is it the *Republic of China*, its official name? Or, *Chinese Taipei*, as it's called in the Olympics? How have Taiwan's leaders fared given such an intrinsic question of identity? Let's first take a quick look at Taiwan's unique history.

HISTORY

Taiwan was initially inhabited by Austronesians[1] millennia before being incorporated into China when it was made a prefecture of Fujian Province in 1684.[2] In fact, Chinese migrants didn't start arriving on Taiwan until the 15th century. At different times, Taiwan has also been under varying degrees of Dutch, Portuguese, Spanish and Japanese control. But Taiwan, as we think of it today, has been operationally in a state of *de facto* independent limbo since 1949. That's when, after

---

*The author is a senior vice president at Park Strategies, which represented Taiwan's Ministry of Foreign Affairs in the United States from 2009 to 2012. The author's also a University of Notre Dame Liu Institute for Asia & Asian Affairs Affiliated Scholar.

[1] Taiwan's aboriginals, who today comprise 2% of the island's population, are descendants of these Austronesians.

[2] John S. Bowman (2000), *Columbia Chronologies of Asian History and Culture*. New York, NY: Columbia University Press, p. 230.

losing the Chinese Civil War to Mao Zedong's communists, Chiang Kai-shek's Nationalist Republic of China (ROC) Kuomintang (KMT) regime fled the Chinese mainland and set up shop on Taiwan in quasi-domestic exile.

CHIANG KAI-SHEK (1949[3]–1975)

Chiang died in 1975 but, until 1991, Taipei's ROC government claimed to represent not only Taiwan but also mainland China. It occupied many world body seats as *China*, including the Chinese seat in the United Nations (until 1971). Taipei refused to recognize any government that recognized what it called Beijing's *communist bandits*. Washington held to Taipei as the sole Chinese government until 1978. Seoul didn't flip Beijing's way until 1992. And, although Taipei's *now* willing to recognize any government that recognizes it, Beijing's unyielding claim to Taiwan's terra firma means Beijing won't recognize any government that recognizes Taipei. Hence, Taipei has formal diplomatic relations with only 15 governments and is sadly shut out of many international organizations, especially those that require statehood for membership.

Taiwan's leaders thus end up *leading*, as best they can, in a kind of parallel geopolitical universe, officially cut off from much of the world. The same goes for many Taiwanese civil servants, unable to directly interact with their contemporaries in most other countries. This means Taiwan officials miss out on many of the latest global trends, best practices and irreplaceable face time that other government representatives and diplomats take for granted. It also means Taiwanese citizens, and anyone who travels there, could face higher risks than need be, as the island's exclusion from entities like the World Health Organization and International Civil Aviation Organization, to cite just two examples, unnecessarily imperils its health and aviation safety, respectively.

Chiang Kai-shek was, until he arrived on Taiwan, a *leader* in the traditional sense. He led China through World War Two and his wife, ROC First Lady Madame Chiang Kai-shek (aka Soong Mei-ling), addressed a joint session of the United States Congress in 1943. Chiang even sat alongside US President Franklin D. Roosevelt and UK Prime Minister Winston Churchill at the 1943 Cairo Conference.[4] But after retreating to Taiwan in 1949, Chiang was a man without a country, forever looking to reclaim the Chinese mainland to which he never returned. He was wracked by anxiety that he'd be abandoned by friendly powers.

---

[3] Chiang actually became ROC president in 1948 but the years listed here indicate the years that he ruled the Republic of China (ROC) while physically on Taiwan.

[4] Encyclopedia Britannica, Cairo Conference World War II [1943], https://www.britannica.com/event/Cairo-Conference, Last updated: November 25th, 2018.

His fears bore out as, one by one, the world's major democracies (e.g. Great Britain, Canada and Japan) dumped Taipei for Beijing. Chiang didn't live to see Washington's New Year's Day 1979[5] switch, but did suffer the indignity of Richard Nixon's 1972 Beijing visit to meet Chiang's arch-rival, Mao Zedong.

Chiang presided over the launch of Taiwan's economic miracle alongside those of fellow *Asian Tigers* Hong Kong, Singapore and South Korea. It should be noted that Taiwan's economic metamorphosis was greatly aided by America's security guarantee and American private sector investment, which helped to unleash its meteoric growth and industrialization amidst Chiang's economic policies and reforms.

But Chiang also ran an oppressive dictatorship on Taiwan, the fault of lines of which have not yet fully closed. Chiang empowered newly arrived mainlanders over *native* Taiwanese (i.e. ethnic Chinese[6] already on Taiwan before 1949). Martial law remained in effect until 1987. Only then, *thanks* to Chiang's son, Chiang Ching-kuo (who became president in 1978 and who himself had mercilessly run Taiwan's secret police from 1950 to 1965[7]), were opposition parties legalized and the first seedlings of Taiwan's eventual democracy and free media allowed to take root.

YEN CHIA-KAN[8] (1975–1978)

Before Chiang Ching-kuo assumed the presidency, Vice President Yen Chia-kan served out the remaining 3 years of Chiang Senior's term. Born in Jiangsu Province on the mainland, Yen was an economist and former premier without a military background. He was considered a very capable administrator but lacked any political power base of his own. Nonetheless, Yen oversaw an orderly constitutional transfer of power and introduced incentive plans to establish the Hsinchu Science-based Industrial Park, which has contributed to Taiwan's position as a worldwide technology leader. Yen's transitional tenure was brief, but he certainly did Taiwan no harm while in office and also backed then-Premier Chiang

---

[5] U.S. Department of State, Office of the Historian, Foreign Relations of the United States, 1977–1980, Volume 1, Foundations of Foreign Policy, https://history.state.gov/historicaldocuments/frus1977-80v01/d104.

[6] No matter when they came, 98% of Taiwan's population is ethnically Chinese.

[7] Selig S. Harrison, *Taiwan After Chiang Ching-kuo*, Foreign Affairs, https://www.foreignaffairs.com/articles/asia/1988-03-01/taiwan-after-chiang-ching-kuo, Spring 1988.

[8] GlobalSecurity.org, *Yen Chia-kan*, https://www.globalsecurity.org/military/world/taiwan/yen-chia-kan.htm.

Ching-kuo's ambitious Ten Major Construction Projects that addressed Taiwan's infrastructure shortfalls in regards to highways, seaports, airports and power plants.[9]

CHIANG CHING-KUO (1978–1988)

Chiang Junior was in poor health and could see the world changing around him, realizing it would be even harder for anyone (in particular, the United States) to continue supporting Taipei if its government didn't start listening to its own people. This included providing more opportunities and rights for native Taiwanese both within Taiwan at large and within the KMT. Chiang Junior began localizing the KMT, going so far as to hand-pick native Taiwanese Lee Teng-hui as his successor, who assumed power upon the younger Chiang's death in 1988.[10] Was this *leadership* as we think of it, or was Chiang Junior just being forced to face up to new realities? Maybe it was both. But that's often how it is with momentous historical change; an almost irresistible combination of virtue and need. Other examples of such *leadership* include Soviet leader Mikhail Gorbachev in Eastern Europe and P.W. Botha in South Africa.

LEE TENG-HUI (1988–2000)

Now 96 years old,[11] Lee entered government as an agricultural economist with a doctorate from Cornell University.[12] He had also studied in Japan when Taiwan was a Japanese colony and was suspected of being a Trojan horse for Taiwanese independence within the KMT. These suspicions were on the mark, as Lee now calls for a referendum on Taiwanese independence. Lee's affection for all things Japanese tracks with his pro-independence views, as independence backers tend to be very Japan-friendly because Taiwan's Japanese colonial era (1895–1945) speaks to a time before the Nationalists arrived on Taiwan and helps further differentiate it from the mainland. What's more, native Taiwanese were long since gone from mainland China during its brutal World War Two conflict with Japan

---

[9] Revolvy, *Ten Major Construction Projects*, https://www.revolvy.com/page/Ten-Major-Construction-Projects.

[10] Shullen Shaw (2008), "The Death of Chiang Ching-kuo Leaves a…," *United Press International*, January 14th, 2008, https://www.upi.com/Archives/1988/01/14/The-death-of-Taiwan-President-Chiang-Ching-kuo-leaves-a/7663569134800/.

[11] Encyclopedia Britannica, Lee Teng-hui/President of Taiwan, https://www.britannica.com/biography/Lee-Teng-hui, May 13th, 2019.

[12] Cornell University Graduate School, Notable Alumni, https://gradschool.cornell.edu/about/history/notable-alumni/lee-teng-hui-68-agricultural-economics/.

and don't share mainlanders' first-hand memories from that time. Lee's not only prone to speaking Japanese on television when visiting Osaka for his medical treatments but has even dressed in Japanese Cosplay costume and opined that Taiwan has no claim to Japan's Senkaku Islands.[13]

Most significantly, however, Lee was in office for Taiwan's first *true* legislative election in 1991, held after Taiwan's Legislative Yuan finally abolished its seats *in absentia* for long ago-lost mainland constituencies. Aside from being Taiwan's first native Taiwanese leader, Lee also became its first directly elected president when he was re-elected in 1996 after having stared down mainland Chinese missile tests (with a big assist from America's 7th Fleet). It is for reasons like these that Lee has been called Taiwan's "Father of Democracy". He also made a landmark 1995 visit to his Cornell reunion and, in 1999, famously designated Taiwan–PRC relations as "nation-to-nation, or at least as special state-to-state ties, rather than internal ties within one China,"[14] earning him Beijing's ire forever. His Mainland Affairs Council Chairwoman, who oversaw fraught relations with Beijing at the time, was none other than current Taiwan President Tsai Ing-wen.

CHEN SHUI-BIAN (2000–2008)

Taiwan's first opposition president, former Taipei Mayor Chen Shui-bian of the Democratic Progressive Party (DPP), followed Lee. Chen won with only 39.3% of the vote in 2000 because independent candidate and former Taiwan provincial governor James Soong split the KMT vote,[15] gaining more support than party standard bearer and former Premier Lien Chan. Chen campaigned as a moderate on cross-Strait issues (by DPP standards) but promptly moved toward a harder independence line while in office.

Chen's flip-flop on Taiwan's fourth nuclear power plant[16] hurt him at home while he also found himself caught out *vis-à-vis* Washington. When US President George W. Bush entered the White House in 2001, he talked tough on Beijing and

---

[13] Kyodo, Taiwan president slams Lee for saying Senkakus belong to Japan, https://www.japantimes. co.jp/news/2015/08/03/national/politics-diplomacy/taiwan-president-slams-lee-for-saying-senkakus-belong-to-japan/#.XPaWFhZKi70, August 3rd, 2015.

[14] Shirley A. Kan, China/Taiwan: Evolution of the 'One China' Policy – Key Statements from Washington, Beijing and Taipei," Congressional Research Service Report for Congress (Code: RL 30341), p. 59, Updated August 17th, 2009, https://www.eapasi.com/uploads/5/5/8/6/55860615/appendix_100_--_taiwans_lee_teng-hui_on_special_state-to-state_relations_1999_.pdf.

[15] New Taiwan Ilha Formosa, *The Website for Taiwan's History, Present and Future, Year 2000 Presidential Elections*, https://www.taiwandc.org/elec2000.htm, Updated: February 24th, 2004.

[16] Nicolas Freschi, *Taiwan's Nuclear Dilemma*, The Diplomat, https://thediplomat.com/2018/03/taiwans-nuclear-dilemma/, March 14th, 2018.

was openly supportive of Taiwan, perhaps leading Chen to assume that Bush shared Chen's increasingly separatist agenda. But after the September 11 terror attacks, Bush suddenly needed Beijing not to oppose his Afghanistan invasion. America had newly urgent priorities beyond Taiwan, which Beijing was in a position to block but, thankfully, did not. Taiwan was now a secondary concern at best.

Chen's second term ended with his wife, First Lady Wu Shu-chen, under arrest on corruption charges. She was eventually convicted, as was Chen after leaving office. (However, he's now out on medical parole.)

Taiwan formally joined the World Trade Organization on Chen's watch, but it was also at a time when mainland China's economy was truly taking off, irrevocably reshaping the world while technology-dependent Taiwan disproportionately suffered the consequences of the global dot.com bust. Taiwan's own restrictions on mainland trade, investment and travel, not unreasonable given the security threat that Beijing poses, resulted in more and more companies and businesspeople leaving Taiwan, or just avoiding it altogether. In economic terms, the 2000s have thus been dubbed *Taiwan's Lost Decade*.

MA YING-JEOU (2008–2016)

Another former Taipei mayor, the KMT's Ma Ying-jeou, succeeded Chen in 2008. In fact, Ma had dethroned Chen in the latter's 1998 re-election bid for mayor. Ma took Taiwan in a completely opposite direction from Chen, lifting many of its mainland trade, investment and travel restrictions while embracing Beijing's sacred 1992 Consensus that allegedly states both the mainland and Taiwan belong to *One China* but theoretically allows each side to interpret exactly what *One China* means. Whether any such consensus ever existed, and whether Beijing still even believes in it, is a matter for debate. But whatever Ma said at the time was enough for Beijing to bless his administration and directly engage Taipei in ways never before seen. As Ma saw it, and explained at the University of Notre Dame's 2016 Liu Institute Asia Leadership Forum, Taiwan can choose between confrontation and rapprochement when it comes to dealing with mainland China. He chose rapprochement, as he put it, *under the rubric of the 1992 Consensus.*[17]

Ma's low-key cross-Strait posture also meant fewer headaches for America after the tumultuous Chen Shui-bian years and may have even given then-US President Barack Obama the peace of mind to launch his *Asia Pivot's* harder line on Beijing. With Ma not rocking the boat in Taipei, Obama could rest assured that

---

[17] Speech by former Taiwan President Ma Ying-jeou, Taiwan's New Role in Asia and the World, The University of Notre Dame Liu Institute Asia leadership Forum, November 20th, 2016, https://www.youtube.com/watch?v=jeyLr4TabOE&amp=&feature=youtu.be.

however much he pushed back on Beijing, it wouldn't end up being about Taiwan (Beijing's *third rail* as it were).

In 2010, Ma signed the Economic Cooperation Framework Agreement with Beijing that, among other things, cut tariffs on goods back and forth across the Strait but favoured Taiwanese *exports*[18] (so as to curry favour with suspicious islanders). In 2014, Ma's KMT tried ramming through a 2014 services agreement without a full reading in the legislature, bringing the island to a standstill. The activist student sit-in Sunflower Movement sprang up in response and the bill was shelved. The services agreement, and the way the KMT promoted it, was a bridge too far too soon for many Taiwanese who felt the island was moving too close to Beijing. Voters responded by overwhelmingly electing the DPP's Tsai Ing-wen as president in January 2016.

TSAI ING-WEN (2016–PRESENT)

Tsai, reelected in January 2020, is the antithesis of Ma and is Beijing's professed bête noire, even though she's governed and spoken in a rather moderate and restrained manner. Tsai tried to make clear in her 2016 inauguration speech that she's not seeking to alter the status quo in the Taiwan Strait, but Beijing remains unconvinced. Like Chen and Lee before her, Tsai is native Taiwanese. But most ominously for Beijing, she refuses to endorse the 1992 Consensus, which means the PRC won't talk to her and has since poached seven of the 22 governments that had still recognized Taipei when she came into office.[19]

Tsai's stuck across the Strait, facing an increased military buildup by mainland Chinese President Xi Jinping, the poaching of Taipei's diplomatic partners and a drastic reduction in PRC tourists visiting Taiwan since she came into power.[20] But, Tsai has so far found a friend in US President Donald Trump. Trump signed the 2018 Taiwan Travel Act into law, lifting all restrictions on high-level governmental visits between the United States and Taiwan and afforded Tsai the red carpet treatment on her Los Angeles and Houston transits that same year. In March 2019, US Ambassador to Palau, Amy J. Hyatt, conspicuously attended Tsai's banquet there, signalling America's stated desire that Palau not flip on Taipei. Tsai also seems to be where most Taiwanese are on cross-Strait issues.

---

[18] Lucy Hornby, *Taiwan and China sign trade pact*, Reuters, https://www.reuters.com/article/us-china-taiwan-signing/taiwan-and-china-sign-trade-pact-idUSTRE65S17Z20100629, June 29th, 2010.
[19] Katherin Hille, Taiwan shifts gears as China poaches diplomatic allies, *Financial Times*, https://www.ft.com/content/5187cf44-c513-11e8-8670-c5353379f7c2.
[20] Syaru Shirley Lin, *Xi Jinping's Taiwan Policy and Its Impact on Cross-Strait Relations*, China Leadership Monitor, https://www.prcleader.org/lin, June 1st, 2019.

That is, don't rock the boat by declaring *de jure* independence but, at the same time, don't bend to Beijing's will. Tsai's leadership on *domestic* issues has won her fewer plaudits however, as her controversial pension and labour reforms greatly contributed to the DPP's across the board wipeout in the November 2018 local elections.

BUSINESS

Taiwan is the world's 21st largest economy,[21] but very few, if any, of its brands are known by name. For every Taiwan Semiconductor Manufacturing Company (TSMC) and Acer, there are several original equipment manufacturers whose products we use but whose names most of us will never know. It can't be easy for any company to brand itself when it comes from a place that can't even come to terms with its own name. Corporate branding issues are in effect a metaphor for Taiwan's identity crisis as a whole.

Taiwan's global non-standing means its business leaders, rather than government officials, are sometimes called on to represent the island at major international meetings. For example, TSMC's Morris Chang represented Taiwan at the 2018 Asia-Pacific Economic Forum meeting in Papua New Guinea where he met US Vice President Mike Pence.

Taiwan's businesses and governmental leaders have to be more nimble than most, always navigating Taiwan's mostly unofficial existence, constantly evolving global supply chains and rivalrous US–PRC relations. Taiwan's political leaders have leaned heavily on US congressional support in lieu of formal US Executive Branch relations while its businesses have, perhaps counterintuitively, invested heavily in mainland China. In fact, Taiwan is the PRC's number one offshore investor. This gives Taiwanese companies access to the global supply chain and vast internal mainland Chinese market but also leaves them vulnerable to mainland political pressure as well as the ebbs and flows of Beijing's often contentious trade relations with the rest of the world.

CONCLUSION

Chiang Kai-shek held off Mao from invading Taiwan and locked in US support for his Nationalist government. But that was perhaps more in spite of his often corrupt and heavy-handed leadership than anything else, as the United States only truly committed to Taiwan's security after realizing the island's strategic import during the Korean War. Chiang Senior presided over Taiwan's breakout economic

---

[21] Countryeconomy.com, GDP TAIWAN 2018, https://countryeconomy.com/gdp/taiwan.

development, as authoritarian leaders can sometimes do,[22] but the island's still coming to terms with the divisions that he sowed. Yen Chia-kin may have done little more than set the table for Chiang's son, Chiang Ching-kuo, who himself may have merely been forced into reforms by the tide of history. But Chiang Junior did what he did when he had to do it. That's what counts. The reforms he undertook also meant more coming from a KMT mainlander.

Chen Shui-bian couldn't read the political tea leaves in Washington and his legal troubles marred the opposition's prized first chance at governing.[23] Ma opened Taiwan's economy to mainland China, and — by extension — to the world, but misread the public mood as to how far and how fast to open further. The story's far from written on incumbent Tsai Ing-wen and, while she has struck just the right tone on cross-Strait affairs, some of her missteps at home diminished and jeopardized her first term. But Hong Kong's extradition bill controversy and Xi Jinping's hardline unification remarks in his 2019 New Year speech gave Tsai new political life which she rode to reelection.

Lee Teng-hui, among all others, stands out to me as Taiwan's prime leadership example. He came to power at the tail end of Taiwan's authoritarian era, oversaw the island's transition to full democracy, was its first freely elected leader and shepherded his homeland through the almost calamitous Third Taiwan Strait Crisis. Honourable mention goes to Chiang Ching-kuo, whatever his true motivations, for the brave decisions he took in his final years.

---

[22] Harry Harding, "Four Styles of Political Leadership: What Works When?" (University of Virginia/ The Sorensen Institute, Charlottesville, Virginia, December 10th, 2010).

[23] Former presidents Lee and Ma were also both indicted after leaving office and Ma was even sentenced to 4 months in prison in a political leaks case. But Ma's sentence was revoked in January 2019. Hence Chen remains the only former Taiwan president to have gone to jail. Chen's case was also heavily covered while he was in office.

Chapter 9

A CASE STUDY OF POLITICAL LEADERSHIP IN TAIWANESE ELECTION CAMPAIGNS: A BRIEF ANALYSIS OF THE HAN KUO-YU PHENOMENON

T. Katherine

East Asian Institute, National University of Singapore

BACKGROUNDER: THE 2018 MUNICIPAL ELECTION

Han Kuo-yu, a former Nationalist Party (also known as Kuomintang, KMT) legislator and general manager of Taipei Agricultural Products Marketing Corporation, has unexpectedly navigated himself successfully to become the Kaohsiung city mayor, by winning a significant margin of 150,000 votes in the 2018 municipal election (Central Election Committee (ROC/Taiwan), 2018). Han, from a KMT veteran family in New Taipei city, changed his household registration to Kaohsiung area only in April 2018. His unexpected victory can be attributed to a combination of the following reasons: a charismatic personality, successful self-rebranding as an unconventional KMT politician, widespread social media outreach and the promise of a mandate of reform and change. When contextualized in terms of party politics, Han's victory has further implications beyond just the election outcome, such as the emergence and introduction of non-conventional campaigning and the competition between older generation patriarchal authoritarian figures and younger generation liberals within the party to fight for self-determination and the future direction of Taiwanese politics.

The "Han wave" was believed to be one major reason behind the unexpected KMT victory in the 2018 municipal election. The ruling Democratic Progressive Party (DPP) in Taiwan suffered a major defeat in the municipal election held in November 2018. In the 22 local government posts, DPP-controlled strongholds dropped from 13 (2014 municipal election) to six (2018 municipal election), while retaining only two out of six special municipalities, Taoyuan and Tainan cities.[1] One of the biggest surprise is the defeat of a policy-oriented DPP mayoral candidate in Kaohsiung city, deemed to be a stronghold base for DPP. DPP also lost Taichung municipality to KMT, an unexpected defeat due to the remarkable policy achievements of an incumbent mayor. Even in Tainan, another long-term staunch supporter to DPP, the DPP mayoral candidate won a narrow victory, with a slim margin of only 5.65%.[2]

Heavyweight figures and leading factions in the ruling DPP party had to immediately respond to the election outcome, including this Han Kuo-yu[3] phenomenon (also known as the "Han wave", referring to the surging popularity of Han among the Taiwanese public).

In a press conference on 7 December 2018, the then-Premier William Lai addressed DPP's self-reflection of the election outcome. They attributed the defeat to a number of factors, namely, miscommunication between the government and society of policy goals and DPP political reform impacts, incomplete policy deliberation in several politically sensitive reform topics, disinformation disseminated by foreign actors and the incongruence between executive and legislature governmental departments resulting in complications to policy implementation.[4] Lai only implicitly addressed the "Han wave" as a factor for the election outcome when analyzing the defeat, repudiating the explanation for the election outcome as a signal for the Taiwanese to embrace the narratives that prioritize economic growth and Chinese market, a view held by Han himself and within the KMT.

DPP understood that it was facing a formidable new political actor known as the "Han wave" that was dreadful for the political future and destiny of the party and also understood from its perspective that the "Han wave" was boosted by disinformation and other forms of implicit influences of foreign intervention.

---

[1] Central Election Committee (Government of the Republic of China, ROC/Taiwan), 2018. "2018 Taiwanese Local Elections", https://www.cec.gov.tw/mobile/en/. Accessed 10 April 2019.

[2] *Ibid.*

[3] Han Kuo-yu had sworn in as Kaohsiung City mayor on 25 December 2018.

[4] Executive Yuan (Republic of China/Taiwan), 2018. "Premier Lai Ching-te's remarks on 2018 election results", https://english.ey.gov.tw/News_Content2.aspx?n=8262ED7A25916ABF&s=904AC88 C1A077BD9. Accessed 10 April 2019.

China was deemed, in DPP's views, the biggest suspect of the undue foreign intervention.[5]

DPP's understanding of the "Han wave" emergence had evolved along this line, and its self-styled economic growth priorities rhetoric was a growing threat to extinguish Taiwan's democracy and the nativist Taiwanese identity. In this post-election context, it is fair to conclude that DPP has now branded Han Kuo-yu as the new symbolic figure of a local collaborator to the Chinese influence and a rival vision to DPP-style Taiwanese democracy. The campaign theme for the 15th presidential election scheduled in January 2020 has been pivoted to the level of re-securing Taiwan's national security and robust defence of democracy, namely, a battle for Taiwanese political survival and the Taiwanese identity.

ANALYZING DPP'S VIEW AND CONTEXTUALIZING "THE HAN WAVE"

After suffering landslide defeats in the 2018 municipal election, DPP and its former leader Tsai Ing-wen have devoted themselves to regaining the electoral support, while recovering DPP's political reputation in policy-making. Meanwhile, DPP's reflection on the severe defeat in the 2018 municipal election has evolved from a self-absorbed re-examination of its weaknesses to one aimed at securing Taiwan's democracy in the face of China's cross-straits unification efforts.

Further, DPP's views on the "Han wave" reflected two things, despite the relative disregard of the elections outcome as a subset to the Chinese factor. First, DPP's focus is on defeating Han Kuo-yu, but not his party, KMT. Second, DPP has depicted any possible DPP loss in future elections as a devastation to Taiwan's democracy, and Han is being branded as the biggest rival of this democracy and a collaborator with China.

The fact that DPP has viewed Han as a major rival, rather than KMT, implies that the long-term bimodal polarization of party politics in Taiwan may have experienced some fundamental transformations. Han has become a *de facto* leading figure in the pan-blue camp, which can be verified by the prevailing surging enthusiasm of pan-blue camp supporters and swing voters, who see Han as the most appropriate presidential candidate of KMT.

---

[5] The *New York Times* reported on the eve of the election, 23 November 2018, that China was using "a Russia-style campaign" to meddle in this election. Yet, a research fellow in Academia Sinica, Nathan Batto, observed that "it's difficult to determine exactly how much influence Beijing is having on the Kaohsiung race ... because discussions often take place in closed, private groups." Staff Writer, "2018 ELECTIONS: China using 'Russia-style influence campaign': report", *Taipei Times*, 24 November 2018.

However, it is too early to say that Han has also garnered support of the KMT comrades. Han is deemed to be a non-mainstream KMT figure, who has been marginalized from KMT central organizations and public attention for around 17 years before his unexpected victory in the 2018 municipal election. Therefore, he received very little KMT assistance in the early campaign period in 2018. Even in the pre-election period, Han refused to have KMT party figures rally for him, worrying that KMT would become a burden for his campaign and distance him from the electorate.

Therefore, relations between Han and the KMT central are intriguing, which should be deemed as one borne out of strategic pragmatism and far from one built on long-term mutual trust. In plain terms, KMT's major goal is to win the 15th presidential election scheduled in January 2020, in which the "Han wave" is now an important tactical factor.

However, Han's position on the cross-straits relation does not seem to deviate from the traditional KMT narrative. In his recent visit to the US, Han stresses on the importance of a peaceful cross-strait relation and unimpeded economic and personnel bilateral exchanges for Taiwan,[6] which largely mirror KMT's position, particularly, during the Ma Ying-jeou era (2008–2016). Therefore, without new narratives and ideational prescriptions, what distinguishes Han from KMT is Han's unconventional way of conducting campaigns and eliciting empathy from the people when interacting with the public, through the use of folkloric language and slogans and a lot of doggerel. Han has a charismatic personality as well, which is the main reason for his surging popularity despite his controversial behaviours; for example, Han's meeting with the Chinese Communist Party Liaison Office Director in Hong Kong during his visit to Hong Kong, Macau and Xiamen in March 2019.[7]

DPP's evolving narratives, seeing its loss in future election as a signal for more Chinese inroads to take over Taiwan, merit some elaboration here. In other words, DPP has self-appointed itself as the guardian of Taiwan's democracy, whereby Tsai and DPP's officials have spared no efforts to form a staunch alliance with liberal democratic countries to push back against the geopolitical siege laid down by thriving authoritarian regimes, like China and Russia.

DPP's re-branding is reified again in an interview by Tsai in a mainstream US media outfit, CNN, on 21 February, 2019.[8] Tsai presented voluminous evidence in

---

[6] Chung, Lawrence (2019). "Taiwanese mayor Han Kuo-yu heads to US as he seeks to boost profile". *South China Morning Post*, 8 April, https://www.scmp.com/news/china/diplomacy/article/3005272/taiwanese-mayor-han-kuo-yu-heads-us-he-seeks-boost-profile. Accessed 10 April 2019.

[7] Liu, Kuan-ting and Kao, Evelyn (2019). "Bashing of Han for meeting Chinese official in Hong Kong stepped up". *Focus Taiwan News,* 24 March, http://focustaiwan.tw/news/acs/201903240006.aspx. Accessed 10 April 2019.

[8] Rivers, Matt, Jiang, Steven and Westcott, Ben (2019). "Facing an aggressive Beijing, Taiwan's president issues a warning to the world". *C.N.N.*, 21 February, https://edition.cnn.com/2019/02/19/asia/tsai-ing-wen-china-us-interview-intl/index.html. Accessed 10 April 2019.

the interview on the growing Chinese threat constraining the room for Taiwan's participation in the international community and extinguishing Taiwan's democracy. Tsai further listed three issues when elaborating her duties as a president and her ideals of Taiwan's prospect, namely to safeguard democracy, to deliver policy performance and to tackle the intrusion of foreign intervention and spread of disinformation via both new media and conventional channels.

In this context, Han's position on the cross-strait relation — which welcomes exchanges of cross-straits by upholding the 92 Consensus, while avoiding addressing the relations between the 92 Consensus and "One Country, Two Systems" — sends alarming signals to pro-democrats and liberals for two reasons.

First, Han has stressed on the instrumental effectiveness of the Chinese market in wealth creation and the economic revival of Kaohsiung, in a changing context where China has explicitly re-configured cross-strait relations based on "One Country, Two Systems", whereby the term "92 Consensus" has been replaced. Han's position in adhering to cross-straits relations appears quite abrupt and insensible in the situation of a changing political context. Second, amid unfurling Sino-US rivalry and increasing criticisms of western countries on Chinese sharp power in motivating business dealings with China, Han's position actually triggers more doubts on whether he has the required and competent capability to steer through dangerous waters of the cross-strait relations. Han's mayoral performance in Kaohsiung will become the litmus test of Han's leadership capability.

Despite pending clarifications from Han on these issues, the Taiwanese public seem to support Han more than Tsai and other political figures, who have launched their participation, or started showing their political will/intentions, to join in the fray for the Taiwanese presidential election.

Survey results in the bimonthly period (February to March 2019) show that Han remains the most popular presidential candidate among the Taiwanese. In four possible combinations of a campaign pair (a presidential candidate plus another vice presidential candidate), the pair adopting Han as the presidential candidate always gets the highest support. See Table 1 for the survey outcome.

The prevailing "Han wave" seems to imply that the Taiwanese have held a rather tolerant attitude to Chinese influences. Intriguingly, this is echoed in the increasing portion of the Taiwanese, who maintain "unification" as their choice for future cross-strait relations. During the 2016–2018 period, those supporting unification have surged from 10.2% in 2016 to 15.9% in 2018, while the proportion of people supporting independence has decreased from 22.9% in 2016 to 20.1% in 2018.[9]

---

[9] "Taiwan Independence vs. Unification with the Mainland (1992/06–2018/12)", Election Study Centre (National Chengchi University), 28 January 2019, https://esc.nccu.edu.tw/app/news. php?Sn=167. Accessed 10 April 2019.

116   *T. Katherine*

Table 1. The electorate support to different combinations of candidates, February to March 2019.

	TVBS (pan-blue) 14–20 February 2019	Taiwan brain trust (pan-green) 12–13 March 2019	My-Formosa (mild green to the middle) March 2019
Ko	41%	30.9%	32.4%
Chu (KMT)	29%	33.9%	24.6%
Tsai (DPP)	16%	29%	23.2%
Ko	35%	27.9%	27.8%
Han (KMT)	**37%**	**35.4%**	**35.4%**
Tsai (DPP)	16%	30.6%	22.6%
Ko	39%	27.9%	32.8%
Chu (KMT)	27%	31.8%	24.8%
Lai (DPP)	19%	35.1%	25.1%
Ko	33%	24.1%	28.3%
Han (KMT)	**36%**	**34.7%**	**32.1%**
Lai (DPP)	19%	35.3%	26.8%

Notes: Chu: Eric Chu (former New Taipei city mayor, KMT); Han: Han Kuo-yu (Kaohsiung city mayor, KMT); Ko: Ko Wen-je (Taipei city mayor); Tsai: Tsai Ing-wen (president, DPP); Lai: William Lai (former premier, DPP).

Source: Piled by the author. Data retrieved from, TVBS: https://cc.tvbs.com.tw/portal/file/poll_center/2019/20190221/f9e86e1f970925d485787b5e42275c8c.pdf; Taiwan Brain Trust: http://braintrust.tw/wp-content/uploads/2019/03/190312總統選情評估TBT_選項報表.pdf; My-Formosa: https://www.chinatimes.com/cn/realtimenews/20190401004089-260407?chdtv. Accessed 10 April 2019.

An explanation regarding the prevailing popularity of Han (and his business-oriented and relatively friendly attitudes to China) and the rather mild position of the Taiwanese to China on future cross-strait relations is that a significant portion of the Taiwanese has grown tired of talking about the intractable identity issue. Moreover, this issue has been conflated with Taiwanese nationalism and is characterized by polarizing politicization and state political–social engineering efforts. The Taiwanese have been confounded/confused by lofty words of identity politics, and Taiwanese nationalism is affected by the pragmatic problems of slow-paced process of economic restructuring, current reality of low wages, extensive working hours and tough challenges of competitions in international markets.

Han quickly understood these social pulses and focused on economic and management issues domestically, while not egregiously repudiating the core principles of democracy, autonomy/self-governance, economic growth and job security. Most importantly, he has created more political space for Taiwan's *de facto* independence by shunning away from issues that would imply, let alone explicitly state, any form of declaration of *de jure* independence. This explains why and how the "Han wave", by prioritizing economic growth to the divisive

Taiwan identity politics, has resonated widely among the Taiwanese public in the post-election period.

THE IMPLICATIONS OF THE "HAN WAVE"

Political Leadership

The prevailing popularity of Han among the Taiwanese can be explained from the perspective of political leadership. In the course of democracy consolidation, it is common to find pleas for a strong, determined and visionary leadership in political life in Taiwan, particularly at a juncture when economic structural transition is stagnant and slow paced and cross-strait relations is in one of the lowest ever ebbs after the 1990s.

Political leadership has emerged and gradually honed to become sophisticated and be the most critical factor that influences the popularity of political parties, voting patterns and electoral outcome. This personalistic characteristic is a frequent phenomenon in Taiwan's politics, as shown previously in the society's reverence to Lee Teng-hui (president (KMT), 1988–2000), viewing Lee as the founding father of Taiwan's democracy and hailing Chen Shui-bian (president (DPP), 2000–2008) as the "Son of the Taiwanese".

After 2008, some international factors of political leadership and universal trends/traits are introduced into Taiwan's constantly evolving political leadership styles/concept. Ma Ying-jeou (president (KMT), 2008–2016) serves to reify how ideal political leadership is being projected by the Taiwanese to its people and to the world, which comprises a Taiwanese identity, the Taiwanese–Chinese cultural hybridization,[10] multicultural cultivation, international experiences and universal ideational values.[11] Further, with Tsai Ing-wen sworn in, the burgeoning Taiwanese civil society consciousness has added another criterion, by asking Tsai to deliver political leadership having the sensibility and capability to handle the thriving demands for more constructive interactions between the government and civil society.

This political leadership perspective provides one explanation for the DPP's defeat in the 2018 municipal election. Due to the failure of the Tsai government in delivering the much-hoped leadership in responding to the burgeoning civil

---

[10] On 10 October 2009, Ma proposed the construction of "the Chinese culture with Taiwanese characteristics", which addressed mainly the ethnic, social and geographic aspects. Shu-ling Ko, President Touts Chinese Culture, *Taipei Times*, 15 October 2010, at 1.

[11] Ma signed two international covenants on human rights issues, to substantially incorporate Taiwan into contemporary human rights-themed international order. Flora Wang, Legislature Ratifies UN Rights Treaties, *Taipei Times*, 1 April 2009, at 3.

society in Taiwan and more younger voters embracing progressive and liberal ideals, the electorate, particularly younger generations, has abstained from voting completely, let alone turn up at the voting booths to vote for DPP, which is a long-term collaborator with civil society and youth groups.

The fact that the Tsai government had not devoted itself to strongly advocating DPP positions in the 10 referendum initiatives was one example of dissonance with the younger voters. Another example was Tsai Ing-wen's hesitancy to support the legalization of same-sex marriage before the 2018 municipal election. This led to the Tsai administration's marginalization of the Taiwanese holding conservative views on the issue of same-sex marriage, which not only put a halt on the accelerated pace of legalization of same-sex marriage but also rejected the broader liberal and progressive values enshrined therein.

The confused civil society and younger generation voters in Taiwan appeared to have lost clear ideological directions and the political complications have left a void in their prevailing value system. This partially explains the rise of Han, the politician, and the prevalence of the "Han wave", which brings back the developmental rhetoric/narrative that prioritizes economic growth as the main goal of political leadership and instrumental pragmatism.

Therefore, whether DPP and Tsai government's strategic reconfiguration of the administration and party as a guardian of Taiwan's democracy could potentially earn back the electorate's trust and mitigate excessive emphasis on economic developmentalism, particularly to revive younger voters' enthusiasm in DPP's political principles, remains to be seen. Similarly, to what extent the "Han wave" can continue to attract voters is also a daunting challenge for Han, particularly in the absence of a clear ideological narrative that distinguishes Han from conventional KMT principles, in an environment surrounded by opportunistic KMT comrades who prioritize factional and personal interests over party cohesiveness.

The Politico-economic Reality Confronting Future Leadership

The "Han wave" has reified one developing trend, which is that economic difficulties have been greatly felt among the Taiwanese electorate in the post-Sunflower Movement era. This has become one reality powerful enough to compromise the continued enthusiasm of civil society consciousness and advocacies among the Taiwanese public. Despite Tsai government's efforts in restructuring domestic industries and reviving growth impetus for the local economy, the progress is slow-paced and the outcome is barely satisfactory for her critics.

Taiwan's economic growth has been stagnant, due to the following internal structural crises. First, Taiwanese enterprises have generally followed the subcontracting and export model, which needs to seek overseas bases that provide more advantageous manufacturing conditions. Taiwan's GDP growth (to which these enterprises make considerable contributions) is consequently de-linked from economic development in Taiwan. Second, the shrinking domestic industries and ominous economic outlook have entrapped many Taiwanese in economic difficulties, especially those in the middle to lower level groups and the younger generations of voters.

In larger numbers, the baby boom generation has dominated most of Taiwan's economic resources and political agenda-setting power, and they are relatively less affected by the economic difficulties/challenges for many Taiwanese. These challenges are intensified by the process of globalization, greater worldwide competition among workers/employees and the shifting focus/outsourcing of Taiwanese manufacturing industries. These middle to lower income electorates and Taiwanese youths feel that they are not duly represented in Taiwan's politics, which results in a political system vulnerable to dissatisfactions expressed by certain demographic groups.

On top of such generational issues, economic difficulties catalyze the polarization of the Taiwanese electorate. On the one hand, many Taiwanese, regardless of age and party preferences, would actively defend the reality and status of factual *de facto* independence and autonomy of Taiwan at critical junctures when there is a need to do so. This is reified in the increasing consensus among Taiwanese to defend the status quo and factual *de facto* independence of the Republic of China in Taiwan. On the other hand, the Taiwanese expect to have a capable leader, who focuses on rational policy deliberation and genuine efforts in strengthening Taiwan's overall national development, rather than playing the cards of identity politics and nationalistic issues. Those who can best read this dualistic characteristics of the electorate mentality would most likely win the 2020 presidential election.

However, after several rounds of disappointments with perceived incapable political leadership by various ideological factions among the voters, the Taiwanese electorate seems to be trapped in a deep sense of helplessness, with growing resentment to the rhetoric and perceived arrogance held by party elites and bureaucratic cadres. This therefore causes the electorate to de-emphasize political issues, while looking for political figures who show sympathies to their practical difficulties/challenges and endear them to political promises that could immediately deliver policy performance in the economic aspects.

An overall assessment is that among those who have, in whatever form, demonstrated their willingness to run for the 2020 presidential election, they are able to partially respond to the multidimensional and fickle electorate mindset. For Han Kuo-yu, potential challenges in his political campaign would be that Han would need to re-elaborate his positions on the 92 consensus, which is strongly interlinked with the "One Country, Two Systems" policy. This is deemed by most of the Taiwanese to be a threat to status quo and a denial of factual *de facto* independence of Taiwan.

Furthermore, Han's understanding of Taiwan's future is characterized by economics-centred thinking, a narrative that ignores the newly minted political culture by the electorate that embraces de-centralization and power-sharing in the governance system. By holding on to a top-down perspective and patriarchal thinking, Han seems to be insensitive to the dualistic political mindset of the Taiwanese electorate, which then puts into question if Han can truly read and respond to the consolidating aspirations of Taiwanese-style democracy among the electorate.

Taiwan is standing at a critical juncture in the course of democratic consolidation. The "Han wave" reifies that after three decades of democracy consolidation efforts, political identity does matter to the Taiwanese, but only when Taiwan's economy and the overall development of the country could grow and become sustainable.

Chapter 10

LEADERSHIP IN HONG KONG: THE FRAGILE "ONE COUNTRY TWO SYSTEMS" AND THE CHINA FACTOR

H. Y. Li

Institute for International Strategy,
Tokyo International University, Tokyo, Japan

HONG KONG LEADERSHIP AFTER THE HANDOVER

Hong Kong has been regarded as a distinctive international city. Though the political system is not fully a democratic one, Hong Kong people enjoyed rule of law; free flow of people and information; academic, press and mass media freedoms; as well as rights for demonstration. But after Hong Kong's handover from the United Kingdom to China in 1997, there is increasing concern on the mainlandization of Hong Kong for enormous Chinese political, social and economic influence.[1]

A major reason is that the current leadership is not accountable to the ordinary people of Hong Kong. First, the Chief Executive (CE), the head of the Hong Kong Special Administrative Region (HKSAR), is elected by the Election Committee instead of universal suffrage, and the 1,200 Election Committee members are selected from 38 different professional sectors and district organizations.[2] Beijing

---

[1] Sonny S. H. Lo (2008). *The Dynamics of Beijing-Hong Kong Relations: A Model for Taiwan?* Hong Kong: Hong Kong University Press, p. 10.

[2] See the website of Election Committee Subsector Elections, https://www.eac.hk/en/ecse/ecse.htm. Accessed on 1 May 2019.

has even manipulated the CE election processes such as pre-nomination, nomination, campaign and post-election stages.[3] Besides, Beijing has maintained the British colonial "executive-dominant" system by keeping the executive strong and the legislature diversified and weak, while the CE as the head of the executive must not belong to any political party according to the Basic Law.[4] Such institutional arrangement makes the CE less relevant to the ordinary people and political parties in Hong Kong, which naturally drives the CE to take care of the concern of the pro-Beijing Election Committee on Chinese national interests.

Another reason is the rapid expansion and penetration of Beijing's influence in Hong Kong, which further weakens the Hong Kong leadership under the CE.[5] Apart from the Chinese manipulation in CE election, Beijing's influence can also be found in the Legislative Council (LegCo) elections since early 1990s, which later stimulated pro-independence and self-determination movements in Hong Kong.[6] Also, the business elites in Hong Kong have enjoyed great influence over Hong Kong's policy for their access to the Chinese government, this not only puts the CE into a difficult position but also compromises Hong Kong's autonomy.[7]

While the China factor is crucial for "one country, two systems", the definition and scope of Hong Kong leadership in this book chapter mainly refer to the CE and the administration under the CE. Different from other democratic countries, the Hong Kong political system is a relatively closed system for the "executive-dominant" system. The most powerful actor is the Chinese government who designs the rules of the game using the Basic Law (which is also known as a mini-constitution of Hong Kong) and manipulated the CE and LegCo elections with the support of Hong Kong business elites. The CE is a dependent actor or a proxy for keeping Hong Kong in line with Beijing's interests. Other supporting actors of Hong Kong leadership include the politically appointed secretaries who are similar in status to the Western ministerial government, the Executive Council (ExCo)

---

[3] Sonny S. H. Lo (2017). "Factionalism and Chinese-style democracy: the 2017 Hong Kong Chief Executive election". *Asia Pacific Journal of Public Administration*, 39 (2), 100–119.

[4] Brian C. H. Fong (2014). "Executive-legislative disconnection in post-colonial Hong Kong: The dysfunction of the HKSAR's executive-dominant system, 1997–2012". *China Perspectives*, (1), 5–14.

[5] Hak Yin Li (2011). "Two key stumbling blocks for Hong Kong's democratization: Personal vote and Beijing's policies". In: Liang Fook Lye and Wilhelm Hofmeister (editors), *Political Parties, Party Systems and Democratization in East Asia*, World Scientific Publishing, pp. 291–319.

[6] Ngok Ma (2017). "The China factor in Hong Kong elections: 1991–2006". *China Perspectives*, 3, 17–26.

[7] Brian C. H. Fong (2014). "The partnership between the Chinese government and Hong Kong's capitalist class: Implications for HKSAR governance, 1997–2012". *The China Quarterly*, 217, 195–220.

as well as the civil servants. The Principal Officials Accountability System (POAS) was established by the first CE Tung Chee Hwa in 2002. The political appointees are very often senior civil servants or pro-Beijing politicians who are appointed by the CE. Thus, the political appointees are not leaders indeed, but they advance the CE's agenda. Currently, the Chief Secretary for Administration, Financial Secretary and Secretary for Justice are the top three political appointees, and there are 13 other politically appointed secretaries who are responsible for overseeing various sectors from education and environment to labour and welfare. The 16 principal officials in total thus form the POAS under the CE. Nevertheless, the POAS is still regarded as underdeveloped after more than a decade.[8] The ExCo is composed of 32 members with 16 principal officials, while the remaining 16 members are appointed by the CE. The ExCo is mainly an advisory body for facilitating the CE's decision-making process.[9] The civil service in Hong Kong has been regarded as one of the best in the world for its efficiency. However, civil servants are supposed to be neutral, which distinguishes them from the politicians who offer political leadership.

Given the importance of the China factor in "one country, two systems", this chapter explains Beijing's institutions in Hong Kong from an institutional perspective. The incapable Hong Kong leadership in resisting Beijing's influences will also be examined with empirical evidences. Last but not least, this chapter points out some relevant policy implications to mainlandization and Hong Kong leadership.

BEIJING'S INSTITUTIONS IN HONG KONG

After the handover in 1997, Beijing has expanded and enhanced its institutions to manage the affairs of Hong Kong. At the state level, Beijing strengthened the Hong Kong and Macao Affairs Office (HKMAO) and established the Institute of Hong Kong and Macao Affairs (IHKMA) under the Development Research Center (DRC) of the State Council in 2003 since a half of a million Hong Kong people took to the street for demonstration. At the local level, the Hong Kong Branch of Xinhua News Agency was renamed as The Liaison Office of Central People's Government of China in the HKSAR (LOCPG).

---

[8] Eliza W. Y. Lee and Rikkie L. L. Yeung (2017). "The 'Principal Officials Accountability System': Its underdevelopment as a system of ministerial government". *Asia Pacific Journal of Public Administration*, 39(2), 120–134.

[9] See the website of Executive Council, https://www.ceo.gov.hk/exco/eng/index.htm. Accessed on 1 May 2019.

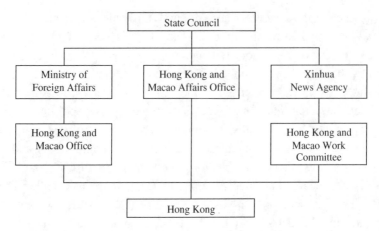

Figure 1. Beijing's institutions in Hong Kong before the handover.

Beijing's institutions in Hong Kong can be traced back to the era before the handover. Figure 1 shows that Ministry of Foreign Affairs (MFA), HKMAO and Xinhua News Agency all assisted Beijing regarding Hong Kong issues. The latter two institutions played a more important role during the discussions of Hong Kong transition. First, the HKMAO was responsible for investigating and reporting the situations in Hong Kong to Beijing as well as promoting patriotic propaganda among the Hong Kong people.[10] The Hong Kong and Macao Work Committee (HKMWC) was the *de facto* Chinese Communist Party in Hong Kong under the cover of Xinhua News Agency. The committee had various affiliated members such as the Bank of China, China Resources Corporation, the China Merchants Group and China Travel Service, which had certain network and influence in Hong Kong.[11] The Hong Kong and Macao Office under the MFA were relatively inactive when compared with the other two institutions.

After the handover, Beijing has modified its institutions in Hong Kong as shown in Figure 2. The modification can be classified in two stages. The first stage took place from late 1999 to mid-2003. In December 1999, the State Council decided to alter the name of the Hong Kong Branch of Xinhua News Agency to the LOCPG. It means that the HKMWC works publicly nowadays rather than underground as during the British colonial rule. The LOCPG is mainly responsible for helping Beijing to manage the Chinese corporations in Hong Kong; promoting exchange and cooperation between Hong Kong and the mainland; building up network between Hong Kong and the mainland for mutual interactions; reflecting

---

[10] Norman Miners (1998), *The Government and Politics of Hong Kong*, Hong Kong; New York: Oxford University Press, 1998, p. 262 and John P. Burns (1990). "The Structure of Communist Party Control in Hong Kong", *Asian Survey*, 30(8), 756–757.

[11] Steve Tsang (1996). "Maximum flexibility, rigid framework: China's policy towards Hong Kong and its implications". *Journal of International Relations*, 49(2), 415–416.

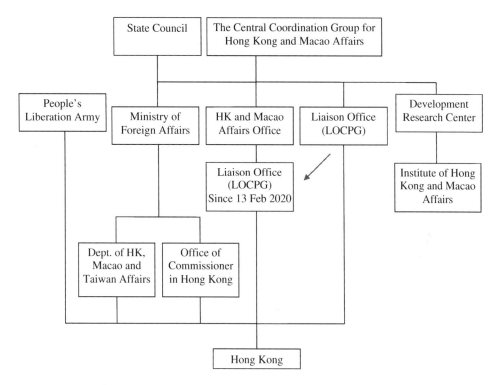

Figure 2. Beijing's institutions in Hong Kong after the handover.

the opinions of the Hong Kong people to the mainland; handling anything that is related to Taiwan; and implementing the policy which is laid down by the central government.[12]

The Office of the Commissioner of the MFA of the People's Republic of China (PRC) in HKSAR (Office of Commissioner) was also established under the MFA. Its major responsibility is about managing diplomatic functions in Hong Kong. For example, assisting Hong Kong in participating in international organizations or conferences, helping international organizations in setting up offices in Hong Kong, supporting Hong Kong in organizing intergovernmental conferences, authorizing HKSAR to negotiate bilateral agreements with other countries and managing the scope and application of international covenant in Hong Kong.[13] Another sub-organ within the MFA, Hong Kong and Macao Office was transformed into the Department of Hong Kong, Macao and Taiwan Affairs. But this organ remains quiescent in dealing with Hong Kong affairs.

---

[12] See the website of the Liaison Office, http://www.locpg.gov.cn/zjzlb/2014-01/04/c_125957082.htm. Accessed on 13 March 2019.

[13] See the website of the Special Commissioner, http://www.fmcoprc.gov.hk/chn/zjgs/gszn/t661847.htm. Accessed on 13 March 2019.

The People's Liberation Army (PLA) is another new institution after the handover. The symbolic significance for sovereignty is indeed greater than its function for safeguarding Hong Kong's security. Some PLA barracks are open for public visits annually in order to increase the Hong Kong people's understanding of the military forces of the PRC, which may help to promote a sense of national identity among Hong Kong people.

The second stage of modification of Beijing institutions in Hong Kong began after the 1 July protest in 2003. Half a million Hong Kong people took to the streets to protest the legislation of Article 23 in banning treason, secession, sedition and subversion. The protest not only showed the inability of Tung Chee Hwa leadership as the CE of Hong Kong but also Beijing's will in implementing a national security law in Hong Kong. The Chinese government then established the Central Coordination Group for Hong Kong and Macao Affairs (CCGHKMA), which is now being chaired by a national leader Han Zheng, who is a Politburo Standing Committee member and Vice-Premier of the State Council. The CCGHKMA is indeed a supreme institution above the other established institutions in guiding Beijing's policies on Hong Kong. Such an institution gives Beijing direct control over Hong Kong affairs.

Besides, the IHKMA was set up under the DRC of the State Council. The IHKMA was founded probably because of the inability of the HKMAO and LOCPG in evaluating/coping with the social problems in Hong Kong, which ultimately led to the mass demonstrations. Thus, the IHKMA examines the latest developments in Hong Kong in the fields of politics, economics, society, culture and even religion in Hong Kong and Macao.[14]

In addition, the recent rise of localism and the independence movement in Hong Kong have caught Beijing's attention. The PLA organized military drills and war games in Hong Kong during the 20th anniversary of the handover, while the Chinese Communist Party's Publication *Qiushi* offered a clear explanation of the military exercises that "Hong Kong is a forefront of the east-west clashes of ideology and values… The soldiers face long-term grim challenges of ideology and debauchery".[15] The presence of PLA in Hong Kong is no longer a symbolic gesture, but it can also be used to deter any forces that aim at separating Hong Kong from China.

Nevertheless, Beijing further polished its institutions in Hong Kong after the anti-extradition bill movement. Around two million Hong Kong people joined a mass rally in June 2019 for protesting a proposed bill by Hong Kong government

---

[14] See the website of Institute of Hong Kong and Macao Affairs, http://en.drc.gov.cn/2013-09/06/content_16949967.htm. Accessed on 13 March 2019.

[15] See Brad Lendon, "China makes its military more visible in Hong Kong". *CNN*, 29 June 2017, https://edition.cnn.com/2017/06/27/asia/china-military-hong-kong/index.html. Accessed on 1 May 2019.

that criminals in Hong Kong may be extradited back to mainland China. Thereafter, social unrests can be seen in Hong Kong for months, and confrontations between police and protestors have not even entirely stopped in early 2020. Also, Hong Kong people showed their grievances in District Council elections in late 2019, the pro-Beijing political parties suffered a disastrous defeat. Then in February 2020, Beijing upgraded the HKMAO by absorbing the LOCPG. The new head of the HKMAO is Xia Baolong, who is the Secretary General and Vice-Chairman of the Chinese People's Political Consultative Conference. Xia is indeed a national leader, and he is expected to work with another national leader Vice-Premier of State Council Han in CCGHKMA. The two national leaders in charge of Hong Kong affairs demonstrates the increasing attention of Beijing.[16]

The Hong Kong leadership is inherently weakened by the "one country, two systems" since Beijing institutions are already managing Hong Kong's foreign and military affairs according to the Basic Law, while the CE does not enjoy much flexibility in managing various influences from Beijing.

BEIJING'S INFLUENCES

Under the "one country, two systems", Beijing is not supposed to interfere in the internal affairs of Hong Kong except issues related to foreign affairs and national defence. However, the strengthening of the Beijing's institutions related to Hong Kong suggests that Chinese leaders aim to gain more control over Hong Kong issues. Such trend inevitably drives Hong Kong towards "one country" rather than "two systems", which further limits the autonomy of Hong Kong leadership.

Beijing has attempted to strengthen its ties with the Hong Kong executive administration and civil servants. On the 10th anniversary of the handover, the CE and some senior secretaries were invited to Beijing for a seminar on Basic Law. The seminar aimed to provide a better understanding of the Basic Law to the administration such as the nomination power of Beijing over the CE selection/ appointment process and the principle of executive-dominant governance in Hong Kong.[17] A similar event was also held in 2017 for the commemoration of the 20th anniversary of the handover.[18] In addition, the Hong Kong government has

---

[16] See William Zheng and Echo Xie, "China upgrades Hong Kong affairs with new chief", *South China Morning Post*, 13 Feb 2020, <https://www.scmp.com/news/china/politics/article/3050401/china-appoints-new-director-hong-kong-and-macau-liaison-office>, accessed on 14 Feb 2020.

[17] See "China marks 10th anniversary of HKSAR Basic Law". *China Daily*, 6 June 2007, http://www.chinadaily.com.cn/china/2007-06/06/content_888463.htm. Accessed on 1 May 2019.

[18] See the website of Basic Law Promotion Activities, "Basic Law Seminar in Commemoration of the 20th Anniversary of the Establishment of the Hong Kong Special Administrative Region", https://www.basiclaw.gov.hk/text/en/activities/seminar.html. Accessed on 1 May 2019.

consigned to the Chinese Academy of Governance in Beijing the assignment of organizing the Advanced National Studies Programme for instructing Hong Kong's civil servants since 1999.[19] The programme is taught by mainland scholars and some senior Chinese cadres in various topics like Chinese public administration, governance, state-owned enterprises, economic and financial reforms, and the relationship between different levels of governments in China.

The criteria of the CE have also been discussed and shaped informally by Beijing. The discussions on highlighting the good qualities of a CE emerged in 2007 when the pro-democratic camp first nominated a candidate for the post. Various Beijing leaders openly addressed the prerequisite requirements of the CE such as Jia Qinglin, Chairman of Chinese People's Political Consultative Conference (CPPCC) in March 2007,[20] and Wang Guangya, the Director of HKMAO in July 2011, respectively.[21] They said that the CE should be loyal to the PRC and Hong Kong, should advocate the Basic Law and should have certain capabilities in governance. Such statement helps to ensure that the Election Committee picks up the "right" candidate to be the CE.

Beijing's influence can also be found in the debate of political reform in Hong Kong. Wu Bangguo, the Chairman of the National People's Congress (NPC) Standing Committee, reminded Hong Kong people in June 2007 that the power of Hong Kong government comes from the central government; thus, the Hong Kong government does not enjoy any residual power. And Hong Kong should not simply copy the separation of power from the West.[22] Wu's statement is widely interpreted as stating that any democratization development in Hong Kong should be proposed according to the Basic Law in a progressive manner. Zhu Yucheng, the Director of IHKMA, also pointed out bluntly right after Wu's speech that the political reform in Hong Kong is part of China's national interest. Hong Kong should be ruled by Hong Kong people who are loyal and patriotic to the PRC.[23]

While Beijing has cautiously manipulated the "one country, two systems", its policies could not satisfy the demand for democratization by the Hong Kong people. The Occupy Central Campaign and Umbrella Movement broke out in Hong Kong in 2014 with the protestors blocking major roads in the central business district area for 79 days in the hope of securing Beijing's approval for universal suffrage in the CE election. The movement ended with police clearing the crowds

---

[19] See the press releases of Hong Kong government, "Civil Service Bureau signs memorandum of cooperation with Chinese Academy of Governance", 27 May 2010, https://www.info.gov.hk/gia/general/201005/27/ P201005270091.htm. Accessed on 1 May 2019.

[20] See *Ming Pao Daily*, 7 March 2007.

[21] See *Ming Pao Daily*, 12 July 2011

[22] See Jimmy Cheung, "NPC warns on HK autonomy". *South China Morning Post*, 7 June 2007, https://www.scmp.com/article/595867/npc-warns-hk-autonomy. Accessed on 1 May 2019.

[23] See *Ming Pao Daily*, 17 June 2007.

and Beijing never accepting the request from the protesting masses. Chinese President Xi Jinping further clarified the role of Hong Kong in "one country, two systems" in the 20th anniversary of Hong Kong's handover that "one country" is more important than "two systems", and "one country" is just "like the roots of a tree".[24] It is also the first time a top Chinese leader emphasized that Hong Kong must act according to the Chinese national interests. Xi said: "[a]ny attempt to endanger China's sovereignty and security, challenge the power of the Central Government and the authority of the Basic Law of the HKSAR or use Hong Kong to carry out infiltration and sabotage activities against the mainland is an act that crosses the red line, and is absolutely impermissible".[25]

Thus, in the overall picture, Beijing's influences can be seen from its ties with Hong Kong's administration and civil servants, its expectation on the CE and political reform in Hong Kong as well as the role of Hong Kong in facilitating Chinese national interests. These influences by Beijing have not directly intervened in the internal affairs of Hong Kong; however, the Hong Kong leadership could be shaped according to Beijing's values and interests. There are increasing empirical evidences that the Hong Kong leadership has worked on behalf of Beijing interests instead of the majority interests of the Hong Kong people.

The changing Hong Kong leadership has caught the attention of the United States. The US Department of State publishes *Hong Kong Policy Act Report* annually. The report in May 2018 regarded Hong Kong's "one country, two systems" as having been blurred by growing Chinese influences. The report cited evidences such as the jailing of civil disobedience activists, banning human rights activist Benedict Rogers' entry to Hong Kong and barring pro-independence candidates from running for elections.[26]

Another example is the rejection of Victor Mallet's working visa renewal in October 2018. Victor is a veteran British news editor of *Financial Times*, and he worked in Hong Kong for a long time without having any trouble in renewing his working visa previously. But the rejection came after Victor's invitation to the leader of the pro-independence Hong Kong National Party for a talk at the Foreign Correspondents' Club of Hong Kong.[27] The Hong Kong government did not

---

[24] See "Full text: Xi's speech at meeting marking HK's 20th return anniversary, inaugural ceremony of 5th-term HKSAR gov't". *China Daily*, 1 July 2017, http://www.chinadaily.com.cn/china/hk20threturn/2017-07/01/content_29959860.htm. Accessed on 2 May 2019.

[25] *Ibid*.

[26] Bureau of East Asian and Pacific Affairs, "Hong Kong Policy Act Report", US Department of State, 29 May 2018, https://www.state.gov/p/eap/rls/reports/2018/282787.htm. Accessed on 6 March 2019.

[27] Ben Bland (2018). "Financial Times journalist's visa renewal denied by Hong Kong". *Financial Times*, 7 October 2018, https://www.ft.com/content/5240ecda-c870-11e8-ba8f-ee390057b8c9. Accessed on 2 May 2019.

explain the rejection in detail, but the international community has raised concern over the declining mass media freedom in Hong Kong.

Even in the economic realm, the increasing Chinese economic capabilities have left little autonomy to Hong Kong leadership. In February 2019, Beijing announced the "Greater Bay Area" plan, incorporating Hong Kong with nine cities in Guangdong province into a giant economic area. In the past, Hong Kong feared peripheralization by the emerging economies in the Peral River Delta region, but now some Hong Kong legislators voiced the concern of Mainlandisation and wonder whether Hong Kong's economic policy is being planned and governed by Beijing.[28]

POLICY IMPLICATIONS

There are mainly two reasons for the deterioration of Hong Kong's leadership under the "one country, two systems" framework. The first is an institutional one. There is lack of legitimacy of the Hong Kong government because the CE seems to be responsible/answerable to Beijing rather than the Hong Kong people through a limited election by the pro-Beijing Election Committee. Second, Beijing has strengthened its institutions in Hong Kong for better preserving the political order and social stability in Hong Kong after 2003, while there is increasing influence from Beijing after 2007 for managing the expectation of the CE candidate, political reform and even the role of Hong Kong according to Chinese national interests.

The Hong Kong leadership has compromised on the issues of protection of human rights, political equality and mass media freedom in order to tackle the rise of localism and pro-independence movement. In February 2019, the Chinese government issued an official letter to Hong Kong to endorse the Hong Kong administration's effort in banning the pro-independence Hong Kong National Party and requested for a report on the issue. It is the first time Beijing issued an official letter to Hong Kong after the handover, which raised the concern of more direct and formal interventions from Beijing in the coming future.[29] Mainlandization is currently happening in Hong Kong as the Hong Kong government's policies are moving towards "one country" rather than maintaining "two systems".

---

[28] Alvin Lum and Sum Lok-Kei (2019). "Hong Kong legislators seek details from Carrie Lam on Beijings Greater Bay Area' plan". *South China Morning Post*, 20 February 2019, https://www.scrup.com/news/hong-kong/politics/article/2186983/hong-kong-legislators-seek-details-carrie-lam-beijings.

[29] Phoenix Un (2019). "Beijing takes Lam to task over indy party ban". *The Standard*, 27 February 2019, http://www.thestandard.com.hk/section-news.php?id=205391. Accessed on 6 March 2019.

The fading of the "one country, two systems" has several implications. Hong Kong is regarded as a model for the people in mainland China in promoting democracy. But the mainlandization in Hong Kong has probably led to the disappointment of many Western countries. And Chinese leaders have been very cautious with Hong Kong as though it will be used to democratize mainland China. In the 15th Report of the NPC, the Chinese President at that time, Jiang Zemin, stated that China cannot allow any foreign intervention that may harm the model of "one country, two systems". In the 17th Report of the NPC, the Chinese President at that time, Hu Jintao, even made it clear that China does not allow any foreign influence in manipulating the affairs of Hong Kong and Macao. The current Chinese President Xi Jinping firstly defines the role of Hong Kong in that it cannot be used to challenge the central authority. Thus, the future development of Hong Kong is in doubt as Beijing is very likely to manipulate Hong Kong leadership continuously such as the expectation that the CE should be loyal to the PRC and the form of Hong Kong government should remain an executive-dominant one rather than the separation of powers in the West. Under this political structure, Hong Kong leadership can never enjoy a high degree of autonomy.

Besides, due to the lack of legitimacy, the Hong Kong government is facing more and more challenges nowadays from political parties, non-governmental organizations and political and environmental activists. The mainlandization in Hong Kong boosts further discontent among Hong Kong people. After the handover, there are increasing regular and frequent protests against the Hong Kong government for its incapability in preserving the rule of law and various freedoms in Hong Kong. The inclination of formulating policies towards Beijing's priorities inevitably further damages the credibility and legitimacy of the CE as well as the whole Hong Kong leadership.

Paradoxically, just when Beijing and the Hong Kong leadership have worked closer together for maintaining political order and social stability, some civil society activists remind Beijing about Hong Kong's aspirations for a democratization process. These activists do not belong to any pro-democratic political parties, but they organize social movements on their own initiatives including the Occupy Central Campaign and Umbrella Movement. Mainlandization has exerted strong political pressures on the Hong Kong leadership as they are no longer on the same ideological page with Hong Kong people.

Section B

COMMUNITY LEADERSHIP

Chapter 11

COMMUNITY LEADERSHIP AND SOCIAL DEVELOPMENT IN SINGAPORE

W. Kenneth

Institute of Technical Education, Singapore

INTRODUCTION

Community leadership and social development are intertwined together.[1] The type of community leadership demonstrated is largely dependent on the extent of the social development and inclusion within the society. Discussions surrounding social development and inclusion in Singapore have rarely drifted far from the focus on its multiculturalism and social integration. Since Singapore's independence in 1965, multiculturalism, especially relating to ethnicity and religion, has been one of the most important building blocks for nation-building. Essentially managed by the state, the legislations and policies implemented by the government have been arguably rather successful to a certain extent with ethnicity, religion or language overly emphasized in public policies or favouring one group or another.

It is worth noting that for any country that officially proclaimed a particular ethnicity, religion, language as their national or official ethnicity/religion/language, the rest of the existing non-national ethnicity/religion/language will always be marginalized or de-privileged. This is especially true for Singapore as a melting pot of different cultures, religions, ethnicity and languages since the founding of the country by Sir Stamford Raffles in 1819. The British Empire made Singapore

---

[1] Phillips, R. and Pittman, R. H. (eds.) (2008). *An Introduction to Community Development*, London: Routledge.

a free trading port for traders and merchants from the East and West to converge and conduct trading, although the divide-and-rule policy was instituted to keep the races apart for effective British rule as the ultimate adjudicator of racial communities.

However, social development and inclusion were not being emphasized during the early days of self-government.[2] Social unrests caused by racial tensions during the early 1950s result from the lack of mutual understanding and racial tolerance among the different ethnic groups in Singapore. This is evident with the development plan implemented during the early colonial period by British planners with many immigrants settling down in Singapore according to a Town Plan organized into functional and ethnic subdivisions under the Raffles Plan of Singapore. Since then, ethnicity was "divided" geographically. Soon after independence in 1965, the Singapore government's approach to remove ethnic enclaves was integrated into the public housing policy whereby ethnicity was then slowly "mixed together" with the social integration plan by the Housing Development Board (HDB).

SOCIAL DEVELOPMENT: INCLUSION OR EXCLUSION

The formation of ethnic enclaves has created strong solidarity within each ethnic group but at the same time, resulting in alienation and lack of mutual respect and understanding between the Chinese, Malays, Indians and others. With all the efforts taken by the Singapore government to remove ethnic enclaves and promote racial harmony, no doubt that racial riots and violence have been successfully avoided, but whether Singaporeans are really racially harmonious or living under the ambit of racial tolerance is a subject matter that needs to be examined further.

In Singapore's contemporary society, the relevance of social development and inclusion to its social harmony is greater than before, and it goes beyond integration and racial harmony. Globalization and migration have a direct impact on the social development and inclusion, which are damaging to the society.[3] Although Singapore's social development approaches have been arguably successful in working towards achieving the goals laid down under Sustainable Development Goals (formerly known as Millennium Development Goals), including poverty

---

[2] Vasoo, S. (2001). "Community Development in Singapore: New Directions and Challenges". *Asian Journal of Political Science*, 9(1),

[3] Midgley, J. and Conley, A. (eds) (2010). *Social Work and Social Development: Theories and Skills for Developmental Social Work*, New York: Oxford University Press.

eradication, jobs creation and social integration,[4] it is undeniable that there is room for more improvement. For example, more effort can be put into social management by all stakeholders to address the issues faced by the socially marginalized groups such as the ethnic minorities, people with disabilities, special needs, LGBT (Lesbian, Gay, Bisexual and Transsexual), foreign migrants, new citizens, elderly, asset-rich cash-poor, economically vulnerable, and low-skilled workers to achieve a more inclusive society.

Most of the initiatives used to promote social development and inclusion are state driven — ranging from maintaining ethnic ratios in the public housings to careful promotion of social harmony messages by grassroots organizations. It is widely agreed that the government is taking a strong stand in ensuring multiculturalism and social integration in Singapore. However, in the recent years, it has become more visible that groups within the society are taking more ownership in shaping the type of community that they want to see. Thus the focus of this chapter is to look at community-driven initiatives and policies for community integration and cohesion.

SHAPING THE SOCIETY THROUGH COMMUNITY LEADERSHIP — PERSPECTIVES FROM COMMUNITY AND CIVIC SOCIETY ORGANIZATIONS

Leadership is not a fixed concept; scholars and academia have their own set of theory, belief and argument. Patterns of leadership traits, behaviours and theories vary from time to time and across different cultures and societies, it is important within the context of social development[5] in a nation-state.

During Singapore's pre-independence period, several riots and strike took place in the colony such as the Maria Hertogh Riot in the 1950, which sparked the riot between ethnic Malay, European and the Eurasian communities, in which at least 18 people were killed and 173 were people injured; racial riots between Malays and Chinese communities occurred in which 22 people were killed and 454 were injured.[6] Hence, to counter racial tensions and foster closer ties among the different ethnic groups, upon achieving independence, the new government established The People's Association (PA) in 1960 to promote social inclusion

---

[4] Ang, B. L. and Tan, N. T. (2002). "Social Development in Action: The Case of Singapore". *Social Development Issues*, 21(1), 68–75.

[5] Bass, B. M. (1990). "Bass and Stogdill's Handbook of Leadership". *A Survey of Theory and Research*, New York: Free Press.

[6] Riots Inquiry Commission (1951). Report of the Singapore Riots Inquiry Commission, 1951: Together with a despatch from His Excellency the Governor of Singapore to the Right Honourable the Secretary of State for the Colonies. Singapore: Government Printing Office.

through citizens' participation in community and integration activities for both new and existing citizens.[7] Under the ambit of PA, community centres/clubs (CCs) were set up to create common spaces for people of all races and socio-economic status to come together, build friendships and promote neighbourliness among fellow residents.

CCs also serve as a platform to connect and bridge residents and the government by providing relevant information and gathering feedback on national concerns and policies. Each CC serves about 15,000 households or an average of 50,000 people.[8] Over the years, more people became active in community work after the establishment of the Citizens' Consultative Committees (CCCs) in 1965 and, later on, the Residents' Committees (RCs) and Neighbourhood Committees (NCs) as well. RCs and NCs were set up in 1978 and 1998, respectively, to promote neighbourliness, racial harmony and social cohesion in the community and to gather feedback and support the last-mile delivery of government policies and initiatives before implementation. People of different racial, language, income and age groups participated in a wide range of activities at the CCs. Such multiracial participation promoted unity despite the diversity in race, culture and religion in Singapore.

Today, PA continues to bring people together through a wide range of activities organized at more than 100 CCs, 550 RCs and 100 NCs all across Singapore. PA has grown from strength to strength and is constantly seeking ways and avenues to continue its role in strengthening the community and nation-building. Community leaders, who are also residents in the neighbourhood, step forward to volunteer their time and efforts by organizing events and conducting house visits to get to know their neighbours well and attending to any of their issues which may arise during the interactions. In this way, we hope to re-instil the "kampung spirit" within the community whereby neighbours will look after one another, and in time of need, everyone will chip in and lend a helping hand to those in need of help. More than often, these community leaders go beyond their call of duty to attend to residents' enquiry and issues and to provide assistance to them. More importantly, these community leaders also act as voices of people to gather feedback from residents through house visits, dialogues, community gatherings and share residents' feedback with the relevant ministries and agencies so as to improve public policies and neighbourhood cohesiveness. At the same time, community leaders also act as

---

[7] Prime Minister's Office Singapore (2010). *Speech by Mr Lee Hsien Loong, Prime Minister, at People's Association's 50th Anniversary Grassroots Appreciation Dinner. Presented at Suntec Convention Centre*. Retrieved 13 July 2014 from http://www.pmo.gov.sg/content/pmosite/media centre/speechesninterviews/primeminister/2010/July/speech_by_mr_leehsienloongprimeministerat peoplesassociations50th.html#.U8ObAfmSySo.

[8] The People's Association (2018). Our Networks: Community Clubs. Retrieved 1 August 2018 from https://www.pa.gov.sg/our-network/community-clubs.

a bridge between the government and the people to mobilize residents to do their part for the community and assist the government to distribute resources to targeted residents effectively and promptly. Community leaders also play an important role when the government needs to implement tough policies.

Singapore, as a melting pot for diverse cultures, religions and languages, required efforts in strengthening a sense of nationhood among fellow Singaporeans of different creed through National Education (NE, one of the many educational initiatives for fostering a multiracial society). NE was implemented as part of the teaching syllabus in primary and secondary schools to inculcate the importance of maintaining racial harmony and deeper understanding about the history of Singapore to instil the sense of patriotism in the younger generations of Singaporeans. To promote stronger interaction among Singaporeans, there is no segregation of children from different ethnicity background when they enrol in the Ministry of Education-managed or mandated schools.

To remove ethnic enclaves, HDB ensures that, through their high-rise public housing schemes, there is appropriate ethnic mixture in the allocation of apartments through the use of a quota system for various racial groups residing in the apartments. However, Vasoo[9] pointed out that such high-rise living environments caused some social implications such as alienation among neighbours, lack of community ownership and mutual support. To counter this, the residents' committees step in to organize and support social bonding activities to encourage neighbours to join in and get to know one another.

To enhance peace and religious harmony, the Inter-Religious Organisation (IRO), Singapore was founded in 1949 representing 10 major religions. Over time, IRO organized activities in line with its objectives and participated in local and international forums to learn more about what is being done in the region to promote religious harmony. IRO also regularly conducted interfaith prayers and blessings at the launching ceremonies of public and private institutions. Increasingly, IRO became recognized as a force for good. To further promote and enhance racial harmony, OnePeople.SG, a national body for inter-racial and inter-religious understanding in Singapore, was established in 1997 to spearhead programmes and initiatives to bring the different ethnic communities together and champion racial harmony initiatives in Singapore. OnePeople.SG organizes regular camps, training programmes and dialogue sessions to engage Singaporeans in understanding the importance of racial harmony and, at the same time, explore possible avenues for the message to reach more fellow Singaporeans.

To encourage more ground-up initiatives and introduce interfaith activities at the community level, the Inter-Racial and Religious Confidence Circles (IRCCs)

---

[9] Vasoo, S. (2001), *op cit.*

was set up to target the local-level interfaith platforms in every constituency, formed to promote racial and religious harmony. The work of the IRCCs is instrumental in strengthening our social cohesion and supports the SGSecure movement.[10] The IRCCs serve as important bridges between religious, ethnic and community groups at the local level. Religious leaders from these groups come together to join the IRCC networks to build friendship and trust and deepen people's understanding of the various faiths, beliefs and practices through interfaith and interethnic themed activities such as heritage trails, interfaith talks and various ethnic and religious celebrations. In addition, the IRCCs are trained to respond quickly to racial and religious tensions by remaining calm and resilient on the ground during crises. The IRCCs will also assist in the recovery process, to help their communities and the nation return to normalcy.

Socially, although Singapore does not adopt a standard poverty line,[11] the government has greatly invested in poverty eradication and assistance schemes for the needy, which includes national schemes such as Compulsory Education System, Comcare and Public Assistance, Central Provident Fund and heavily subsidised education and housing grants, to improve the quality of lives for its citizens. For employment, low-skilled workers are encouraged to upgrade themselves through continued adult education and support provided by the various trade unions (NTUC's Employment and Employability Institute, Progressive Wage Incentive, Union Training Assistance Programme just to name a few), SkillsFuture Singapore and Institute of Adult Learning and intensified through progressive wage packages and workfare schemes.

Family service centres and social service organizations were set up to address the different needs in the society — ranging from financial, parenting to relationship issues. Self-help groups — such as the Chinese Assistance Development Council, Yayasan Mendaki, Singapore Indian Development Association and The Eurasian Association, Singapore — were also set up to render support and assistance to Singaporeans of different ethnic groups. Moving away from state driven to community driven, more and more different stakeholders are coming together to form a community. It is not just about grassroots being in charge but also others who operate within the community — social service organizations, schools, religious organizations and local merchants.

Over time, it is evident that there has been an increase in the number of people and organizations who eschew traditional "top-down" volunteering channels for ground-up initiatives that tend to be more organic, cause based and informal.

---

[10] SGSecure (2018) Home. Retrieved 2 August 2018 from https://www.sgsecure.sg/.
[11] Ministry of Social and Family Development (2013). *Poverty Line in Singapore*. Retrieved 13 July 2014 from http://app.msf.gov.sg/PressRoom/PovertyLineinSingapore.aspx.

For instance in 2014, Ms Priscilla Ong, an infant-care teacher, realized that children at her centre lacked clothes and toys. Ms Ong started collecting and getting donation for these items and over time, her effort turned into a community initiative called "Project Love Lunch" — besides giving clothes and toys, the project also provides food and groceries to more than 70 needy households on a regular basis.[12] Another community initiative worth mentioning is "Running Hour", an inclusive running club, promoting integration of people with special needs through running. People who are passionate in running activities can serve as running guides for friends who have mild intellectual impairment, who have physical impairment, who are hard of hearing, and with visual impairment to facilitate their interests in picking up the sport to keep fit.

While individuals are taking ownership of such initiatives to make a difference to the community, many civil organizations are also being set up to champion or advocate the social causes. *The Straits Times* Singaporean of the Year Award 2017 recipient, Dr. Goh Wei Leong, saw a need to provide support for migrant workers in the community. Henceforth, he co-founded HealthServe to provide medical care, counselling, case work, social assistance and other support services to them. Over the years, HealthServe developed partnerships and collaborations with regulatory authorities, agencies, schools and corporate organizations to initiate public health awareness programmes and research projects.

Another ground-up initiative which was set up to address marginalized group of sex workers in Singapore is Project X. Established in 2008, Social Worker Wong Yock Leng recognized that sex workers in Singapore are among the most marginalized and discriminated individuals in society and saw a gap in providing social services for the sex workers community. She started with a small team of committed volunteers who would walk the streets of Geylang regularly to speak to sex workers and close the gap between sex workers and non-sex workers in the general rubric of providing social services. Since then, Project X has grown to become a community-based organization where former sex workers are hired as staff members and are directly involved in the planning and execution of the programmes.

Project X believes that sex worker's rights are the same fundamental human rights applicable to everyone else. They wish to challenge the social stigma and discrimination that sometimes results in physical, verbal, emotional and financial violence. While there are multiple reasons for entering into the sex industry, the bottom line for doing so is generally related to bread-and-butters issues like making a living in an urban setting and economy where costs of living is going up.

---

[12]Yuen Sin (2017). "More Turn to Ground-Up Volunteer Projects". *The Straits Times*. Retrieved from https://www.straitstimes.com/singapore/more-turn-to-ground-up-volunteer-projects.

In recent years, emphases on climate change and environmental protection have gained international awareness and interest. Locally, the Environmental Challenge Organisation (Singapore), or ECO Singapore, a non-government youth environmental social enterprise, was set up to encourage youths aged 17–35 to adopt sustainable lifestyles and actively engage in environmental issues.

To this end, ECO Singapore works to promote and support youth engagement in sustainability and environmental decision-making by creating environmental leadership opportunities for Singaporean youths, educating and empowering youth to engage with key environmental issues (such as climate change) and instilling a sense of ownership in the local and global environment. ECO Singapore also drives and supports local and global environmental initiatives in collaboration with other environmental and youth stakeholders. Through all these community initiatives and efforts, it is heartening to see that volunteerism and philanthropy have grown in popularity. The volunteerism rate has doubled from 18% in 2014 to 35% in 2016 and donations have increased by over $200 million from $2.5 billion in 2013 to $2.7 billion in 2015 (MCCY, 2018).

ROLES OF CIVIL SOCIETY IN COMMUNITY LEADERSHIP — EMPOWERING THE COMMUNITY

The definition adopted by the World Bank[13] for describing civil society is "non-governmental and not-for-profit organizations that have a presence in public life, expressing the interests and values of their members or others, based on ethical, cultural, political, scientific, religious or philanthropic considerations". Civil society organizations (CSOs) refer to a wide of array of organizations (civil society actors) such as community groups, non-governmental organizations, religious organizations, labour unions, non-profit organizations, ethnic-based organizations, and associations and foundations.

Several authors and intellectuals from academia conceptualize civil society through various aspects and perspectives — from analyzing civil society through civic engagement based on small-group interaction to developing a proper macro policy framework in empowering social movement and eventually holding the civil society accountable for their actions. Fine and Harrington[14] emphasize the importance of civic engagement through small-group interactions, conceptualizing

---

[13] World Bank (2013). Defining Civil Society. Retrieved on 13 November 2015 from http://web.worldbank.org/WBSITE/EXTERNAL/TOPICS/CSO/0,contentMDK:20101499~menuPK:244752~pagePK:220503~piPK:2204/b~theSitePK.228717,00.html.

[14] Fine, G. A. and Harrington, B. (2004). "Tiny Publics: Small Groups and Civil Society". *Sociological Theory*, 22(3), 341–356.

small groups as incubators of the bigger civil society. In many societies, the physical presence of CSOs may be interpreted as a dysfunctional signal that challenges the authorities (often politically related) and social norms. However, their existence can be a good representation of a holistic development in democratic societies, creating a wide network of association, intersecting webs of allegiance and building bridges across various groups to strengthen social networks between people from various community groups. They also generate alternative ideas, worldviews and social schemes/assistance for the state and society and empower more individuals to come forward to have their voices heard.

With the necessary empowerment, CSOs can become mechanisms to attract and mobilize people and resources which can eventually translate into actions through framing and mobilizing, drawing crowds and creating their own citizen's identity and enhance their civic mindedness. Villeval[15] elaborated on the concept of empowerment through partnership and capacity-building. Precisely because resources are limited, knowledge and authority are unevenly distributed, empowerment is necessary to equalize inequality in the society. Social movement always starts small. Partnership and networking among smaller groups promote a high degree of centralization of efforts — giving greater and louder voices in the movement.

For instance, in the past, Singapore's society has been resistant towards accepting the "Freedom of Love" mindset when it comes to the LGBT (Lesbian, Gay, Bisexual and Transgender). However, over the past years, the LGBT Movement (also known as the Pink Dot Movement) has gained attention by attracting a greater mass/audience and people are becoming more comfortable in expressing themselves. However, Pink Dot Movement also inevitably creates an alternative counter movement (Wear White Campaign) by Christian Groups which are antithetical to the LGBT Movement. This exemplifies that small movements created by CSOs can eventually become a national movement through the necessary empowerment and civic engagement. Other movements that are attracting social attention are the rights of migrant workers, environmental conservation, care for animals and people with disabilities, etc.

With regard to the issues on empowerment, there are four areas of practice identified by the World Bank[16] in promoting advocacy and capacity-building: (1) access to information, (2) inclusion and participation, (3) local organizational capacity and (4) accountability. In particular, for the aspect of accountability, when CSOs grow in the society, a certain level of trust and accountability

---

[15] Villeval, P. (2007). "Towards a Policy Framework for the Empowerment of Social Movements". *Development in Practice*, 18(2), 245–257.

[16] World Bank (2013), *op cit.*

(be it moral accountability or procedural accountability) must be maintained and upheld while advocating for greater opportunities for voices to be heard from the affected. Ultimately, CSOs are not voted by the people, and hence, their legitimacy can be questionable.

Kaldor[17] highlighted the importance of the necessity to maintain accountability in the CSOs so that trust can be gained from the public. For instance, the abuse of authority, embezzlement of public fund, fraud and actions that undermine the integrity of CSOs will weaken public trust entrusted to the CSOs in providing voices and alternative ideas/policies to society. They serve as a "check-and-balance" on public policies and governance and raise concerns and feedback on behalf of the affected and marginalized groups in the society. However, there may be instances where CSOs used their 'voices' to convey misleading information to achieve their own objectives, thus abusing the trust given to them by the people and the authorities. A closer relationship among donors, beneficiaries and the CSOs will help to increase the accountability of the organizations.

Putnam's[18] definition of civic engagement eloquently sums up the key important concepts raised in the three articles that "trust, norms, and networks that can improve the efficiency of society by facilitating coordinated action among civil society groups" (p. 343). In some societies, the hardball management methodologies by the authorities against CSOs prevent them from growing in ways that are not necessarily beneficial to the society at large. The ability of a society to encourage the growth and development of CSOs-driven activities is an indication of the state of civic health in allowing civil society groups to grow its membership base. Regularly held civic engagement with CSOs through group discussions and debates are necessary for creating collective actions. Such participation by the individual citizens will strengthen their desire and encourage them to continue their involvement with the organizations. This may also strengthen the social capital of the society.

However, while stakeholders/government encourage civil society to grow, they also have to be aware of the possibility of the excessive concentration of power and authority, which will essentially lead to a decline in civic engagement. In addition, there will always be certain groups in civil society that promote and encourage anti-social or "deviant" behaviour and attitudes such as youth gangs, terrorists group and extreme religion groups which are unfavourable to the growth of the civil society and may advocate its members to take up detrimental actions

---

[17] Kaldor, M. (2003). "Civil Society and Accountability". *Journal of Human Development*, 4(1), 5–27.

[18] Putnam, R. (1995). "Tuning In, Tuning Out: The Strange Disappearance of Social Capital in America." *Political Science and Politics*, 28, 664–683.

to civil society. Every civil society group sets up their own set of objectives, missions and agendas for advocacy and/or providing assistance to the public. While legitimacy and empowerment should be given to civil society groups that are contributing to the nation-state, due care and accountability must be taken by the authorities and members of the public to ensure that the public interest of the society is being safeguarded.

Whatever social welfare and social caring systems that are put in place are by no means perfect — there is always room for improvement. The government's commitment towards forging strong social inclusion and improving the lives of its people through social investment and schemes are indeed reasonably successful and focus on "people-centred" development (Eade, 1997; MCCY, 2018) rather than on demagogue populist approaches. While the state may take the lead in strengthening and improving the social development and inclusion, nothing beats having the community take ownership of these functions to make a difference.[19,20]

---

[19] Eade, D. (1997). *Capacity Building: An Approach to People Centred Development.* Oxford: Oxfam Publications.

[20] Ministry of Culture, Community and Youth (2018). *Speech by Ms Grace Fu, Minister for Culture, Community and Youth at the 2018 Committee of Supply debate. Together, making Singapore home.* Retrieved on 6 August 2018 from https://www.mccy.gov.sg/news/speeches/2018/Mar/together-making-singapore-home.aspx.

Chapter 12

UNDERSTANDING COMMUNITY LEADERSHIP — A CASE STUDY OF YOKOHAMA CHINATOWN

W. Elim

Chinese University of Hong Kong, Hong Kong

INTRODUCTION

Very often, when the concept of leadership is discussed, institutionalized political leadership in the case of the government and business leadership in the corporate sector are vigorously discussed. But, equally important, is the idea of community leadership, which may involve local residents, civil society groups, non-profit organizations, ethnic associations, neighbourhood groups, non-governmental organizations, local business associations, local businesses and other stakeholders in local community well-being. The chapters in Section B examine this concept of community leadership and its impact on community well-being. Several specific case studies will be examined in depth. Unlike Section A which tends to examine political leadership from a macro theoretical and empirical perspective, Section B adopts historical-anthropological perspectives to analyze case studies. Other case studies in Section B will also examine policy formulation and implementation to look at the role of government in handling community-level issues.

One of the reasons for picking Yokohama Chinatown as a case study is due to its rich tapestry of ethnicities, civil society groups, local and overseas visitors and its sheer scale and size. The second largest Chinatown in the world — Yokohama Chinatown — hosts the largest population of overseas Chinese and the largest number of overseas Chinese associations among the three Chinatowns in Japan. The community is also home to two overseas Chinese schools, more than 250

Chinese restaurants and shops and the two Chinese temples — the Temple of Guandi and Temple of Mazu. These heritage sites as tourist assets enable Yokohama Chinatown to be ranked among the top three most-visited sightseeing spots in Japan among domestic tourists for over 10 years. Such accomplishments in getting into high-profile national rankings by Yokohama Chinatown are partly due to the efforts of its community leaders.

This chapter discusses the state of community leadership in Yokohama Chinatown. Yokohama Chinatown, according to existing scholarly literatures, is considered as a model community since the Chinatown is a well-developed and self-sustainable ethnic community that brings a sense of belonging to its overseas Chinese residents. The community is led by a few overseas Chinese leaders, and one particular community leader from Yokohama Chinatown is studied as an example to investigate how a community leader has contributed to the development of Yokohama Chinatown. This chapter and the next one on the Yokohama Chinatown case study are divided into five parts: first of all, the definition of community and community leadership is highlighted for the readers to understand the basic elements found in a community and its mobilization by the leaders.

The second part of the chapter investigates the complexities of the Yokohama Chinatown's society and how the community leaders coped with the difficulties faced by the community in the Chinatown. This is followed by a brief background of community leader Jin, whose biographical details are examined in this research. This chapter examines three major contributions of Jin in developing Yokohama Chinatown with fieldwork material, including the integration of the overseas Chinese residents, introduction of Chinese folklore to the host society (referring to mainstream society in Japan) and the promotion of Tokyo/Yokohama/Japanese tourism industry using Chinese culture as an attraction. Up to the point of this writing, this is the first oral interviews and fieldwork observations-based research focusing on a major Chinatown in Japan that provides new perspectives on community leadership in understanding the development of Yokohama Chinatown.

COMMUNITY AND COMMUNITY LEADERSHIP IN YOKOHAMA CHINATOWN

The overseas Chinese community in Yokohama Chinatown serves as a significant migrant community in Japan for research purposes due to their established community foundations. The notion of community has been discussed by various scholars. In one such literature, Yokohama Chinatown is regarded as a well-developed self-sustaining community that allows the Chinatown to maintain its vibrancy for more than a century. As early as 1978, Doolittle and MacDonald suggested six major factors that contributed to the construction of community neighbourhoods: supportive

Understanding Community Leadership 149

climate for community building (frequent interactions with other residents), family life cycle (concerns about the community and participation in local area community life), safety issues, informal interaction within the community (socialization and expressive communication), neighbourly ties and localism.[1]

Based on such definitions of a community, the overseas Chinese community in Yokohama Chinatown can be regarded as a model neighbourhood. It hosts more than 30 informal associations and organizations based on clan and dialect group ties (for example, the Cantonese Club), interest groups (for example, the Yellow River Women's choir), occupation (for example, the Association of Chinese Chef in Tokyo and Yokohama), gender (for example, Yokohama Overseas Chinese Women's Association) and so on.[2] These associations and organizations are open to all overseas Chinese migrants, and some of them welcome Japanese residents as well, especially those who share the same interests or occupations. The establishment of these self-sustaining informal associations and organizations provides a common space for the members in the community to interact and communicate with their fellow residents. Through cooperation and interactions among individuals and organizations, neighbourly integration is encouraged. This creates a sense of identity among the members who show "a desire for involvement in community or neighbourhood-based organizations."[3]

Moreover, overseas Chinese migrants in Yokohama Chinatown share a sense of local identity that enables members in the community to be closely associated with each other. According to Doolittle and Macdonald, when the residents in a community "engage in frequent and satisfying informal interactions among themselves", a sense of unity is formed.[4] This statement is proven by the active involvement of the overseas Chinese migrants in Yokohama Chinatown in community-wide activities and events. Not only does the community host the largest number of overseas Chinese associations in Japan but also the overseas Chinese members in Yokohama Chinatown organize and participate in a large number of traditional Chinese culture-related activities and folklore practices.

These activities and practices are often studied by scholars when investigating how overseas Chinese migrants maintain their local identity and traditions by being involved in the community-wide events. For example, Zhang focuses on lion dance performances in the overseas Chinese schools and the running of two

---

[1] Robert J. Doolittle and Donald Macdonald (1978). "Communication and a Sense of Community in a Metropolitan Neighborhood: A Factor Analytic Examination". *Communication Quarterly*, 26(3), 5–6.

[2] See Xiongpu Fang (1995). *Haiwai qiaotuan xunzong* (The search of overseas Chinese associations), Beijing: Zhongguo huaqiao chubenshe.

[3] Doolittle and Macdonald (1978), *op cit.*

[4] *Ibid.*

temples in Yokohama Chinatown.[5] She argues that the Chinese folklore is a way for the old overseas Chinese migrants to maintain their ethnic identity and a channel that enhances community integration in Yokohama Chinatown. In her academic writing, Shiho Arisawa mentions lion dance practices followed in Yokohama Chinatown to argue that the Chinese tradition is preserved as a means to express identity and build up the community.[6]

Nevertheless, Yokohama Chinatown can be considered as an ethnic quarter with a sense of community since the overseas Chinese community has a high social bonding, an important element to study sense of community, as suggested by Riger and Lavrakas.[7] To Riger and Lavrakas, if the members in a community have the ability to identify with their fellow members and are willing to participate in community-wide affairs with their neighbours,[8] they are essentially a community with community bonds. This social bonding is not limited to those who are active participants to the community. An ideal community with high social bonding is one in which the neighbourhood children are familiar with each other and the environment is favourable for the young generation to have a sense of belonging to their immediate community.[9]

Yokohama Chinatown is a location where community leadership passes from one generation to the next, since most of the overseas Chinese members of these association (including the Chinatown residents) share social bonding. For example, the author spent 6 years in Yokohama Chinatown for fieldwork and interviewed a few community leaders, such as chairpersons from clan association, heads of folklore organizations and the representatives of the two temples in the Chinatown. One commonality is that the community leaders in Yokohama Chinatown share a strong sense of social bond: they knew fellow leaders and members in the associations from a very young age, attended the same schools and they commit themselves in organizing community-wide festivals and events aimed at boosting "neighbourly integration".

This chapter introduces the personal experience of the former chairperson in Yokohama Chinatown as a case study to discuss leadership in an overseas Chinese

---

[5] See Yuling Zhang (2008). *Kakyō Bunka no Sōshutsu to Aidentiti: Chūka Gakkō, Shishimai, Kanteibyō, Rekishi Hakubutsukan* (Creation of Culture and Identity of Ethnic Chinese in Japan: Chinese School, Lion Dance, Guandi Temple, Overseas Chinese history Museum). Nagoya: Unite Press.

[6] See Shiho Arisawa (2012). "Lion Dance in Yokohama Chinatown: A Study of Identity Expression and Community Building". *Journal of Overseas Chinese Studies Takushoku University*, 1, 130–150.

[7] See Riger, S. and Lavrakas, P. J. (1981). "Community Ties: Patterns of Attachment and Social Interaction in Urban Neighborhoods". *American Journal of Community Psychology*, 9, 55–66.

[8] *Ibid.*

[9] *Ibid.*

community. Mr. Jin, the second-generation resident of the Chinatown, is a well-known community leader in Yokohama Chinatown.[10] To Sullivan, a community leader not only acts as an influencer on his/her followers but also acts as a form of symbolism for change and progress within the community.[11] Zanbar and Itzhaky further elaborated on Sullivan's narrative by suggesting that the actions of community leaders in the Chinatown are based on voluntarism.[12] Jin has been devoting more than 40 years in community-wide affairs as a member of the Chinese associations and a voluntary community leader. In the past 20 years, he was elected as the chairperson of the largest pro-mainland Chinese overseas Chinese association, served as a committee member in several clan associations and Chinese folklorist organizations and introduced changes to the overseas Chinese community. One of the significant changes in the overseas Chinese community in Yokohama Chinatown is its integration with host society through traditional Chinese cultural exchange, which will be discussed with examples in the following section.

This chapter relies on the seven elements of successful community leadership as suggested by Onyx and Leonard in studying Jin's leadership experience in Yokohama Chinatown. These seven elements potentially enable Jin's case study to be an example of effective leadership in an overseas Chinese community. Based on case studies on five different communities, Onyx and Leonard categorized the seven following characteristics that a good community leader could have: embedded, shared decisions, open systems, vision, practical management skills, succession planning, and energy, commitment and perseverance.[13] To summarize the above points, a successful community leader should have "strongly embedded within the formal and informal networks of the community", who never made decisions alone.[14]

At the same time, the energetic leader, who has a strong commitment to the community, has a "broad vision for what is possible in the future for the community", is able to identify paths to achieve such goals, engages with the other community members with good coordination and communication skills and at the same time always has a plan for choosing successors from the community.[15] These

---

[10] The real names of informants in this chapter are replaced by pseudonyms in order to protect their privacy.

[11] Helen Sullivan (2007). "Interpreting 'Community Leadership' in English Local Government". *Policy Political*, 35, p. 142, 146.

[12] Lea Zanbar and Haya Itzhaky (2013). "Community Activist's competence: The Contributing Factors". *Journal of Community Psychology Banner*, 41(2), 249.

[13] Jenny Onyx and Rosemary Jill Leonard (2011). "Complex Systems Leadership in Emergent Community Projects". *Community Development Journal*, 46(4), 503–505.

[14] *Ibid.*

[15] *Ibid.*

seven elements are the mark of a good community leader, according to Onyx and Leonard, and this set of evaluation formulas, which is also known as complexity leadership theory, will be used as a measurement tool to prove Jin's qualification as a community leaders.

This chapter aims to suggest an answer to the following two questions: Why/how can this case study on Jin represent a typical example/model of community leader? Why/how can Yokohama Chinatown, under the leadership of Jin, become an ideal overseas Chinese community with a high sense of community belonging? This research is a cross-disciplinary project based on historical and anthropological frameworks, the two major disciplines of migration studies. Trained as a historian, the author intended to learn about how community leadership contributes to the development of Yokohama Chinatown. As suggested by Brettell and Hollifield, "historians tend to focus more on individual migrants as agents" which they show is "less concerned with explaining how social structures influence and constrain behavior."[16] The case study on Jin is the author's human agent in this research. It is the analytical lens used to investigate the lives of Cantonese migrants in Yokohama Chinatown in this chapter. Due to the limited first-hand materials found in the Chinatown, which was either largely destroyed in the Great Kanto Earthquake in 1923 or went missing during the air raids in the Second World War, the author plans to compare existing newspapers, limited official records and secondary scholarly works with the oral narratives collected from interviews. This chapter is the first scholarly work written in English on community leadership in overseas Chinese community in Japan, and it sheds light on Chinese diasporic studies by suggesting a new angle to study overseas Chinese community.

MISSIONS FOR THE LEADERS: THE COMPLEXITY OF OVERSEAS CHINESE COMMUNITY IN YOKOHAMA

The city of Yokohama, until April 2018, is populated by 38,292 individuals with mainland Chinese nationality and 2,758 with Taiwanese nationality, while 10,093 of them live in Naka-cho, where Yokohama Chinatown is located.[17] The number does not reflect the actual number of overseas Chinese population since the statistic does not include those who naturalized to Japanese nationality. Yokohama

---

[16] Caroline B. Brettell and James F. Hollifield (2000). "Migration Theory: Talking across Disciplines". In: Caroline B. Brettell, James F. Hollifield *et al.* (editors), *Migration Theory: Talking across Disciplines*, New York: Routledge, p. 4.

[17] "Foreign population of the City of Yokohama (until April 2018)". Civic Affairs Bureau, http://www.city.yokohama.lg.jp/ex/stat/jinko/non-jp/new-j.html. Accessed 10 May 2018.

Chinatown stands out as a landmark historical icon of local community history as well as the largest Chinatown in Japan. The Chinatown was established in 1859 after the port of Yokohama was opened for trade. Although the Chinatown has been well developed by the overseas Chinese residents, given the complicated history between its overseas Chinese residents in the previous 60 years, Yokohama Chinatown is different from the other two Chinatowns in Japan in terms of the relationship between ethnic Chinese individuals with opposing political preference.

Going back to the early 1950s, the Chinatown had experienced a turbulent time when there was dissension over political factors between the pro-People's Republic of China (PRC) and pro-Republic of China (ROC) ethnic Chinese individuals. In 1951, two groups of ethnic Chinese argued over the right of possession of the only overseas Chinese school, Yokohama Chūka Gakkoū (Yokohama Chinese School), in the Chinatown. This historical hostile confrontation/situation is still a problematic issue in the community as both camps are less willing to either communicate or cooperate with the opposite camp when compared to the days before this so-called "School Incident". The School Incident in 1951 is considered as the beginning of the spilt of Yokohama Chinatown. From the insiders' point of view, the Incident is described as a "violent protest against the ownership of overseas Chinese education". The former pro-PRC Yokohama Yamate Chinese School (YYCS) school principle Chen provides a brief background on the establishment of YYCS after the School Incident:

> After the establishment of PRC on 1 October 1949 and the retreat of the Kuomintang (Chinese Nationalist Party) in Taiwan, with the protection of the US, the Taiwanese wanted to expand their influence [in overseas Chinese education] in Japan. On 1 August 1951, the Taiwanese people, with the backup of Japanese police, took over the authority of the only ethnic Chinese school [Yokohama Overseas Chinese School] … all teachers and students who came from mainland China were expelled [from the school], and that is why we needed to build a new school for the expelled [mainland Chinese students]. This is the primary reason why YYCS was built in 1953.[18]

Based on the above explanation provided by Chen, the "School Incident" can be understood as an event that strongly related to political situation. The overseas Chinese residents in Japan, along with the change in the political environment in mainland China in 1949, were divided into two hostile camps based on the individuals' choice of ideological idea. Ideological divisions became a sensitive topic in Yokohama Chinatown, especially among the ethnic Chinese

---

[18] Chen (2012). Interview by the author. Personal Interview. A Restaurant at Yokohama Chinatown, Japan, 6 March 2012.

students in the overseas Chinese school. The choice of self-defined nationality represented the migrants' identity formation processes. Some overseas Chinese families in Yokohama Chinatown gave up mainland Chinese nationality in favour of the Taiwanese nationality. However, those who applied for Taiwanese nationality feel undue peer pressure from others in the overseas Chinese school, since the school was mostly managed by the pro-PRC teachers and school principal.

As a result of continuing tussle between the two groups, the pro-ROC individuals eventually took over the management board of the school with the assistance from the Japanese police (since Taiwan was officially recognized by the Japanese government in the 1950s). They forced the pro-PRC school principal to step down from his position and expelled all pro-PRC teachers and students from the school on 1 August 1951.[19] The two parties have parted ways with communication revived only in the late-1980s when the Temple of Guandi was destroyed by a great fire and both pro-PRC and pro-ROC groups in the Yokohama Chinatown agreed to put aside their differences to rebuild the temple together. However, aside from rebuilding the Temple of Guandi in the early 1990s, on other issues, the two factions were back to having a hostile relationship once again. Until today, the unification of the entire ethnic Chinese population in Yokohama Chinatown remains a critical challenge to all community leaders, regardless of ideological or political factions.

Community leaders have the responsibility in maintaining the traditional cultural fabric of the community. Cantonese culture is one of the major areas useful for sustaining Yokohama Chinatown's cultural ballast for over a century. From folklorist practices like the lion dance to local material culture such as Cantonese cuisines, Cantonese culture plays a prominent role in building up the image and feel of Yokohama Chinatown. Nowadays, most of the Chinese festivals, such as the Chinese Lunar New Year (LNY) celebration and the birth of Guandi, are still celebrated in the Cantonese cultural traditions. The practice of southern-style lion dance in the festivals is an example.

Writer Arisawa considers lion dance as the key to the maintenance of cultural cohesion in the Yokohama within overseas Chinese community as well as essentially forming a cultural bridge between the Chinatown and its host society

---

[19] The School Incidents can be understood through the lens of the pro-PRC individuals and the pro-ROC individuals. Both sides have included the incident in their school history. See Hengbin Shanshou Zhonghua (2004). *The Hundred Years of History of Yokohama Yamate Chinese School, 1898–2004*, Japan: Yokohama Overseas Chinese School; and Liang Wang (1995). *Yokohama Overseas Chinese School 100th Anniversary Commemorative Volume*, Yokohama: Yokohama Overseas Chinese School.

(mainstream Japanese population).[20] At the same time, the lion dance is a cultural property that promotes a sense of belonging to the hometown culture.[21] Community leadership in Yokohama Chinatown, therefore, is a role that advocates the transmission and promotion of the culture of Yokohama Chinatown. The leaders have to make sure local folklore in the Chinatown is well preserved and encourage the young generation to participate in such symbolic culture of the local community.

Last but not least, the most challenging task for community leaders in Yokohama Chinatown is to manage the above-mentioned cultural affairs and other internal community issues, while maintaining a friendly relationship with the host society and promoting tourism in Yokohama Chinatown. The overseas Chinese community in Yokohama has been living with the mainstream Japanese host society for over 150 years. Although the Chinatown is established and maintained by ethnic Chinese individuals, the community itself is a long-standing component of the city of Yokohama. Therefore, maintaining the connection and social interactions with mainstream Japanese society and residents is essential and important for migration experience, since Japan is the host country for all overseas Chinese in Japan, including those who have naturalized. Moreover, the tourism industry in Yokohama Chinatown is another connection between the ethnic quarters of Chinatown with the host society as well. By increasing the number of visiting domestic tourists, the Yokohama Chinatown can have further channels to introduce their culture to their neighbours in order to enhance integration. As a result, working hand-in-hand with Yokohama city government and local organizations in promoting tourism is high on the agenda of Chinatown's leaders.

CASE STUDY — JIN AND HIS LEADERSHIP IN YOKOHAMA CHINATOWN SINCE THE 1990S

Jin is the second generation in the family. His father arrived in Yokohama in the early 1920s, along with a few friends from Canton China. Jin's father was a chef who served in various Cantonese restaurants before the outbreak of the Second World War. After the war, the first generation of the Jin family opened a Cantonese restaurant on the main street of Yokohama Chinatown in early 1950s. At very young age, Jin knew that he would need to take over the Cantonese restaurant from his father someday, but he did not know that, years later, he inherited not only the family business but also his father's leadership role in overseas Chinese associations.

---

[20] Arisawa Shiho. *Lion Dance in Yokohama Chinatown: A Study of Identity Expression and Community Building*, pp. 144–145.

[21] *Ibid.*

Although the daily operations of the Cantonese restaurant were hectic, Jin's father devoted all his spare time to preserving folklorist practices and community affairs in the Chinatown. He was one of the founding members of a clan association, which he joined in the early 1930s, later rising to become a committee member in the 1950s, compelling him to become involved in the management of the community affairs. Also, the first generation of the Jin family organized the first lion dance team in Yokohama Chinatown. The team does not exist today; nevertheless, it sowed the seeds in the Chinatown that encourage the young generation to continue this Cantonese folk practice as a way to preserve aspects of the ethnic Chinese identity. Given the 60-year experience of the Jin family in associational affairs, the family understood the needs of the community, and most important of all, made them realize what makes a good community leader in the Chinatown.

Inspired by his father, Jin took up important roles in the Chinatown community by joining various Chinese community organizations in the Chinatown. But the second generation of Chinatown residents (of which Jin was a contemporary peer) decided to put more efforts in community affairs, so he decided to take on management roles in a number of community associations. That kickstarted his active role in community affairs. Since the early 1990s, Jin was first elected as a committee member in the biggest overseas Chinese association in the Chinatown — Association A (the acronym used in this chapter). In Association A, Jin was responsible for organizing large-scale celebrations and festivals such as the annual Chinese LNY festivals and Chinese National Day's celebrations. Since the early 2010s, Jin became the chairperson of Association A for six consecutive years. Jin continued to practice lion dance with his father for over 30 years, and he was chosen as the coach in one of the leading lion dance team in Yokohama Chinatown in the 1980s.

Lion dance is an indispensable cultural element in Chinese folk religion events in Yokohama Chinatown. In most of the folk religion events in the Chinatown, Jin assumes a leading role in managing folklore performances, including lion dance and other forms of religious performance. In this work, Jin fully understands the integration among ethnic Chinese residents and how the Japanese neighbours (i.e. mainstream society) are important to the development of Yokohama Chinatown itself. Being a community leader in the Chinatown, he intends to build the bridge between the two different groups/factions of Chinese residents (i.e. the pro-PRC/pro-ROC and new/old overseas Chinese). Based on his community experience in organizing lion dances, Jin utilizes the folk practices as a medium to not only promote Chinese culture to the Chinese residents (as a unifying factor) but also incorporate the participation of interested Japanese members too.

INTEGRATION AMONG ETHNIC CHINESE RESIDENTS IN YOKOHAMA CHINATOWN

The pro-PRC and pro-ROC migrants in Yokohama Chinatown are mostly elderly overseas Chinese. Therefore, before establishing good relationships with the new-comers in the Chinatown, the community leader needs to resolve and overcome the difficulties in integrating the pro-PRC and pro-ROC groups within the Chinatown. After the outbreak of the School Incident in 1951, the two hostile groups were less willing to communicate with each other. A few high-profile dis-putes between the pro-PRC and pro-ROC residents were even featured in the Japanese mass media. For example, *Yomiuri Shimbun* reported that the pro-PRC residents suspected the pro-ROC migrants of stealing one of the two PRC flags that were placed at the entrance of Chinese restaurant *Taipinglou* on the night before the PRC National Day on 1 October 1958.[22] The disputes between pro-PRC and pro-ROC residents have been a seriously disruptive issue to community peace until a fire destroyed the third Temple of Guandi in 1986. The two groups agreed to put aside their difference and organize fundraising activities together to rebuild the current Temple of Guandi so as to restore spiritual comfort for the ethnic Chinese migrants. After the construction of the fourth Temple of Guandi, the over-seas Chinese migrants made one step forward to increase communication with the opposing camp. In fact, the two groups of elderly Chinese migrants have been longing for a reunion, which resulted in a turning point in the instance of the first case of cooperation between the two Yokohama Overseas Chinese Associations (YOCAs) in the Yokohama Chinatown, steered under Jin's leadership as the chair-person of Association A.

Many of the author's pro-PRC informants revealed that they felt more com-fortable to talk to the pro-ROC migrants since the 1990s, but whenever issues affect the direct community interests of the two camps, there would still be dis-putes brewing between them. Overseas Chinese education in Yokohama Chinatown is essential to both pro-PRC and pro-ROC residents (especially for their kids). Thus, when the pro-ROC school YOCS wanted to expand its campus since 1995, the overseas Chinese community was again split into two rival camps. The dispute started with an unsettled right of ownership of a piece of land located right next to the pro-ROC school.

Before the 1951 "School Incident", the former Chairperson Lee of Association A purchased the land in 1948 for use in the future expansion of the former Yokohama Overseas Chinese School, the only school in the Chinatown at that

---

[22] Yomiuri Shimbun (1958). "The Flag of Chinese Community Party was Stolen". *Yomiuri Shimbun*, 1 October 1958, p. 9.

158   W. Elim

time. After the "School Incident", the campus was divided into two halves each claimed by an opposing camp, while the ownership of the land remained unsettled. When the owner of the property passed away in 1995, both YOCAs in the Chinatown claimed ownership rights to that land. From the death of the former chairperson in 1995 to the time the different factions reached a consensus in 2013, it took almost 18 years for the pro-PRC and pro-ROC groups to come to compromise/ solution, and Jin was a major driving force behind the consensus.

Jin believes that, after all these years, it is time for both parties to put aside the hostility and settle the remaining issue over the use of land. Therefore, Jin met with the Lee family from the opposing camp and the son of Lee revealed his father's wish to Jin:

> My father did not want to see the split of pro-PRC and pro-ROC migrants. He said only if the two parties discuss the issue [expansion of the pro-ROC school] and cooperate with each other, he would consider selling the land to Association A. My father wished to see the overseas Chinese migrants become united again.[23]

The involvement of Jin as chairperson of Association A marks a turning point in this issue. In fact, the discussion of unity in the community started as early as 1997 when four former chairpersons from Association A started communication with the pro-ROC groups but the two parties did not come to an amicable conclusion. Jin explains the reason for the failure:

> The ownership [of the land] cannot be settled for over 18 years because both pro-PRC and pro-ROC hold different opinions over the issue. The pro-ROC consider the issue as their own business, and they want to settle the problem by themselves without any aid from the outsiders [pro-PRC]. Also, the pro-PRC refused to cooperate with the Taiwanese because [the expansion of] pro-ROC school has nothing to deal with them. Since the pro-PRC cannot benefit from the issue [expansion of pro-ROC school], they see no point in offering help to them [pro-ROC]. Although the situation was once improved [the first cooperation on the rebuild of Temple of Guandi in 1987], the fundamental disagreement between the two groups is still affecting the overseas Chinese community.[24]

For over the past 18 years before the agreement was made in 2013, the previous chairpersons from the two parties faced difficulties in bringing the two groups of overseas Chinese in the discussion. The pro-ROC focused mainly on the expansion of pro-ROC school, and they refused to seek for help from the so-called "outsiders" regarded by them. Meanwhile, the pro-PRC saw no responsibility in

---

[23] Jin. Interview by the author. Personal Interview. Yokohama Chinatown, 12 August 2015.
[24] *Ibid.*

helping the opposing group as they rather put efforts into maintaining and upgrading their own school.

When Jin became the chairperson in 2011, one of the most important issues in his agenda was to continue the discussion with the pro-ROC group over the issue of unsettled land issue. From his perspective, the property is not only a piece of land for the expansion of an overseas Chinese school but also a platform for all young overseas Chinese migrants to come together to learn and preserve traditional Chinese languages and cultures:

> We have to solve the unsolved questions left by the School Incident. The pro-PRC are ethnic Chinese migrants, and so do the pro-ROC! It is very important to provide a favorable environment for our young generations to learn Chinese language and culture. If either one of the two overseas Chinese schools in Yokohama Chinatown cannot accommodate all overseas Chinese applicants, they may have to attend other overseas Chinese school to learn Chinese culture. That's a way to preserve overseas Chinese education. We need to consider the future of the young overseas Chinese residents, not the dispute that happened over five decades ago.[25]

Upon his appointment as chairperson of Association A, Jin called for a meeting with the former chairperson from the largest pro-ROC association in Yokohama Chinatown to discuss about the land issue. The two chairpersons evaluated the hostile situation in the Chinatown and came up with a solution: increased communication between their communities. According to Jin, previous discussions hosted by the leaderships from both groups of overseas Chinese in the Chinatown failed to come to a conclusion because they did not get the support/consent from the public (specifically their own respective communities). As a result, Jin decided to communicate with all committee members in Association A on a face-to-face basis and individually before opening up the discussion of community reconciliation to all residents in the Chinatown.

From 2011 to 2013, Jin met with numerous committee members from Association A and a few other overseas Chinese associations to explain the importance of community cooperation. He highlighted the need for cooperation in the overall interest of overseas Chinese education and not for the benefit of either party. "It was very hard to have the understanding from everyone. I failed but I did not give up. If I do not do this [explaining to the public], there will never be a solution, which is harmful to the development of overseas Chinese education," Jin explained.[26] As Jin received the consent from the public, he called for a meeting with the pro-ROC representatives, and an agreement was finally made on July 19, 2013.

---

[25] Ibid.
[26] Ibid.

The pan-Chinese committee, formed by representatives from both pro-PRC and pro-ROC, highlighted three remarkable points on the agreement: (1) the two parties [to the agreement] should share the fee for renaming the ownership of the land, (2) the land can only be used for overseas Chinese education and all profits made from the educational institution should be used on charitable affairs the community, (3) the two parties should provide full support on overseas Chinese education in Yokohama Chinatown, and the two overseas Chinese schools should establish a friendly relationship. All the three points emphasized cooperation between the pro-PRC and pro-ROC groups, and the two parties agreed that overseas Chinese education should be considered top priority in community affairs, regardless of ideological preferences.

The above-mentioned initiative is the most recent case of cooperation between the pro-PRC and pro-ROC led by Jin. The chairperson of Association A is happy to see that the two groups can finally settle the questions that have been discussed for over 18 years. But Jin is not only pleased to see the settlement of land but also the fact that he can finally seek understanding from the public for forging good ties between the two groups of Chinese residents in the Chinatown. He said, "… to sign an agreement may take a minute, but to change someone's mind takes days, months and even years."[27] Jin spent almost 2 years persuading the committee members at the two overseas Chinese schools, Association A and the leaders at the overseas Chinese associations to opt for cooperation within the community. "Sometime the parents [parents of kids from the pro-PRC-operated school] asked me 'why should we help the Taiwanese school?' and I have to spend time and effort in explaining the importance of overseas Chinese education for our young generation," Jin continued.[28] Now that the pro-mainland Chinese and pro-Taiwanese (both groups of elderly overseas Chinese migrants) have experienced community-wide cooperation twice, the next step is to motivate all elderly overseas Chinese (who may have remnants of Cold War-era ideological differences) to establish good relationship with the new overseas Chinese in order to strengthen the Yokohama Chinatown as an unified and harmonious community.

PROMOTION OF CHINESE FOLKLORE IN YOKOHAMA CHINATOWN

Jin's father and Jin are two leading and well-known Cantonese figures in Yokohama Chinatown because of their involvement in the Chinatown's religious activities. Jin's father was an active Chinese musical instrument player in Foshan

---

[27] Jin. Interview by the author. 12 August 2015.
[28] *Ibid.*

(his hometown) and in Yokohama Chinatown. Being an energetic Cantonese opera player in religious festivals, his son Jin has been strongly influenced by his father's dedication to the community. Ever since Jin was 3 years old, his father took him to participate in the celebrations held at the Temple of Guandi and watch his Cantonese opera performance. Jin did not follow his father's path to get involved in the Cantonese opera team. Instead, he was deeply impacted by the lion dance performances at the same event. In addition to devoting more than 30 years to the lion dance team, Jin's interest in the Cantonese rites and the temple have led him to become one of the core members in the Temple of Guandi committee. Since 2002, Jin organized the annual celebration of the birth of Guandi, and under his leadership, the celebrations are rich in diversity with the involvement of both local and overseas organizations.

The author spent two summers in Yokohama Chinatown and observed the 2015 and 2016 celebrations of the birth of Guandi event. Based on these observations, it seems that both celebrations reflected the will to bring about continuation/preservation of Cantonese culture in Japan, just as the overseas Chinese residents in Chinatown intended to maintain the ritual practices inherited from their hometown. Furthermore, as a Chinatown located amidst mainstream Japanese society, the celebrations in the Chinese community aimed to connect with the host society (mainstream Japanese) by inviting Japanese (including those residing in neighbouring areas) to the overseas Chinese events in the Chinatown, which up to that point was not a typical practice among other overseas Chinese communities in Japan. After spending 2 weeks with the Chinatown organizers in the two annual celebrations, the author suggests that her participant observation demonstrates the diversity of Chinese practices in religious events organized in the Chinatown.

The Temple of Guandi has been a religious landmark in Yokohama Chinatown for over 150 years. Since an unknown Chinese migrant brought a statue of Guandi from China to Yokohama in the 1850s, Guandi worship has become an important rite in the daily lives of overseas Chinese. The Temple of Guandi has been rebuilt four times, and the latest temple is regarded as the must-see sightseeing spot among local tourists. To overseas Chinese, the Temple of Guandi serves both emotional and practical functions. The worship of the Taoist God and preformance of the rites provide the overseas Chinese with emotional comfort, while the continuity of the religious festivals and ritual events allow the Chinese migrants to recall and uphold their sense of belonging to the community as well as their hometown. The temple serves as an excellent location for the younger generations to learn about the motherland culture and history as well, so the visits can pique the newer generations of Chinatown residents' interest in learning more about the overseas Chinese culture and thus strengthen their ethnic Chinese identity in the process.

Based on her investigation and participant observation, the author believes that the content of the religious rites and festivals has been modified and localized according to the changing social environment in the host society as well as local conditions, but a great volume of traditional Chinese culture continues to be maintained by Jin, now the major organizer of the Temple of Guandi events. From the story of Jin and his father, one can develop a picture of how the Jin family has placed efforts into the maintenance of local customs and cultures within the Chinatown. Rather than regarding their identities as a creation or an invention of Chinese culture, the author detects a utilitarian purpose for it. There is a use of religious constructs as well as ritual events for maintaining a good relationship between the Chinatown and its host society.

Historically, the Jin family's involvement in the development of the Temple of Guandi began in the late-1940s, when Jin's father joined the committee for discussing the rebuilding of the destroyed temple in Yokohama Chinatown. Large-scale air raids in Yokohama during the Second World War period destroyed the entire Chinatown, including the Temple of Guandi. It took the overseas Chinese approximately 2–3 years to restore the order of the Chinatown. Due to limited financial support from the local overseas Chinese residents, they sought the help of the Chinese communities in Tokyo, Kobe and Osaka.[29] The reconstruction of the temple was finally finished by 1948, and the overseas Chinese continued their daily rites in the temple to pray for peace and harmony in the newly renovated Chinatown.

Unfortunately, the next 40 years of history of the third Temple of Guandi are less well documented by comparison. As the only religious building in Yokohama Chinatown, the temple was influenced by the impact of the 1951 "School Incident". Existing records indicated two important facts: first, the overseas Chinese residents restored the celebration of the birth of Guandi and other religious events immediately after the rebuilding of the third temple. Also, the facilitates of the Yokohama Youth Association established after the Second World War replaced the destroyed *heqin* theatre used for the performance of Cantonese operas in the religious rites. Other than these two historical developments, detailed information on the Temple of Guandi remains very limited due to the split in the overseas Chinese community into two political factors. According to Jin, most of the records are kept by the pro-ROC party which the pro-PRC is unable to access.[30] Nevertheless, the author gathered information from eyewitnesses in order to examine the nexus between the development of the third Temple of Guandi with the

---

[29] *Ibid.*, p. 71.

[30] Jin. Interview by the author. Personal Interview. Yokohama Chinatown, 4 August 2015.

Figure 1. The third Temple of Guandi.[31]

contribution of Cantonese migrants in the overseas Chinese community (see Figure 1).

What was so significant about the newly reconstructed Temple of Guandi was that the temple was not open to all overseas Chinese residents. Unlike the previous two temples, pro-PRC migrants were prohibited from entering the temple after the "School Incident" in 1951. The temple was relocated next to the Yokohama Overseas Chinese School. Along with the only overseas Chinese School, the control of the temple was taken over by the pro-ROC because the location was within the sphere of the pro-ROC. "Our people [the pro-PRC migrants] could not enter the temple because the pro-ROC banned us from entering the area [where the Temple of Guandi was located]. We did not have a choice but to suspend all the religious events and rites in the temple. It was a dark age of the temple," explained Jin.[32]

The author also interviewed Mr. Seki, another witness of the incident. In his description, only the Cantonese opera performances offered by the Yokohama Youth Association in the annual celebration of the birth of Guandi continued, but the regular religious events in the temple were suspended.[33] As a result, the separation in the overseas Chinese community has had a huge impact in the Chinatown not only by separating the associations and the overseas Chinese

---

[31] Photo taken by Minai Katsuyo. Kanteibyō to Yokohama Kakyō Committee Board, *Kanteibyō to Yokohama Kakyō: Kantei teikun chinza 150 shuren kinen* (Temple of Guandi and Overseas Chinese in Yokohama: 150th Anniversary of the Statue of Guandi) (Yokohama: Jizai Company), 74.
[32] Jin. Interview by the author. 4 August 2015.
[33] Kanteibyō to Yokohama Kakyō Committee Board, *Kanteibyō to Yokohama Kakyō: Kantei teikun chinza 150 shuren kinen* (Temple of Guandi and Overseas Chinese in Yokohama: 150th Anniversary of the Statue of Guandi), 74.

Figure 2. Overseas Chinese women worshiped the God of Guandi in 1973.[34]

schools into two but also by destroying the key symbol of unity and spiritual landmark in the Chinese community. Nevertheless, the fundamental function of the temple had not been forgotten as the third Temple of Guandi was visited by the pro-ROC residents who continued their daily worship in the temple (see Figure 2).

On the side of the pro-PRC residents, the migrants could only practice Taoist worship in their own individual way. The expelled pro-PRC migrants maintained their cultural representation of religious figures through public performances of Cantonese opera. The Yokohama Youth Association was established by a group of mostly Cantonese migrants who aimed to preserve Chinese culture, and the Association performed annually to celebrate the birth of Guandi after the temple was put under the control of the pro-ROC. Jin's father was the founding member of the association. Jin followed his father to the religious events in the 1950s, and he remembers his father's performance:

> Since my father could not join the management board of the temple, he participated in the [Yokohama] Youth Association instead. Whenever there were [religious] events, he performed the lion dance or performed in the Cantonese opera. He valued the inheritance of Chinese culture in the Chinatown. I always stood beside the stage and watched my father's performance. And I think this is how I started to get interested in lion dance and the temple where I spent my childhood learning about Chinese culture.[35]

---

[34] The photo was published on *Kanagawa Shimbun* on 13 June 1973. *Ibid.*
[35] Jin. Interview by the author. 4 August 2015.

Jin's father was very determined to continue with his religious worship and practices. The lack of an actual physical temple for worship was not an obstacle for the members in Yokohama Youth Association in practicing for cultural performances. The members built a stage for their Cantonese opera and organized lion dance performances in the Chinatown for those who were banned from entering the Temple of Guandi to celebrate his birthday. As recalled by Jin, his father devoted most of his spare time apart from his family business in *Shatenki* to organizing/practicing lion dances and Cantonese operas with his Cantonese peers.[36] Jin was impressed by the strong will of the Cantonese residents in preserving their culture during the turbulent period in Yokohama Chinatown. His father, Jin claims, made an important impact on him when it comes to formulating his sense of community belonging and maintenance of ethnic Chinese identity.[37] Family education in the Jin family also paved the way for Jin's devotion to religious affairs (see Figure 3).

If the absence of the temple among the pro-PRC migrants was an opportunity for Jin to learn about the essentiality of the local culture, the establishment of the

Figure 3. Jin watched his father's performance in a Cantonese opera in 1956.[38]

---

[36] *Ibid.*
[37] *Ibid.*
[38] Photo kept by the Yokohama Youth Association. Kanteibyō to Yokohama Kakyō Committee Board, *Kanteibyō to Yokohama Kakyō: Kantei teikun chinza 150 shuren kinen* (Temple of Guandi and Overseas Chinese in Yokohama: 150th Anniversary of the Statue of Guandi), 207.

fourth Temple of Guandi was a place where he could continue his father's efforts in religious practice. The year of 1986 is regarded as a critical year that transformed the community. A fire, the cause of which remains unknown, occurred in 1986 and destroyed the third Temple of Guandi. The fire seemed like an unfortunate disaster to the overseas Chinese community but was a blessing to the relationship of the pro-PRC and pro-ROC groups within the Chinatown. The loss of the community's religious center provided a chance for both parties to put aside their feelings of hatred and cooperate with each other.

The day after the fire, the overseas Chinese residents in the Chinatown set up a committee to "Rebuild the Temple of Guandi" to discuss the building of the fourth replacement temple. The committee involved members from the two opposing parties and the associations. This brought about changes in the community's religious activities and also stimulated renewals in committee management and strengthened the promotion of Chinese culture for both residents and visitors and helped in the revival of community-wide events and rites under Jin's leadership. Jin played a key role in this stage of development since he was in charge of their management boards and operational details of the events themselves, driven by his beliefs and actions to revive the local culture in Yokohama Chinatown that helped in understanding the role of Cantonese migrants in religious affairs (see Figure 4).

Jin's participation was a watershed moment in the history of the Temple of Guandi. As a new member of the committee board but an experienced participant in religious events, Jin brought new ideas to the management board in order to revive the pan-Chinese religious affairs and cooperation in the Chinatown that had been suspended for over three decades due to ideological differences. He especially valued the importance of cooperation and the maintenance of community cohesion. In the first council meeting in 2002, Jin suggested that the religious

Figure 4. The fourth Temple of Guandi.

events in Yokohama Chinatown could be seen as an opportunity to communicate with the Chinatown's immediate neighbours and their overseas Chinese peers from other countries, for example, the dragon dance teams from Singapore and Kobe as student exchanges with both overseas Chinese schools and local Japanese schools.[39]

Most importantly, Jin was the one who suggested the organization of the religious events in the playground of the Taiwanese-operated Yokohama Overseas Chinese School, which was the first time in the history of Yokohama Chinatown that the Chinese migrants put political views aside and organized religious events together since the 1951 "School Incident".[40] The author considers this to be a revival of the social function of the temple (like a community hall that pulls residents of all affiliations together). In the early days when the community was not split up, the temple had this function in gathering the overseas Chinese migrants together. As a place where the residents could meet and interact with each other, the temple brought not only religious and spiritual harmony to the community but also provided practical support for the migrants, who have been contributing to the development of the Yokohama Chinatown since its early inception. Having discussed the historical development of the Yokohama Chinatown in this chapter, the next chapter will go on to examine specific cultural activities inside the Chinatown.

---

[39] *Ibid.*, pp. 169–170.
[40] *Ibid.*

Chapter 13

CASE STUDY OF GUANDI'S BIRTHDAY CELEBRATIONS IN YOKOHAMA CHINATOWN IN 2015 AND 2016

W. Elim

Chinese University of Hong Kong, Hong Kong

INTRODUCTION TO THE CASE STUDY

The previous chapter sketched out the broad outlines of community leadership in Yokohama Chinatown and the main human agencies involved in organizing and managing the community events. This chapter will look at the specific case study of a seminal event in the Chinatown — the birthday celebrations of Guandi organized by the local residents. The birthday celebration of Guandi is held every year on June 24 in the Chinese lunar calendar, and the committee board of the Temple of Guandi decided to augment the celebration by adding on different kinds of colourful traditional ritual practices before and after the main celebration, so the entire programme often lasts for a week or longer. The celebration is the second largest Chinese festival event after the Chinese Lunar New Year in Yokohama Chinatown and attracts thousands of visitors from Japan and overseas to experience Chinese culture with the Chinese migrants.

The author attended the 2015 and 2016 celebrations of the birth of Guandi. In order to understand the celebrations better, the author observed the events from two different perspectives: as an insider and as an external visitor. The author was invited by Mr. Jin, the main person in charge of the celebrations, to join the organizing team and was permitted to observe some of the private events, which were mostly Cantonese rites practiced by the overseas Chinese community. The public is not allowed to attend these ritual practices because the rites are intra-community Chinese migrant-oriented and used as blessings for safety, peace and harmony in Yokohama Chinatown. As an insider (a Cantonese and an overseas Chinese), the author was able to observe and collect valuable sources on the Cantonese practices that are still performed by the overseas Chinese in Yokohama Chinatown. The author also observed the festive celebrations as an external visitor. Different from the 2015 celebration, the author joined the crowd of local Japanese visitors and spent most of her time on the streets to watch the performances (i.e. not privy to the making of background scenes).

The main difference between the two experiences was that the author could gather information from two perspectives. As an insider, she viewed the celebration from the perspective of the Cantonese migrants in Yokohama Chinatown, and she focused mainly on the Cantonese ritual practices that are not open to the public. On the contrary, she also learnt about the cultural/religious experience as a visitor and fathomed the meaning of the celebration to the outsiders (external observers). Based on her two participant observations, she interpreted the birthday celebrations of Guandi as having three major symbolic meanings to both the overseas Chinese community and the host society: first, the celebration is a reflection of the practice of Cantonese culture in the contemporary overseas Chinese community. According to Mr. Jin, Yokohama Chinatown is the only Chinatown in Japan that celebrates the birth of Guandi with large-scale ritual performances lasting for a week.

Based on the experience of the first few generations of migrants from Guangdong province, the Chinese migrants understudied the senior members of the community to learn how to perform Cantonese rites. Yokohama Chinatown, therefore, is the only Chinatown where one is able to experience the Guandi birthday celebrations authentically in Japan. Secondly, although the celebration is mostly practiced by the Chinese and tailored to the needs of the overseas Chinese, the event indeed creates new elements to link up the overseas Chinese community with the local Japanese society. Yokohama Chinatown is not a stand-alone community in Japan but an integral component of to the mainstream Japanese host society. The purpose of the celebration, therefore, has become connected to reaching out to the mainstream Japanese society in the last decade. In the interest of increasing tourism revenue, the committee added new elements that are related to popular culture and entertainment. Today, the celebration of the birthday celebrations of Guandi can also be regarded as an amusing and interesting festival for the family in addition to its religious symbolism.

The "crossing the bridge" ceremony is one of the three highlights that were widely promoted by the committee and was advertised on promotional pamphlets and posters for the community. A tiger head gate and a bridge were prepared in

Figure 1. The Tiger Gate in front of the Temple of Guandi.

advance and placed outside the Temple of Guandi (see Figure 1). The "crossing the bridge" rite is a common Cantonese practice in the Taoist tradition. The tiger in Taoist belief has an important status. On the religious level, the animal is believed to have the power to destroy and expel monsters.[1] Local Chinese also believe that the tiger has the ability to bring wealth and power to the people.[2] The image of the tiger is often visible in Chinese society, for example, the locals placed a tiger head image in front of the door to protect their families from evils (see Figure 2).

At around 1 pm, the ceremony started with a Taoist priest who blew a dragon horn. The blowing of the dragon horn has an important role in the Taoist rite in China as the sound from the horn is a signal that invites good spirits to fight

---

[1] Henry Dore (1987). *Chinese Customs*, trans. M. Kennelly, Singapore: Graham Brash, p. 702.
[2] Chen Jinfeng (2008). "Daojiao yu he manshuo (A Talk of Daoism and Tiger)". *Hungdao*, 4, 18–27.

Figure 2. The bridge in front of the Temple of Guandi.

against the bad spirits (see Figure 3).[3] The committee members followed the priest, and they walked beside the tiger gate until they reached the bridge. The bridge, on the contrary, represents forgetting the bad luck in the past.[4] The members walked one by one across the bridge and exited through the tiger gate. The entire ceremony lasted for about 5 minutes. Upon exit from the tiger gate, each member was given incense sticks, and they had to make a final bow at the exit to finish the ceremony (see Figures 4 and 5).

The ceremony was open to the public, but beforehand, the committee arranged a lion dance performance to bless the gate and bridge before the visitors participated in the religious rite. As discussed, the Cantonese southern-style lion dance is seen as a symbol of Yokohama Chinatown and also represented the act of driving away evil. The decision to add a lion dance performance after the Taoist rite is a tailor-made programme especially for the community that is intended to preserve Cantonese culture. The lion dance lasted for a short time, probably less than 5 minutes and the visitors who lined up beside the temple could start crossing the bridge according to the directions of the organizing committee members.

The "protection from evils" ceremony started at the gates at the Chinatown. The committee members brought a burning metal bucket with a carrying pole, while the two main Taoist priests performed the rite. First, one of the priests rang the hand bell, which the Taoists believe can ward off ghosts and evil spirits.

---

[3] "Introduction of the Taoist instruments," Very Taoism , http://verytaoism.com/adder.php. Accessed 23 March 2017.
[4] Dore, *Chinese Customs*, p. 530.

Figure 3. Taoist priest with dragon horn leading the committee members to cross the bridge.

Figure 4. Two committee members exit from the tiger gate.

Figure 5. Crossing the tiger gate.

This was followed by another priest who blew a dragon horn to attract the good spirits, and the priest spat oil into the burning metal bucket creating a larger fire in the bucket. The fire is regarded as a medium that protects the community from evil. The lion dance performance was performed after the Taoist rites which heralded good luck and after the evils are dispersed with the burning fire. The performance was carried out by the students from the overseas Chinese schools in the Chinatown. There were around 10 members in the lion dance team: two students played the lion and the rest were responsible for playing musical instruments such as drums and cymbals. A total number of approximately 40 shops and restaurants registered for the blessing ceremony and the entire schedule ended at around 5 pm (see Figures 6 and 7).

Jin was in charge of the "protection from evils" ceremony. Upon arriving at a shop or restaurant, he gave an introduction of the ceremonial procedure to the owner because the ritual practice required the participation of the shop representative. After the Taoist priests rang the bells and spat into the burning fire, Jin invited the owner to perform the rite along with the priests. The rite was simple: the owner walked from the left to right direction with both hands lifted up and placed above the carrying pole. The Chinese believed the smoke that went through the body of the shop represented the heralding of good fortune to the shop. Other than being the advisor to the participants, Jin helped in every single detail during the ceremony, including the maintenance of the fire's temperature (see Figures 8–11).

After the religious rites, a community-wide parade was held in Yokohama Chinatown. Similar to the "protection from evils" ceremony, the owners of shops and restaurants signed up for the event at the committee beforehand. The parade

Figure 6. The Taoist rite at the Temple of Guandi before the start of the "protection from evils" ceremony.

Figure 7. Lion dance at the Temple of Guandi before the "protection from evils" ceremony.

to commemorate the birth of Guandi in fact represents religious and social functions. For religious purposes, those shops and restaurants in Yokohama that had already signed up for the ceremony had to prepare offerings for the God of Guandi. The offerings were usually fresh fruits, flowers and burning incense sticks. The owner also had to prepare a table that was covered with a gold cloth. On the cloth, the Chinese word *Jinyumantang* (treasures everywhere in the house) was sown in gold thread.

Figure 8. Setting off fire for the "protection from evils" ceremony.

Figure 9. The Taoist priest spat oil into the burning metal bucket to set a larger fire. The smoke is believed to bring good fortune to the shop.

The origins of this cultural display are based on Cantonese belief that Guandi is considered the god of wealth among the locals (especially the small time retailers). When the parade participants arrived at the pre-registered shop or restaurant, each member stopped by the shop and bowed to the shop representative until the sedan chair with the Guandi idol arrived. Every shop representative bowed to the Guandi idol, symbolically making offerings to Guandi. The entire ceremony ended with a Cantonese lion dance performance. The performance at the shop entrances usually attracted a large number of visitors (see Figures 12 and 13).

Figure 10. The "protection from evils" ceremony at a Chinese restaurant.

Figure 11. Representatives from a Chinese restaurant co-performed the "protection from evils" ceremony under Jin's directions.

THE CONNECTION WITH THE JAPANESE SOCIETY

Although the major purpose of the entire celebration is to preserve Cantonese culture, the festival was also designed to reach out to members of the public in the mainstream host society in Japan. Jin explains the special arrangement in the 2016 celebration:

> Next year [2016] will be the 155th anniversary of the celebration of the birth of Guandi. We are planning something big. Bigger than the previous celebrations.

Figure 12. Offerings for Guandi.

Figure 13. Chinese (Cantonese) dance performance in front of a Chinese restaurant.

Moreover, as we are a part of Japanese society, I want to invite the Japanese to join our celebration. This is not an event for only the overseas Chinese. This is for everyone in the community. I hope we can bring the blessing to our neighbors too. So we [committee board] are adding new elements to the celebration that are related to Japanese society.[5]

Since the author attended both 2015 and 2016 celebrations of the birth of Guandi, by comparing the two celebrations, it is discernible that the 155th anniversary of

---

[5] Jin. Interview by the author. 4 August 2015.

Case Study of Guandi's Birthday Celebrations in Yokohama Chinatown 179

the celebration in 2016 was a far richer and colourful programme that catered to the Japanese visitors. The 2016 celebration was one of the largest celebrations of Guandi's birthday in the history of the Yokohama Chinatown. Jin expanded the route of the birth of Guandi parade outside the Chinatown and into mainstream Japanese streets and communities and this, according to Jin, helped to promote overseas Chinese festivals and local community Chinatown culture to members of the public in the host society.[6] The committee decided to expand the parade route to Motomachi, a neighbouring area to Yokohama Chinatown. This was not a common practice in the annual celebration of the birth of Guandi. The last time this occurred was during the 150th anniversary of the birth of Guandi in 2011, which was also the first time when Jin considered an expansion of the traditional parade.

The parade started at around 3 pm after the morning celebrations at the Temple of Guandi. The team of over 300 participants started the parade from the Temple of Mazu, then walked through the Temple of Guandi Road to the exit of the Chinatown. By around 4:15 pm, the team arrived at the entrance of Motomachi, the main shopping street in the Yamate area of Yokohama, and the parade was often preceded by lion and dragon dance performances along the streets. In addition to bringing the performance to Japanese neighbourhoods and areas, the special feature of the 155th anniversary celebration was the visit to a major Japanese shrine during the parade. The entire team stopped by the Miyajima Shrine at Motomachi to greet the Shinto priests.

This arrangement represents the overseas Chinese's determination to maintain a good relationship with Japanese society, as Jin explains, "…we hope to bring good luck to our neighbors as well."[7] The entire parade at Motomachi lasted for about 30 minutes. The author talked to a few local Japanese residents and asked for their opinions on the Chinese parade. Many of them did not know there would be a parade from Yokohama Chinatown but the surprise event brought them much fun and merriment. A Japanese family revealed that they spent a long time at Motomachi watching the parade. A Japanese housewife who brought her daughter for shopping at Motomachi said that she was happy to see the lion and dragon dance since she used to live near the Chinatown and the parade reminded her of her childhood, and she felt pleased to show her facts of her childhood memories to her daughter. The 30-minute parade outside Yokohama Chinatown, especially the lion dance, attracted the local Japanese's attention, and the author saw how most of the visitors looked excited, and some of them took pictures of the performance (see Figures 14–16).

---

[6] *Ibid.*

[7] *Ibid.*

Figure 14. The committee members visited the Miyajima Shrine at Motomachi, Yokohama.

Figure 15. The lion dance team finished its performance at the Miyajima Shrine at Motomachi, Yokohama.

Figure 16. The statue of Guandi was put on a sedan chair and displayed in the parade at Motomachi, Yokohama.

FROM CHINESE RELIGIOUS RITE TO A FESTIVAL FOR ALL JAPANESE

Since Jin became the person in charge of the celebration events for Guandi's birthday, he has added new elements to the traditional Chinese festival. Jin's different roles in the Chinatown encouraged him to introduce changes in the festival to achieve multiple objectives. As the chairperson of Association A, Jin was concerned about the development of the local-area tourism industry, and after he started to organize the religious celebration, Jin attempted to utilize the festival to satisfy both the religious purpose of the event as well as its social role in boosting tourism development. The 2016 celebration is an example of such efforts. As the festival also celebrated the 155th anniversary of the arrival of the Jin statue at Yokohama Chinatown, Jin invited many more participants from Taiwan than the previous celebrations, including the dance team, parade team and Taoist priests. Just like the 150th anniversary, there was an entertainment night on the day before the celebration. Jin welcomed not only the overseas Chinese organizations in Japan but also the Fujianese from mainland China, Hong Kong representatives and Taiwanese guests to perform items in the celebration's entertainment night. The celebration event under Jin's leadership turned into a multicultural event for the public, including the combined participation of ethnic Chinese and Japanese, in activities that included a local religious event for the Chinese migrants in Yokohama Chinatown.

The entertainment night lasted for about 2 hours. All the performances were based on traditional Chinese cultures, such as lion dance, dragon dance, Chinese music and dances. Nevertheless, these performances were recreated and modified with popular cultural elements to increase the popularity of the event. The author participated in the entertainment night of 2016 celebration, and her major aim was to observe how Chinese cultural performances can be combined with popular culture. The 2016 celebration is a breakthrough in the history of Yokohama Chinatown, as the committee used popular culture as a medium for tourism promotion.

These events in Yokohama Chinatown demonstrates significantly how a traditional religious event can be transformed to maintain relevance to contemporary society and also attract young people to join amidst a changing society and social values. In the past, the celebration catered to Chinese migrants and a relatively closed overseas Chinese community within the foreign settlement in Yokohama since the 1870s. Although there were records about foreigners attending the celebration in the early established Chinatown, the religious rites performed in the celebration did not have any connection to the host society or the non-Chinese residents. Today, as the Yokohama Chinatown has turned into a popular tourist spot for the local tourists, the overseas Chinese residents saw the need for a change in the religious festival. Starting from 2016, Jin turned a new page on the religious celebration of the festival by welcoming the participation of the non-Chinese residents in the community as well as visitors by using popular culture to draw the attention of Japanese audiences who may not necessarily be well-versed in traditional Chinese culture.

The entertainment night on 26 July 2016 showcased the use of Korean popular culture (K-pop) in Chinese dance performances. The event included more than 10 Chinese cultural performances by students from the two overseas Chinese schools in Yokohama, a lion dance team invited from the Kobe Chinatown, a dragon dance team from a Kobe high school as well as Chinese dance groups from mainland China and Taiwan. The lion, dragon and Chinese dance performances may not have been as impressive as the popular culture-oriented performances to the audiences because these are regular features in Yokohama Chinatown visible from time to time. However, the musical choices of some of the dance performances brought excitement to the onlookers and became a talking point of the entire event. The event was introduced as a "fun and exciting night" at the greeting session by Jin and the host in the beginning. As a religious festive celebration, the first half of the event, nevertheless, was based on Chinese cultural performances. The lion dance, dragon dance, and Chinese dance performances by the students at Yokohama Chinatown impressed the 200 strong audience with their skilful dance moves. However, everyone's focus was on the second half of the programme, especially on the last three performances by the Taiwanese dance groups.

This was the first time in the history of Yokohama Chinatown that K-pop music was used in Chinese cultural performances. When the music of the Korean male singer Psy's popular song *Gangnam style* was played, the audience was excited to see how the music could complement the lion dance. The lions, despite displaying the usual moves, danced to the tune of *Gangnam style* without caring too much on whether the moves were appropriate for a lion dance performance. This was followed by the Taiwanese dance team's performance of the Korean girl group Girl's Generation's signature song *Catch me if you can*, three mascots in the likeness of Chinese Taoist god Nezha joined the dance team for a performance onstage and offstage gyrating to the K-pop song. The entertainment night ended with a final performance by the three Nezha mascots and the dance team moving to the sounds of a Taiwanese popular song *Little apple* performed by the Chopstick Brothers.

Jin's decision to invite the Taiwanese dance group to the 2016 entertainment night can be considered a watershed moment in the history of the birthday celebration of Guandi. The use of the three mascots of Nezha had been a popular trend in Taiwan since 2009. Nezha worship has been a popular practice in the local Taiwanese folk religion, and its lively and playful image made Nezha a popular local god who provides protection to children. The Taiwanese created the Nezha mascot in the 2000s and used the mascots in local religious events. In all, 32 Nezha mascots, each with a light-emitting diode hairband and driving a motorbike, performed in the 2009 World Games in Kaohsiung that featured Chinese religious figures in modern and contemporary images.[8] Since 2009, the Nezha mascot became known as the Electric Third Prince (the third prince of Vaiśravaṇa who plays electric music) in Taiwan and is famous for its dance performance played to mainly Taiwanese, Japanese and Korean popular music. Today, the Electric Third Prince in Taiwan has a significant social symbolism beyond its former religious connotation. The changing imagery of traditional Chinese religious figure, therefore, is a good fit for contemporary celebrations in honour of Guandi's birthday in Yokohama Chinatown.

In the 2016 celebration, the three Electric Third Princes from Taiwan performed as special guests in entertainment night. After the K-pop songs *Gangnam style* and *Catch me if you can* as well as the Taiwanese pop song *Little Apple*, the three mascots went downstage and danced with members of the audience. From the author's observation, the appearance of the Electric Third Princes received a resounding welcome by Japanese audience members. The three Electric Third Princes continued the K-pop dance performances in the Guandi birthday parade on July 27. The three mascots walked along the streets in Yokohama Chinatown

---

[8] "The search of Electric Third Prince," Taiwanese Folk Culture Studio, https://www.folktw.com.tw/culture_view.php?info=89. Accessed 27 March 2017.

Figure 17. The three Electric Third Princes performed the K-pop group Girl's Generation's song *Catch me if you can* at the entertainment night on 26 July 2016.

and performed their famous K-pop songs in front of the parade participants and onlookers.

Jin added this new element to the parade in order to create a playful environment, further supplemented by two more Sudhana mascots blowing bubbles during the parade as well as dispensing free candies to the audience/visitors/onlookers. Although the two Sudhana mascots are not new additions to the parade, the lively acts put up by these mascots complemented the playful dance performances of the Taiwanese Electric Third Princes. All these new arrangements successfully transformed the religious event from a closed exclusive overseas Chinese community event in the past to a carnival-like event that welcomed all visitors to participate (see Figures 17–20).

PROMOTION OF TOURISM

Yokohama Chinatown has been a popular sightseeing spot since the 1980s, when the Association A shifted its major focus from internal business development to external promotion of the Chinatown. Since Jin became Association A's chairperson in 2011, tourism in Kanagawa prefecture has already matured. The author gathered statistics collected and organized by the Culture and Tourism Bureau of Yokohama City from 2011 to understand the competitive and challenging environment of the tourism industry.

Based on the statistics given in Table 1, developing tourism potential in Yokohama Chinatown is not without challenges. Both the number of Japanese visitors who have heard of and have been to any of the Chinese culture-related

Figure 18. The Electric Third Prince danced with the audience.

Figure 19. Two of the Electric Third Princes performed K-pop songs in front of a Chinese restaurant at the parade for commemorating Guandi's birthday on July 27.

Figure 20. The Sudhana mascot blew bubbles during the parade of the birth of Guandi.

Table 1. Official statistics on Yokohama Chinatown tourism development.[9]

Year	Number of local visitors who have heard of Yokohama Chinatown events (i.e. Chinese Lunar New Year festival, celebration of Birth of Guandi/Mazu)	Number of local visitors who have been to Yokohama Chinatown events (i.e. Chinese Lunar New Year festival, celebration of Birth of Guandi/Mazu)
2011	59.4% (out of 4,777 interviewees)	11.8% (out of 4,777 interviewees)
2012	53.8% (out of 5,963 interviewees)	12.8% (out of 5,963 interviewees)
2013	51.8% (out of 5,636 interviewees)	9.6% (out of 5,636 interviewees)
2014	—	—
2015	51.1% (out of 6,054 interviewees)	9.6% (out of 6,054 interviewees)
2016	—	—

---

[9] "Data and Statistics," Culture and Tourism Bureau, City of Yokohama, http://www.city.yokohama.lg.jp/bunka/miryoku/chosa.html. Accessed 3 March 2017.

Case Study of Guandi's Birthday Celebrations in Yokohama Chinatown   187

activities is decreasing. In 2011, these events ranked the second after sports events that were best known and visited by Japanese tourists. However, the Association A-organized events dropped four places from the second rank to the sixth among all 20 events in the city of Yokohama, which connotes the Chinatown events have become less well-known than other local events, such as the "Thanks to the Port" event that ranked the third in 2011. The downturn in tourism development in terms of Chinatown branding, nevertheless, is not only reflected in Yokohama Chinatown. After the great East Japan Earthquake in 2011, the Japanese economy experienced a challenging period. Mr. Shi, the general manager of a Chinese restaurant in the Chinatown, told the author how the disaster made a huge impact on Yokohama Chinatown:

> We had a tough time after the 3.11 Earthquake. We had four restaurants in the [Yokohama] Chinatown but we only operated one [in the aftermath of the earthquake]. The other three restaurants were in [perpetual] rest mode. The operating cost was too high and we had a very hard time to break even. Another difficulty was that, after the earthquake, a number of our Chinese staff members quit their jobs and went back to China. We have a shortage of staff members. The situation is not getting better now. I think we still need to wait [for a better Japanese economic environment].[10]

The decrease in the number of visitors to Yokohama Chinatown remained a challenge for Association A. The Association takes the mission of tourism promotion seriously, and from the author's fieldwork, it is making an effort to have active participation in community-wide public events.

Besides Chinese cultural promotion, the Association has been seeking ways to reach out to the mainstream host society to attract more tourists to the Chinatown. Participation in Yokohama Sparkling Twilight 2016 accomplished both goals. Yokohama Sparkling Twilight is a community-wide event held by the city government of Yokohama. The concept of the two-day event is marketed as "a summer activity by the sea and harbor at Yokohama city and to create an unforgettable memory for the Yokohama residents."[11] Unlike any other community-building events, Yokohama Sparkling Twilight highlights the participation of the Asian minorities in Yokohama. Hayashi Fumiko, the mayor of the city of Yokohama, hopes to create a unified community and build up friendship between Japanese residents and their neighbours from Asian countries.[12]

---

[10] Shi. Interview by the author. Personal Interview. Yokohama Chinatown, 6 December 2012.

[11] "Concept," Sparkling Yokohama, http://www.y-artist.co.jp/sparkling/#concept. Accessed 4 March 2017.

[12] *Ibid.*

As one of the earliest connecting points between Japan and the world, Yokohama is characterized as an international city made up of residents from a variety of ethnic backgrounds. The event consists of eight major components, and the overseas Chinese from Yokohama Chinatown have signed up to participate in the Sparkling Parade since 2012. The parade is dissimilar to ordinary parade activities in the community because the Sparkling Parade emphasizes cooperation among different parties. In other words, the parade could not have taken place based on efforts by the overseas Chinese residents alone, but only through cooperation with the Japanese public and other Asian minorities in Yokohama. Unlike Chinese cultural activities organized by the Association A, as a new programme feature, Yokohama Sparkling Twilight has lower public awareness comparatively. In the first year when the event was introduced to the society, 14.9% of the interviewees from the 2012 tourism survey claimed that they had heard of the event, while 2.8% of them had participated in it.[13] However, by 2016, there was an increase in visitors who were aware of this event (18.2%) and those who have seen it in person (3.5%).[14]

The author visited Yokohama Chinatown on August 17, 2016 to observe the involvement of the Chinese associations in the parade, with support from Association A. The parade was held at Nihon Ōdori, located near the coast and Yamashita Park. Upon arrival at the venue, the author saw some booths selling different kinds of foods, including Chinese food. The excellent location, just 5-minute walk from the train station or Yokohama Chinatown, attracted hundreds of visitors who stood under the sun for at least 30 minutes before the parade officially began. The parade team members were made up of a number of individuals with different ethnicities. The overseas Chinese team was the first in the line, followed by the Filipino team and then the Indian team. The Chinese team was made up of a few parties from the Chinatown, including the members of the Temple of Guandi, Temple of Mazu, the alumni associations of the two overseas Chinese schools and the CC. Hence, the Sparkling Parade can be conceptuaized as a showcase of Chinese culture performed by the most active Chinese associations from the Chinatown. Before the parade had started, as the chairperson of Association A, Jin was busy greeting the representatives of the other teams (see Figures 21 and 22).

The parade started at 2 pm with the performance of a lion dance by the Yokohama Overseas Chinese School (Taiwanese-operated) (see Figure 23).

---

[13] "The result of statistics on awareness and living activities of Yokohama city," Culture and Tourism Bureau, City of Yokohama, http://www.city.yokohama.lg.jp/bunka/outline/miryoku/ishiki-chosa24.pdf. Accessed 4 March 2017.

[14] "The result of statistics on awareness and living activities of Yokohama city," Culture and Tourism Bureau, City of Yokohama, http://www.city.yokohama.lg.jp/bunka/miryoku/shisetsuandevent.pdf. Accessed 4 March 2017.

Figure 21. The China team in preparation mode.

Figure 22. Representatives from Yokohama Chinatown were greeted by the representative from the Japanese team.

Figure 23. Lion dance performance by the Yokohama Overseas Chinese School team.

Figure 24. Chinese dance performance by Chinese students from Yokohama Chinatown.

This is an important point to note since the team's origin was from China, therefore the involvement of a Taiwanese school was a breakthrough for the Chinatown community after the long period of hostilities since the "School Incident" of 1951. After the lion dance performance, next in line was the Chinese dance team from the pro-PRC overseas Chinese school and a Chinese Gods parade procession organized by the Temple of Mazu team (see Figure 24).

Figure 25. Chinese God parade performed by the Temple of Mazu team.

Jin showed his active participation as the leader of many organizations, not only in playing the role of the chairperson of Association A but also in running the affairs of the Temple of Mazu and the Temple of Guandi. During the 2-hour parade, Jin often offered help to his team members. For example, he led the team by giving directions and guidance, and he sometimes replaced some team members and allowed them to take a break during the long parade. The Sparkling Parade is a one-of-a-kind activity that acts as a channel bringing the residents to the city. As a minority group in Yokohama, the overseas Chinese residents in Chinatown have been living with the Japanese for over 150 years. However, there has been few opportunities for the people to get together to design an activity together. Collective memory stoked among the participants is not only useful for encouraging friendship between the overseas Chinese residents and the Japanese locals but also useful for strengthening the bonds between individuals from the overseas Chinese community, in particular between the old overseas Chinese, the new migrants and the pro-ROC members of the community (see Figures 25 and 26).

(a)

(b)

Figure 26. The Temple of Mazu team.

CONCLUSION

The two chapters on the Yokohama Chinatown case study address two main research questions: (1) What are some features of Community Leader Jin's leadership style/strategies? What are some aspects of Yokohama Chinatown that can create a strong sense of community belonging? The characteristics of a community leader in a model community highlighted by Onyx and Leonard may be useful here. Jin's leadership and organizational features demonstrated strong effectiveness in bringing together the pro-PRC and pro-ROC teams to work on a single community-wide project. In settling the use of an empty land, Jin is visionary in detecting the future shortage of open space for the overseas Chinese school to expand. To him, overseas Chinese education is an important platform for Chinese language and cultural knowledge to be passed onto the young generation. He also had a consultative leadership style and did not make the decision by himself. Instead, he consulted his institution's board members (both pro-PRC and pro-ROC individuals) and the general members of the public. Moreover, Jin promotes the preservation of local culture to strengthen a sense of belonging to the Chinatown.

The birthday celebration of Guandi is an example. The celebration is a mixture of traditional Chinese culture and new religious elements from Taiwan, and it not only helps to promote Chinese religious culture but also serves as a festive event to welcome Japanese visitors to join the Chinese celebration. As a community leader, Jin cultivated formal and informal networks within the community. In the Yokohama Sparkling Twilight 2016, overseas Chinese association (informal non-governmental groups) worked hand-in-hand with the city government of Yokohama (formal institutions related to the state) to promote Yokohama, including Yokohama Chinatown, as a tourist spot. Their cooperation demonstrates the good relationship between ethnic Chinese residents and their Japanese friends. Although Jin has stepped down from his leadership role in Association A, the efforts he put into developing Yokohama Chinatown as an integrated ethnic quarter sowed the seed for his successors in the community, and his leadership remains as a role model for the young generation.

Chapter 14

REVIEW CHAPTER ON IDEAL STUDENT LEADERSHIP AND THE IMPACT ON YOUTH DEVELOPMENT: LEADERSHIP AND PSYCHOLOGY FROM A PRACTITIONER'S PERSPECTIVE

D. Tan

Singapore Chinese Chamber of Commerce & Industry, Singapore

INTRODUCTION

There are tons of books and articles on the subject of leadership which are available to everyone upon a simple Google search. I am sure these works are more than sufficient for the topic of leadership. Therefore, what I write here is a personal perspective on leadership. It is an experiential chapter based on observation studies and practice. Building on my personal experience and perspective, I would like to put up the case on the importance of student leadership and its impact on youth development. I was fortunate to be the president of a student-led society during my university days. It was during this period that, retrospectively, I truly exercised and learnt much on leadership. That said, my knowledge and experiences were gained by looking at and learning from others who have led and reflecting on the subject of leadership. Through these experiences, I developed my personal understanding of leadership, which I practised during my university years.

I would like to set the ground right before we start exploring this chapter. The foundation of this chapter lies in the definition of leadership. There are various definitions/interpretations of what student leadership means, and each interpretation varies from the other. This is expected given that leadership is a complex subject that was never meant to be simple or can be succinctly explained. But, are there some components of leadership which we can identify and the majority will agree to at the very least? I do not seek to add on to a long list of definitions, rather I would like to present an honest and perhaps a practitioner/experiential perspective in defining this subject. I would like to put forth the idea of understanding and exploring leadership as a human-to-human relationship. At the baseline of understanding this subject, a leader and the followers are essentially human beings. The leader is as much a human as the followers. Leadership involves a human-to-human relationship. It exhibits not only our intellectual aspects but also our aspirations, beliefs and emotions. Leadership is indeed as multifaceted as the various characters of a human being, and as such, there is no single definition of leadership. Hence, within leadership, we would find certain qualities or attributes which drive actions and influence the human-to-human relationship. Judgement is thereby passed on the actions of the individuals.

"The whole is greater than the sum of its parts" or "T.E.A.M" which translates to "together, everyone achieves more" are adages we hear often. How did these adages come about and how could these happen? I would like to point out that it is ideal leadership that made it possible. In addition, I would also argue that the impact of leadership, both from holding the position as well as experiencing the leadership of an ideal leader, contributes to development of youth. I encourage people to explore this area by looking at the impact of a positive leadership on their working relationships, impact on society, or in general, how they fare post this experience. My view is that there is a positive relationship between them. It will be too naïve to see the impact as a one-off influence on the individual, for the memories stay within and the relationship cultivated between the individuals could go on for long. Hence, through the experience gained from good leadership, it is possible to see how an individual will first be inspired, then attempt doing something and finally contribute to society or to the areas where one can. In order to create the above-mentioned chain effect, those who led must have some qualities which created the effect.

Leadership should therefore seek to cultivate and improve the human-to-human relationship which then renders a positive influence on the individual within the relationship. With the positive influence supporting and nurturing the relationship, there will be possibilities emerging, thus allowing the identification of potential and the creation of plenary impact on the individual's efforts. This might be how we can achieve the outcome, "the whole is greater than the sum of its parts". In addition, it is necessary to assess what types of qualities will promote the individuals, cultivate the relationships and create the plenary impact to fulfil and achieve the above adage. In this chapter, I further explore some of the qualities which are important to achieving these impacts and what leaders could do to achieve such results. Even though this chapter provides an idealist perspective on the subject of leadership, I believe that having a handful of these characteristics would still help produce a significant impact on someone who is holding a leadership position.

A leader should be humble enough to listen and allow others space to express themselves and speak what is on their mind. Humbleness derives from the understanding that one is finite not only in what one is able to do but also in the amount of knowledge one can hold. Hence, the leader should allow those who are being led to voice their views and concerns, ideas and suggestions. Through the practice of humbleness, the other individuals in the group will be ready and more confident to voice out their concerns. This act has multiple effects on not only the individuals but also the group. The individual gains confidence, experience and learning in the process of the act, while the group gains an additional perspective and consideration for the subject in discussion. Now, if all that the leader does is to allow everyone to speak their views and allow conflict of views to spark endlessly, then the leader will have failed to perform his or her role satisfactorily. Therefore, the next thing which a leader requires is confidence and not arrogance.

A leader should have *confidence* in himself or herself in providing direction and making decisions for the group. Drawing from the situation mentioned earlier, when there is a conflict of views, the leader should be able to pull everyone from the heat of the debate and start exchanging objective views. The leader should also be confident when he or she has made a decision for the group and hold responsibility irrespective of whether the decision is solely made by the leader or is a collective decision. A leader without confidence will only be swayed by the opinions and ideas of the team. Opinions and ideas clash without a leader to provide guidance, resulting in conflicts and the direction being lost. Yet, having confidence does not mean being absolute in the idea of the leader alone. Hence, as a leader, one should listen to what the team has to put forth, assess objectively and give credit where it is necessary. The interplay between a leader who is humble, yet confident, will allow for the team to grow and the most appropriate ideas to surface.

Besides having humility and confidence, a leader needs to have a mission or a dream. A leader should be one who can guide the team and lead it towards and the future which could be shared by all. A leader should be a dreamer, not an idealistic dreamer, but a *practical dreamer*. In order to strive, one will need a destination or a dream that they can hold on to. Destination determines the direction, and with the end in mind, one can work towards the destination. Dream and vision are essential, but a leader has to do more than just dream or set a vision. A leader has to know what is possible and how to progress towards the dream. A leader has to keep his or her sense of realistic expectations and mobilize the team towards the dream. Without this sense, it will always be a dream and the scale of the task in hand will be overwhelming — even if it doesn't show on the leader, it will on the rest of the team. It undermines what the leadership was supposed to cultivate and renders the team to uncertainty and inability to move forward. As the team fails to see how the steps can be taken, the motivation to progress diminishes more and it will only continue till the cycle is broken and the direction is shown.

Now, picture this. An individual is humble enough to listen, confident enough to lead and has the dream and vision in hand with practical plans. Practical plans do not come easy, and at the base, information is required for plans to be generated. These information can be obtained when one seeks to learn and continuously learn. Leadership is not a position of relative ease, nor is it one which offers much unoccupied or idle time. The frontier which confronts a leader is wide and almost endless. *A well-learned and knowledgeable leader* will be able to identify the potentials within the vast amount of possibilities upon the frontier. He or she will be able to bring to fruition a project through the knowledge that he or she possesses, thus boosting the esteem of the team. This will enable the team to progress further under the leadership of one who is learned and knowledgeable. Therefore, it is important for a leader to be learned and knowledgeable in the areas which will expand the capabilities and possibilities of the team. A leader would spend as much effort and time in leading as they would in attaining the knowledge required to bring the team upon a new frontier. This function is not limited to the leader only, as the team members who are knowledgeable and learned will be able to contribute as much to the progress of the team. We could also agree on the point that a learned leader will be able to get the most out of the team.

A learned leader will be able to identify the gaps in the organization or team he or she leads, select those which could be tackled by the team and move the team towards the specific direction. Therefore, a leader should expose himself or herself to the knowledge pool, identify the potentials and align the team towards the selected potentials. As important as the qualities which enable the leader to lead the team, another quality which is essential is trustworthiness. In this human-to-human relationship, the leader needs the assistance and support from the team. How else will the team move together with the leader other than having the trust between them? A *trustworthy* leader is essential to maintain the relationships in the team.

Trustworthy in this context relates to the ability of the team to put their trust in the individual who will lead the team. The team has to percept the individual who is leading the group as one who they can place their trust on. This is important to get the team moving towards the goal or where their vision lies. A team without a trustworthy leader is likely to face challenges and restraints as it works towards its goal or even loses a team member or two. In this situation where the team is unable to trust the leader, time would have been wasted to ensure that the leader is not up to no good or the vision is maintained. Similarly, the same can happen for the leader who is unable to trust the team. The time and energy spent to ensure that no one takes harmful actions against each other again is counterproductive and essentially undermines the progress and development.

My discussion here has been in the static form of examining a one-off situation — extend the time frame by a few weeks or a few years, and the picture starts to change. The duration that is required by a leader to constantly push the boundaries towards the vision varies while learning and unlearning and maintaining the relationships within the team. Aside from these, the unexpected will always happen and the team will have to face these difficulties and handle them effectively. During these challenging times, the leader has to possess the *endurance* to not only maintain himself or herself but also maintain the morale and motivation of the team. As mentioned earlier, leadership is not a position of relative ease. There are many intangible externalities which he or she has to take on. While not all externalities or unexpected events have to be handled fully by the leader, the leader is the individual who will have to internalize the situation and devise a strategy to each of these events.

These qualities or attributes of a leader are essential, yet we should also know that nothing changes unless actions are taken. These qualities influence the actions which a leader would take. A leader has to take actions to express and bring these qualities to influence the team and achieve the desired progress. Here, I would like to refer to Lim Siong Guan's (former Head of Civil Service in Singapore) book on leadership *The Leader, The Teacher & You* (cited in the bibliography). A leader does not always have to be at the front, the leader can adopt multiple positions depending on the situation that he or she is faced with. In his book, he mentions the four positions that a leader can adopt — Front, Side, Behind, and Within. Each position calls for a leader to adopt a different perspective on the team. This is what he refers to as the stages in leadership development process. A good leader will know when he or she will have to shift his or her position and allow others in the team to take the frontline and charge through. "The function of leadership is to produce more leaders, not more followers" is a quote by Ralph Nader that captures the essence of shifting position to allow more to be done.

The shift in position essentially produces or at least exposes the team to more leaders. They will be engaged to think about how best one can execute and manoeuvre forward, thus formulating the direction of the team. What this implies is that a leader does not always refer to the one at the front or to the one who provides all the possible directions. A leader can exist at the side, the back or even within others, thus linking this with the qualities which I determine to be essential for an ideal leader. One of the most important quality will be humbleness. When a leader fails to practice humbleness and listen to his team, he or she will always be at the front doing what he or she determines to be the only or the best way, thereby undermining the process of allowing more leaders to develop. When a leader shifts his or her position, he or she can focus on the other weaker aspects of the team or organization which he or she leads.

This new area which the leader now focuses on undergoes the same process of development and we can expect more development when the team as a whole takes up the lead. Once again the leader is free to focus on the overall direction and orientation of the team. These qualities/actions possessed/performed by the leader will allow for a group of individuals to push the boundaries in all aspects. This might instead be viewed as wasting energy and time as the team tries to explore all the potential areas of interest and little progress can be made. But, it is always the leader who identifies and directs the team towards a certain point to breakthrough. This is why the leader has to gain the trust of his team members, be humble and supportive, allow the team to explore, be confident to direct, be learned to know the potential breakthrough, endure through the process and also yearn to strive towards the vision. An important insight by Lim Siong Guan is "What people want is to taste success for themselves, and realise their potential."[1] Essentially, a leader will progress towards a point where the individuals in the team gain the confidence and knowledge to be future leaders. Therefore, an ideal leadership will encourage the team to cultivate and create the positivity within the team to further drive possibilities, strive towards realizing the potential and create plenary impacts, whereby more leaders surface.

Now that we have established some of the ideal qualities or traits and actions that an ideal leader should possess and take, I want to bring our attention to the impact of such influences on youth development. While we have constantly heard of leadership development in youth, we should also recognize the impact of leadership on youth development. While I believe that this is applicable to all forms of leadership, I will restrict myself to the context of student leadership. Having held the position of a student leader, it would be most appropriate for myself to write on student leadership. I believe that learning and influence happen at all stages of life and the compound effect will only be true if one takes action, and I cannot guarantee that it will happen. I could at most put forth the statement that the chance of such action is higher. Why is my focus on youth development and not development in general?

---

[1] Lim, Siong Guan (2013). *The Leader, The Teacher & You,* World Scientific, p. 247.

The youth are the backbone of the society, and they are the ones who will run the world in the future. If every youth is able to be on track and find areas where they can contribute, then imagine a world where each youth is able to find his or her own purpose and work on it, thereby improving the world. One should keep in mind that we are not including purposes such as the destruction of humanity or anything of that sort. Instead, our focus here is to ensure the continuation of humanity. Those purposes would have rendered this chapter pointless as nothing more could be done when mankind is wiped out. This objective of finding the purpose in life or areas where the youth can positively contribute to is not easy to find.[2] In the process of finding these objectives, it is expected for youth to feel the immense pressure and anguish. The ideal leadership has to assist the youth to cope and handle such situations. If we see youth development as building the abilities of youth to handle the journey towards finding and working to fulfil those purposes, then we should start to realize how leadership, in all its form, is influencing and affecting the development of our youth. Imagine a generation of youth who experienced such leadership improve their personal resources, thereby allowing more of them to overcome the trials which confront them in their life. The impact and improvements to the world will increase as compared with those of the previous generations, and this next generation is likely to achieve more.

So how do the above-mentioned characteristics and actions of leadership make an impact on youth development? I will point this towards the *positivity* that is created from this ideal leadership. This positivity arises from the success and accomplishment of the individual who has now taken the initiative to take lead. Leadership as defined at the start of the chapter refers to human-to-human relationship. Ideal leadership with the above-mentioned characteristics will seek to cultivate and improve *positivity*. The six characteristics mentioned above reinforce one another and cannot work without each other. These characteristics will enable the team to act as one entity with positivity. "Positive emotions appear to broaden people's momentary thought-action repertoires and build their enduring personal resources".[3]

In this scenario, an individual who has experienced positivity will be able to expand his or her views on the different types of situations faced in life, studies and career. The alternative ways of resolving or handling the situations, good or bad, are likely to increase. Instead of a dichotomy, fight or flight, one has at his or

---

[2] While philosophy has been wrestling with this for centuries, I am not here to prove or disprove any of the theories. Yet it will also be untrue should I say that I do not take belief in any of the schools of thought.

[3] Fredrickson B. L. (2004). The broaden-and-build theory of positive emotions, *Philosophical Transactions of the Royal Society of London. Series B, Biological sciences*, 359(1449), 1367–1378.

her disposal an array of options reducing the intensity of the situations and allowing more possibilities to surface. The effect of positivity does not only appear when one is faced with difficult situations but could also produce an effect when one faces failures. It is without a doubt that disappointment and other negative emotions would surface when failures happen, but an individual with resilience will likely be able to see past these immediate emotions and devise action plans for them to review, learn and move on from the failure. Taking a dynamic view, we can expect that one will slowly build upon this pool of resources as they age. A good question which I believe we could explore further is whether this pool of resources will deplete or be eroded over time. Much like how many things are not finite, resilience and these resources should face the same issues.

While it can be argued that having choices does not always lead to better well-being (*The Paradox of Choice — Why more is less* by Barry Schwartz),[4] it is possible that one might be faced with anxiety or passivity to make any decision or action, rendering a downwards spiral towards inactions and negativity. However, we could accept this understanding if we assume that the individual acts like how a magnet will inevitably be attracted to where the opposite pole is located, easily swung by choices and act without an active mind. Yet, when we consider the important attributes of the ideal leader, being knowledgeable and confident, we will not picture an individual who is described as above. Rather, we might picture a captain with a compass in hand (which is also a magnet), yet is able to steer the ship towards where it should. Not being overwhelmed by the waves which sway the ship, the captain makes the decision and steers the ship, confident of his or her ability and knowledgeable about the seven seas and five oceans. Positivity is an important catalyst in connecting leadership to youth development. Leadership with the ideal qualities will assist the development of positivity, which in turn translates to the building of personal resources to overcome trials and tribulations in one's life. Youth development will benefit from the experience of this ideal leadership, where youth discover more and achieve more.

CONCLUDING SUMMARY

I have investigated the practice and idea of leadership itself, adopting a different approach in defining the term "leadership". This approach of understanding leadership as a human-to-human relationship allows us to see the dynamics within and examine the qualities that will bring out the best in others and the best in the team. I have also suggested what the ideal leadership qualities are. In total, there are six

---

[4] Schwartz, Barry (2004). *The Paradox of Choice — Why More is Less*, Chapter 5, Harper Perennial, p. 99.

and in my view all these are essential qualities. The main idea here is to possess the qualities that perpetuate the positivity and the success others see in themselves. I then went on to explore how leadership is key in the adages, "the whole is greater than the sum of its parts" and "together everyone achieve more". Lastly, I have also identified the link between leadership qualities and youth development.

Leadership (which is student leadership in the case of this chapter) generates more value addition by the youth and produces more leaders among the future generations. The influence for youth development does not just stem out from positivity being the sole driver for youth development — the success and positivity felt by individuals and teams (in this case, youth team) performing their best reinforces the initial force. In summary, the ideal leadership allows for cultivation and improvement in the positivity felt by the individuals in the group, which thereby brings about more possibilities and potentials as one internalizes the positive emotions and broadens his or her view on a situation. As one acts upon the agenda and objective that is set, one can see the plenary impact from not only one individual but also the other individuals who experienced these influences and take action to translate these experiences into actualization.

Chapter 15

RELIGIOUS AND SPIRITUAL LEADERSHIP FROM A DEVOTEE'S STANDPOINT PERSPECTIVE: BIOPIC OF A GREAT SPIRITUAL LEADER MASTER CHENG YEN

W. X. Lim

INTRODUCTION

The 2011 *TIME 100* featured the one and only Chinese spiritual leader, Master Cheng Yen, on its annual list, placing her on par with the major iconic religious leaders who have appeared on the *TIME 100* list over the past few years, including Pope Benedict XVI, Pope Francis and the 14th Dalai Lama. Every year, 100 most influential people from different fields around the world are listed on *TIME 100*, the likes of whom include politicians, leaders, scientists, moguls, philanthropists, celebrities, artists, etc. As the one and only Chinese female religious leader to have appeared on the list, the magazine extolled Master Cheng Yen as having "an ethereal quality" and recognized her (organization's) contribution to non-profit humanitarian service at times of calamities.[1]

Having been awarded the Ramon Magsaysay Award (also known as the "Asian Nobel Peace Prize") in 1991 and the Niwano Peace Prize in 2007, Master Cheng Yen is often regarded as the "Mother Teresa of Asia" for her contributions in serving people in need and promoting world peace. However, unlike many other

---

[1] The 2011 *TIME 100*, *Dharma Master Cheng Yen*, http://content.time.com/time/specials/packages/article/0,28804,2066367_2066369_2066393,00.html. Accessed 18 September 2018.

leaders, Master Cheng Yen, at the age of 82, has never travelled outside of Taiwan due to her heart illness. Her health condition however does not limit her unfaltering aspiration for Buddhism as she constantly enlightened her followers through her charisma and wisdom, gaining broad international support over the years. This chapter aims to discuss the role of Master Cheng Yen in the Tzu Chi Foundation and how her teachings, charisma, structured management style and the use of technology help in the formation and expansion of Tzu Chi's influence across the world.

BACKGROUND TO THE TZU CHI FOUNDATION

Originally hailing from Taiwan in Republican China, Master Cheng Yen is the founder of the Buddhist Compassion Relief Tzu Chi Foundation (hereafter "Tzu Chi"), the biggest non-governmental welfare organization in the Chinese-speaking world. Today, the organization has successfully established footprints in 95 countries, with more than 500 offices worldwide in 57 countries and attracting nearly 10 million supporters and followers.

The name Tzu Chi is a translation from the Chinese word "慈济". The word *tzu* (慈) carries the dual meanings of "together/with" or compassion (the ability to empathize with others, to suffer together and to spread care and loving-kindness) in Buddhist terms. The word ji (济) means helping someone to cross a river in the ancient vocabulary, though in the modern context, it refers to providing relief and aid to others. Just as its name depicts, Tzu Chi Foundation is an organization striving to serve the needy, relieving the poor in society and providing humanitarian assistance with the spirit of love, kindness, gratitude and respect. As a non-profit, non-governmental humanitarian organization, Tzu Chi first started as a charity organization and later developed its Four Main Missions: charity, medical care, education and humanistic culture. Adding to the Four Missions are the ongoing efforts in "Bone Marrow Donation, Environmental Protection, Community Volunteerism and International Relief, where these eight concurrent campaigns are collectively known as 'Tzu Chi's Eight Footprints'."[2]

MASTER CHENG YEN AS THE CORE

As the founder of Tzu Chi, Master Cheng Yen is seen as a figure in the core leadership in the organization, where the teacher–student relationship is very much emphasized. In the highly devoted teacher–student relationship, Master Cheng

---

[2] Tzu Chi Foundation, *Tzu Chi Missions*, http://tw.tzuchi.org/en/index.php?option=com_content&view=article&id=293&Itemid=283. Accessed 3 March 2019.

Yen is a spiritual leader who inspires others by her manner of teaching; she is able to influence and win over people by virtue of her words and her actions. Highly disciplined, the religious leader leads a life of quality and value. Breaking the norm of traditional Sangha's practice, Master Cheng Yen made a vow in her early years to not receive any offerings as a Buddhist nun.

Subsequently, when she founded the Tzu Chi Foundation, she laid the rule for all her disciples to strictly abide the principle of "No work, no meal". At the Jingsi Abode where the Master and all her disciples reside, the Sangha lives on their own strength by growing vegetables, doing farm work and handwork. The royalties received for Master Cheng Yen's books are another source of income for the Abode. Even today, not a single cent from the Tzu Chi Foundation is used on the Abode. All the money raised by the Foundation is used to sustain the Four Great Missions of Tzu Chi. The Abode on the other hand has become a site for religious pilgrimage for many Tzu Chi's volunteers who make their "homecoming" trip to Hualien for spiritual cultivation.

In addition, being one of the pioneering Buddhist groups made up of practitioners in the Taiwan brand of Buddhism, devotees are encouraged to embrace and advocate the teachings and self-development of Humanistic Buddhism[3] in the Chinese-speaking world where Master Cheng Yen's disciples spread the word. Master Cheng Yen is able to motivate her disciples to live according to the values of Buddhism in their everyday lives, urging collective efforts to turn the Buddhist value of compassion into pragmatic actions such as international relief, medical service and environmental recycling efforts. In building upon these humanistic ideals, Tzu Chi's teachings, also known as the Jingsi Dharma, transcends traditional Buddhist temple-based teachings and chanting to encourage its followers to place importance on helping the living beings and also praying for the dead. Instead of practicing in solitude, it encourages people to serve the society, thus cultivating and spreading love and care to everyone. In this sense, Master Cheng Yen is highly regarded both as a dharma master and as a dharma practitioner who has greatly contributed in restoring and reviving the tenets of Chinese Buddhism in the modern era.

THE TEACHINGS OF TZU CHI'S MISSION OF CHARITY

As the Jing Si Aphorism[4] says "When the unfortunate cannot find help, those who are blessed must go to them." With this spirit, Master Cheng Yen started the

---

[3] Unlike the conventional teachings in Buddhism, Humanistic Buddhism encourages people to live out the values of Buddhist teaching, integrating Buddhist values in everyday life.

[4] The "Jing Si Aphorism" is a collection of Master Cheng Yen's thoughts on Buddhist teaching and life lessons.

Tzu Chi Foundation in 1966 by carrying out charitable work in the rural city of Hualien in Taiwan. Starting off as a humble organization in the early days, Master Cheng Yen led 30 lay disciples, most of whom were local housewives, to save NT$0.50 from their grocery money and deposit the cash into their bamboo coin bank each day, to kick-start their work of relieving poverty. The initiative later named as the "Bamboo Coin Bank Drive" serves as the backbone of charitable funds for Tzu Chi's mission to help the impoverished and underprivileged even till today.

The teachings of Master Cheng Yen in guiding Tzu Chi's volunteers towards personal and spiritual growth are what differentiate the charitable work of Tzu Chi from other like-minded organizations. Tzu Chi's volunteers are always educated to maintain a heart filled with gratitude towards the Tzu Chi's beneficiaries as the teaching says:

> "It is not about wanting the care recipients to thank Tzu Chi for its help, but rather the volunteers are grateful to the needy for allowing them to witness poverty and illness, which reminds them to be vigilant of the impermanence in life and to be content and cherish what they have."[5]

Master Cheng Yen believes good deeds are a means of sowing the seeds of compassion in everyone's hearts. By witnessing the suffering of others and their will to do something about it, one will tend to appreciate life better and be motivated to help and learn from others. It is often through participation and commitment in Tzu Chi that many have gained increased clarity and wisdom in life.

In addition, unlike many charity organizations that emphasize the rich to help the poor, Tzu Chi has been working towards encouraging and guiding the poor to give to/help each other and do good. One of the most notable cases is the "Rice Bank Movement" in Myanmar, where Tzu Chi's work served to help beneficiaries who were reeling after a recovery from a devastating cyclone. Tzu Chi's relief work garnered support of nearly 1,000 households to give back to the local communities. As reported by the Foundation, "Each month, these villages manage to collect as much as 1,111 kg of rice, which are turned into relief supplies for 66 impoverished families."[6] Giving is thus not the privilege of the rich, but the privilege of the sincere in accordance with their affordability. Through encouraging the giving spirit among all socioeconomic classes, a virtuous cycle of love and

---

[5] Tzu Chi Foundation, *FAQ*, https://www.tzuchi.org.sg/en/about-us/tzu-chi-singapore/faq/. Accessed 10 February 2019.

[6] Tzu Chi Foundation, *"Saving a Hand of Rice" — A Decade of Love and Kindness*, https://www.tzuchi.org.sg/en/news-and-stories/global-presence/saving-a-handful-of-rice-a-decade-of-love-and-kindness/. Accessed 23 February 2019.

kindness is thus formed, cultivating the spirit of compassion within Tzu Chi's Mission of Charity.

THE USE OF MASS MEDIA AND TECHNOLOGY IN PLANTING SEEDS OF COMPASSION AND PROPAGATING DHARMA

As Tzu Chi grows to become a transnational organization, it manifests itself as an institution highly engaged in community responses to globalization with effective use of media and technology. Often, it is through the lens of visual capture technologies that Master Cheng Yen and other followers peer into images of the suffering of the modern world. Every week, Master Cheng Yen hosts a meeting with the departments in the Tzu Chi Foundation to get a snapshot of Tzu Chi charity work across five continents. Relentlessly, she spends hours listening to her volunteers across the globe for timely updates of the cyclone disaster relief situation through videoconferencing and web chat every day.

While mass media and digital technologies transcend distance and boundary to facilitate quick and efficient communication across the globe, they also play an important role in transmitting teachings of the Tzu Chi's religious leader, Master Cheng Yen, worldwide. Tzu Chi's mission of humanistic culture which encompasses various media vehicles such as print media, internet radio, satellite TV and digital multimedia greatly exemplified how media technology, if properly channelled, can serve as a medium for nurturing seeds of compassion and act as an effective means for dharma propagation. Many times, the spirit of Tzu Chi in promoting humanistic values and its footprints of love across the globe were documented and broadcasted through the in-house Tzu Chi Satellite TV Channel — Da Ai TV. Unlike conventional TV channels which seek for higher viewership and commercial advertisements for greater income, the productions of Da Ai TV advocate for positive media influence and truthful portrayal of news and information.

Apart from news, drama series and documentaries, the teachings and sermons of Master Cheng Yen are also broadcast through Da Ai TV. These Dharma Programmes are then used as teaching and training materials for the Tzu Chi overseas offices to propagate the Jingsi Dharma. Notably, the business model of Da Ai TV inherits and passes on the humanistic value as advocated by the mission to adopt a sustainable model of funding. As reported, Da Ai TV Station is "the fruit of the labour of countless Tzu Chi's recycling volunteers in Taiwan."[7] The funds generated by collecting recyclable items from the communities are rechannelled

---

[7] Tzu Chi Foundation, *Tzu Chi's Global Media*, https://www.tzuchi.org.sg/en/news-and-stories/tzu-chis-global-media/. 20 February 2019.

to help sustain the running of the Da Ai TV Station. Tzu Chi's mass media approach coupled with the good deeds and dharma teachings that the organization constantly cultivates among its members thus portray and strengthen Master Cheng Yen's image as a living Bodhisattva, which helps to reinforce the teacher–student relationship and constitute a shared belief and collective identity within Tzu Chi's family of members.

THE ORGANIZATIONAL STRUCTURE OF TZU CHI

While religious belief is not a prerequisite for one to become a Tzu Chi member, it has enabled the organization to flourish and prosper even in a non-Buddhist setting. With the growing Tzu Chi's membership across the globe, Master Cheng Yen has designed a comprehensive and effective Tzu Chi's membership structure in organizing Tzu Chi's volunteers. Besides Master Cheng Yen, who is the founder and the main figure in Tzu Chi, the organization is managed by lay practitioners and staff members with a Chief Executive Officer spearheading religious awareness activities within the confines of the country in which it operates in. Tzu Chi, with its organized and systematic volunteer recruitment system, shows how a religious institution can be effectively run by lay persons while continuing with the overseas expansion with the backing of its networks of volunteers.

Tzu Chi's volunteers can be categorized into several functional tiers, including senior commissioners, commissioners (female), Tzu Cheng Faith Corps (male), Tzu Chi's volunteers, Tzu Ching youth groups, etc. Specifically, there are three stages of training that a volunteer needs to undergo, namely the "attachment", "trainee" and "certification" in the Tzu Chi's training system. After appropriate training, these volunteers undertake different duties and responsibilities to support and execute Tzu Chi's internal activities and community services.

As stated by the organization, the objective of training is to "help volunteers develop a common understanding of Tzu Chi's Missions, protocols, and philosophy", which helps them to integrate better in the Tzu Chi's family as well as promote cohesion and collaborative spirit among the volunteers.[8] Training attachments and trainee volunteers who study the Tzu Chi spirit will help to promote and serve the Four Missions. Subsequently, those who affirm the Tzu Chi teachings and assume the responsibility of a community leader are able to become certified commissioners or Tzu Cheng Faith Corps upon completion of training hours and

---

[8] Tzu Chi Foundation, *FAQ*, https://www.tzuchi.org.sg/en/about-us/tzu-chi-singapore/faq/. Accessed 4 March 2019.

recommendation by volunteer leaders.[9] These volunteers are then invited to Taiwan to attend a certification ceremony where Master Cheng Yen will personally certify the volunteers who have finally arrived at the new milestones in their Tzu Chi's journey (which normally take 3 years or more). Certified volunteers are normally touched by the words and advice dispensed by Master Cheng Yen when they meet her in person during the certification ceremony and are inspired to become more committed to walk the Dharma path and carry out the Tzu Chi's mission. In this way, the multi-layered membership structure, systematic and periodic training as well as well-organized recruitment system not only enable volunteers to work in efficient and harmonious coordination but also serve as an effective system to cultivate deeper teacher–student relationships in walking the Bodhisattva path.

Singing together at the end of every major training session, "The Vow" composed by the Tzu Chi's volunteers greatly depicts how the teacher–student relationship is being reinforced and weaved into the Tzu Chi's training and recruitment system:

立愿文

The Vow

传承法脉心相系，

With our hearts united, we vow to pass on Tzu Chi's Dharma.

弘扬宗门志不移。

Steadfastly, we vow to bring the Path to others.

慈济因缘会珍惜，

This karmic affinity with Tzu Chi, we shall treasure.

静思法髓无量义。

The essence of the Jing Si Dharma is the teaching of innumerable meanings.

吾等弟子当谨记，

We, your disciples, shall never forget.

敬请上人莫忧虑。

So, dear Master, please do not worry.

CONCLUSION

As a concluding remark, this chapter discusses the many aspects of Tzu-Chi's identity and how it is closely linked to the spiritual leader, Master Cheng Yen, thus

---

[9] Tzu Chi Foundation, *FAQ*, https://www.tzuchi.org.sg/en/about-us/tzu-chi-singapore/faq/. Accessed 4 March 2019.

forming an intimate teacher–student relationship between the leader and her followers. This relationship is constantly strengthened through the profound teachings of Master Cheng Yen where she has demonstrated great determination, wisdom and charisma in preaching the Dharma. Master Cheng Yen and her life-long project/creation, the Tzu Chi Foundation, is thus a great example of what a faith-based organization can achieve through employing modern organizational and leadership strategies and methodologies in the 21st century.

Chapter 16

POLITICAL/COMMUNITY LEADERSHIP AND SINGAPORE'S MULTI-RELIGIOUS SCENE

J. Xue

East Asian Institute, National University Singapore

INTRODUCTION

Singapore has achieved fame as one of the most religiously diverse and harmonious countries in the world. According to the Singapore Census of 2015, the most followed religion is Buddhism (33.1%) followed by Christianity (18.8%), Islam (14.0%), Taoism (11.0%) and Hinduism (5.0%).[1] About 18.3% of the resident population are non-religious, while 0.6% follow other religions such as Sikhism, Zoroastrianism and Jainism.[2] Considerable intra-religious diversity exists, with sub-groups and denominations within the religious categories.

Certain religions are more commonly practised within each of the four major racial groups of Singapore. For example, the bulk of ethnic Chinese residents/citizens follow Buddhism and Taoism while most ethnic Indian residents/citizens follow Hinduism. Most Malays adhere to the Islamic faith, while many Eurasians are Christians. As a result, certain religions tend to be associated with certain racial groups, although overlaps across racial lines exist, such as Christian minorities within the Chinese and Indian communities, and small numbers of

---

[1] Department of Statistics, Ministry of Trade and Industry, *General Household Survey 2015*, Singapore, Department of Statistics, 2016, Online, https://www.singstat.gov.sg/-/media/files/publications/ghs/ghs2015/ghs2015.pdf. Accessed 20 November 2018.

[2] *Ibid.*, p. 22.

non-Muslims among the Malays. There are also non-religious Singaporeans among all the four major racial groups.[3]

As certain religions are being associated with certain racial groups, interfaith tensions can potentially acquire a racial dimension. In turn, racial conflict could also escalate into a religious conflict. In the turbulent decades after Second World War, Singapore experienced a few major riots along the lines of race and religion. This includes the Maria Hertogh riots in 1950 during the turbulent post-war years, and the racial riots of 1963 and 1964 when Singapore was part of the Federation of Malaysia.

Since independence in 1965, Singapore has placed great efforts in cultivating harmonious relations between the different ethnic groups and religious communities, adjusting their approaches over the years in response to its effectiveness within evolving social contexts. Apart from the "hard measures" of legislating against speech and activities that harm race and religious harmony (Sedition Act, Section 298 and 298a, etc.) as well as policies aimed at improving integration (Housing Development Board ethnic quotas), there are also "soft measures" aimed at promoting interfaith dialogue between different religious groups.

INTERFAITH DIALOGUES IN SINGAPORE

Founded in 1949, the Inter-Religious Organization of Singapore has a long history of organizing inter-religious activities. It has promoted religious education in schools, took up issues related to morality, addressed tensions over religious proselytization, supported public education and promoted religious harmony in general. Religious leaders from the major religions in Singapore are often seen together in the public, wearing religious robes and praying openly together for the good of the society at large.[4]

After the September 11 terrorist attacks in the United States, the government increased existing efforts to strengthen interfaith relations. In 2002, the Inter-Racial and Religious Confidence Circles (IRCC) were set up as local-level interfaith platforms across all constituencies in Singapore, promoting racial and religious harmony through interfaith and inter-ethnic themed activities such as heritage trails, interfaith talks and various ethnic and religious celebrations.[5]

In an event where racial and religious tensions are heightened, the IRCCs are trained to respond quickly to racial and religious tensions by remaining calm and

---

[3] *Ibid*, p. 25.

[4] Ah Eng, L. (2008). *Religious Diversity in Singapore*. Singapore: ISEAS/IPS, pp. 605–641.

[5] IRCC. About Inter-Racial and Religious Confidence Circles (IRCCs)." Ircc.sg. https://www.ircc.sg/ABOUT%20IRCC. Accessed 22 November 2018.

Political/Community Leadership and Singapore's Multi-Religious Scene 215

resilient on the ground during crises. As important bridges between religious, ethnic and community groups at the local level, the IRCCs assist in the recovery process and help different communities and the nation return to normalcy.[6]

Yet, a 2008 study of interactions among youth leaders of different faiths by Charles Phua, Anita Hui and Yap Ching Wi suggests that interfaith youth leaders want a deeper appreciation and implementation of interfaith work, with dialogues that allow deeper and more genuine understanding, beyond mere tolerance.[7] The desire for deeper and more meaningful interfaith dialogue was one of the reasons why a unique interfaith group called Explorations into Faith (EiF) was set up in 2007 as an initiative under the South East Community Development Council (CDC), one of the five CDCs in the five districts of Singapore. EiF aims to build greater religious understanding, respect, trust and tolerance among a diverse group of people from different faiths.

EXPLORATIONS INTO FAITH (2007–PRESENT)

Over the years, the EiF has developed unique facilitation techniques that aim to foster deeper interfaith dialogue. This chapter focuses on EiF facilitation as a form of leadership, with techniques that are especially useful when managing small and diverse groups. This author interviewed three facilitators at EiF, Farid Hamid, Khee Shihui and Aaron Maniam. Farid, one of the founders of EiF, has over two decades of experience in experiential learning, training and development. Maniam and Khee have been volunteering with EiF for 11 and 3 years, respectively.

The facilitators shared that since 2007, EiF has held an average of six interfaith dialogue sessions per year for the past 11 years, with 30 participants each. EiF interfaith events are usually centred around an aspect of life in which religious faiths exert their influence. For example, there are dialogues regarding "faith and music" and "faith and art." Each of these interfaith gatherings is typically attended by people from a diverse range of backgrounds. In addition, the flagship event of the EiF since 2014 is the UnConference, a ground-up conference that attracts more than 100 participants each year, with four students in every five participants. There was also one interfaith youth camp that attracted 30 participants.

Within the larger interfaith scene, EiF is the only organization in Singapore that provides specialized training for interfaith dialogue facilitators. EiF provides valuable support to other interfaith organizations by providing facilitators at National IRCC Conferences, *Ask Me Anything* series by the Ministry of Culture,

---

[6] *Ibid.*

[7] Ah Eng, L. (2008). *Religious Diversity in Singapore*. Singapore: ISEAS/IPS, pp. 642–660.

Community and Youth (MCCY) and the Common Sense-Common Space programme by Southeast CDC.

Facilitating interfaith dialogues is a challenging task and contains a unique set of leadership skills not commonly found in organizations governed by top-down authorities. According to the facilitators, EiF has organized 11 EiF Facilitators Courses where interested participants are trained to lead and facilitate EiF dialogues. Since 2008, more than 400 working adults have participated in this programme.

The facilitating skills of EiF are designed to handle very delicate interactions at interfaith gatherings. Religious beliefs are often very private and emotional to individuals, and many Singaporeans regard religious teachings as part of their moral values, personal identity and racial identity. Any criticism of religious ideas, even if made with good intentions, can easily come across as an attack on one's identity and entire community.

WHAT IS LEADERSHIP?

In the process of describing the nature of leadership in EiF interfaith facilitation, this chapter will refer to a series of highly influential studies on leadership by Peter Northouse. According to Northouse, leadership is a process whereby an individual influences a group of individuals to achieve a common goal. Northouse also assumes that leadership occurs in groups that serve as a context in which leadership takes place.[8] Northouse identifies two common forms of leadership, assigned and emergent. He defines assigned leadership as one "based on a formal title given to the individual within the organisation."[9] On the contrary, emergent leadership is built from "what one does and how one acquires support from followers."[10]

In addition to leadership, Northouse also examined the concept of power, since leadership requires the ability to influence too. He divides power into two kinds: position and personal. Position power is further subdivided into legitimate, reward and coercive power.[11] Personal powers, in contrast, are given to leaders by their followers when they see their leaders as likeable and knowledgeable.[12] Personal power is built on referent and expert power. Table 1 summarizes the different types of powers that Northouse has defined.

---

[8] Northouse. P. G. (2007). *Leadership: Theory and Practice*, 4th edition. London: SAGE Publications, p. 3.

[9] *Ibid.*, p. 13.

[10] *Ibid.*

[11] *Ibid.*, p. 7.

[12] *Ibid.*

Table 1. Different types of powers.

Type of power	Consisting of
Position power	*Legitimate power*: Associated with having status or formal job authority.
	Coercive power: Derived from the capacity to penalize or punish others.
	Reward power: Derived from the capacity to provide rewards to others.
Personal power	*Referent power*: Based on followers' identification and liking for the leader.
	Expert power: Based on followers' perceptions of the leaders' competence.

Source: Adapted from French Jr, J. R. and Raven, B. (1962). "The Bases of Social Power". In D. Cartwright (ed.), *Group Dynamics: Research and Theory*. New York: Harper & Row, pp. 259–269.

ANALYZING THE EiF FACILITATION PROCESS USING NORTHOUSE'S FRAMEWORK

According to Farid, the primary role of a facilitator is to enable meaningful and authentic interfaith dialogue between participants from different religious traditions.[13] Placing Farid's definition in the context of Northouse's definition of leadership — a process whereby an individual influences a group of individuals to achieve a common goal — this author defines

- the individual as the EiF facilitator (facilitator),
- the group of individuals as the interfaith participants (participants),
- the common goal as meaningful and authentic interfaith dialogue (meaningful and authentic dialogue).

Given the considerable amount of fault lines that exist between different faith traditions, the facilitator's task is a challenging one. Nonetheless, EiF facilitators are particularly adept at distributing position leadership in a way that paradoxically strengthens their goal. Secondly, these facilitators are also skilled in cultivating personal power and emergent leadership within a short time.

This chapter will now explore the three main techniques used by EiF facilitators, namely the Full Value Commitment (FVC), Modelling of Vulnerabilities and Affirmation. These techniques are a common feature across all EiF dialogues, and budding trainee facilitators are taught these techniques during 4-day training workshops periodically conducted by EiF to train new facilitators. The following observations are based on interviews with Farid, Khee and Maniam, as well this author's experience as a trainee in the facilitator workshop (Cohort 12) that took place from 19 to 20 August and 26 to 27 August, 2017.

---

[13] Farid Hamid, Interview by Author, Singapore, November 28, 2018.

218   *J. Xue*

THE ASSIGNED LEADER DISTRIBUTING POSITION POWER

The EiF dialogue always begins with establishing FVC. This stage lasts about 10–15 minutes and involves the facilitators helping the participants negotiate the rules of the dialogue, cultivating "root culture" for the dialogue based on negotiated values.[14] For example, participants can agree on the values of the dialogue, such as the following:

1. showing respect for each other,
2. being open-minded and non-judgemental,
3. honesty and authenticity.

At the FVC, participants are the ones setting the level of privacy, not the facilitator. The participants can choose between "completely secret," "Chatham House" and "full disclosure." In most of the dialogues, participants usually opt for the Chatham House option. As tensions are expected in an interfaith dialogue, participants can pre-set some deconflicting rituals. For example, participants can agree to follow the "law of two feet," where participants can choose to join any conversation they like or choose to withdraw temporarily if they feel uncomfortable. In addition, participants are encouraged to indicate warning signs, such as saying the word "ouch", to demonstrate discomfort so that other participants are aware of the need for restraint.

The benefit of holding the FVC is that the facilitator, as the assigned leader, distributes the burden of exercising position power away to the participants at large. The facilitator is more of a guide than an authority, gently steering people back to the topic when necessary. At the very start of each dialogue, the facilitator encourages the participants to learn from each other.

Paradoxically, distributing the position power strengthens group cohesion and facilitates discussion. Firstly, as the rules are negotiated from the ground up, it achieves legitimate power in the eyes of the participants. Secondly, given that participants always outnumber facilitators, the bigger numbers by themselves exert a degree of coercive power on anybody that breaks the FVC and disrupts the space needed for meaningful and authentic dialogue.

That does not mean the facilitator completely delegates all authority to the crowd. The facilitator also plays the role as a steward of the integrity and safety of the discussion space. If necessary, the facilitator may call for a timeout and invite a seemingly disruptive participant to notice the impact of their rudeness or

---

[14] *Ibid.*

Political/Community Leadership and Singapore's Multi-Religious Scene   219

disrespect. The participant may also be invited to elaborate on the intentions behind what they said, to clear any misunderstanding between the participant and the rest.

Cultivating Emergent Leadership and Personal Power

After the FVC is set, the actual dialogue begins. A considerable amount of effort is needed to help the participants warm up. Religion is a sensitive issue and bringing up thorny issues too quickly could result in anger or defensiveness on the part of the participants. Depending on the length of a dialogue, icebreakers can range from simple introductions that involve people introducing their name and something interesting about themselves to more sophisticated social games that involve people rapidly grouping according to neighbourhoods where they reside and the schools they attended. In the process, participants become more familiar and comfortable with each other, setting the stage for deeper dialogue.

A powerful way of warming up the group involves the facilitator "modelling his/her vulnerabilities."[15] The facilitator starts the ball rolling, sharing an example of what is a meaningful and authentic dialogue, becoming a role model for other participants to follow. The facilitator will share about his/her personal faith journey and clarify doubts over certain religious teachings, inner struggles and their current stage of the journey. The level of disclosure is not predetermined, and facilitators are given the authority to decide how much they want to reveal about themselves. Having led by example, the facilitator encourages others to follow his/her approach.

To the facilitators, EiF is a space where participants can understand each other at a deep, interpersonal level. At the end of each dialogue, participants should be able to relate to each other as peers and friends, without having the burden of representing their respective faith traditions (or secular value systems for non-religious participants). EiF also avoids direct discussions over religious doctrines and interpretations. Such discussions could become distant and theoretical, or in worst cases cause conflict, hurt and unhappiness if not managed carefully, said the facilitators.

Modelling vulnerabilities is a powerful way of cultivating referent power and sets the stage for more inclusive and welcoming discussion spaces. In multi-religious Singapore, religious communities are not monolithic and beliefs within individuals are not monolithic either. Over the course of a lifetime, an individual could have explored different religious teachings and different interpretations

---

[15] *Ibid.*

within their own faith and cultural/religious traditions. By taking the first step to sharing their own spiritual journey, facilitators provide a means for interfaith participants to find common ground with the facilitator.

Reward Power as a Form of Personal Power, Instead of Position Power

Another way of cultivating emergent leadership is towards the development of reward power. To enable this, EiF facilitators practice a strong culture of affirmation. If an interfaith participant follows the facilitator's lead and shares his vulnerabilities that resulted in a "meaningful and authentic dialogue", the facilitator will affirm the participants' efforts through swift and generous praise. Common phrases include: "Thanks for sharing", "I really appreciate it", "It was very brave of you to share that".

These encouraging praises are a form of emotional reward that, while not tangible in nature like material rewards, are powerful means to encourage more sharing within the group. Here, reward power does not fall neatly into the category, position or personal power. After all, giving affirmation is an emotional reward that anyone can do and does not require an assigned leader with position power to give. All the facilitator needs to do is start the ball rolling. The rewarding of affirmation thus contributes towards personal power and overall development of the emergent leadership.

Overall, once the EiF facilitator sets the rules of the dialogue and distributes his legitimate and coercive power among the larger group of participants, the facilitators rely primarily on referent and reward power to develop emergent leadership among a group of strangers in a quick manner. The emergent leadership, while temporary, is crucial in enabling a diverse group of strangers to achieve the organizations' goal — meaningful and authentic dialogue. Table 2 sums up the different powers used by the three EiF facilitation techniques.

Table 2. EiF facilitation techniques and the powers it uses.

Technique	Type of power involved	Leadership
Full value commitment	*Position power*: Legitimate *Position power*: Coercive (but distributed)	Assigned leadership
Modelling vulnerabilities	*Personal power*: Referent	Emergent leadership
Affirmation	*Position power*: Reward *Position power*: Referent	Assigned leadership Emergent leadership

CONCLUSION

Although Singapore has achieved considerable success in ensuring religious and racial harmony between different racial and religious groups over the decades, this harmony remains a constant work in progress. From time to time, key leaders in the Singapore Government, such as Prime Minister Lee Hsien Loong and Minister for Home Affairs and Law, K. Shanmugam have cautioned that tensions and fault lines between different racial and religious communities still exist.[16] Thus, interfaith dialogue remains highly relevant to Singapore, and the city-state's rich experience in interfaith work serves as a reference for other countries in the world that grapple with racial and religious tensions arising from diverse demographics.

The techniques developed by EiF facilitators over the years are highly valuable for organizations and individuals involved in community-building, mediation and other forms of conflict resolution around the world, especially in areas where racial and religious relations have been torn apart by terrorist attacks or years of prolonged warfare. The careful use and blending of different leadership styles (assigned and emergent) and the different types of power used in the facilitation process (position and personal powers) can help create a warm and inclusive environment where different racial and religious communities can slowly overcome their differences and build the much-needed trust.

---

[16] Tan, Jeanette (2012). "Religious, Racial Fault Lines Still Exist: K Shanmugam". *Yahoo! News*, November 20, 2012, https://sg.news.yahoo.com/religious--racial-fault-lines-still-exist--k-shanmugam-074716875.html. Accessed 20 October 2018 and Lee, H. L. (2017). "In Full: PM Lee on Race, Multiracialism and Singapore's Place in the World". *TODAY*, September 29, 2017, https://www.todayonline.com/singapore/full-pm-lees-speech-race-multiracialism-and-singapores-place-world. Accessed 25 October 2018.

Chapter 17

COMMUNITY SERVICES, SERVICE-LEARNING AND SERVICE LEADERSHIP IN HONG KONG

Carol Ma

Singapore University of Social Sciences, Singapore

INTRODUCTION

Hong Kong, as an international city, focuses not only on financial development but also on social welfare and services development. Hong Kong citizens always care for vulnerable groups and people in need, especially to address social injustices and tackle issues of inequality in the society. The spirit of volunteerism is very strong. Since the early days of British colonial administration till handover to Mainland China in 1997, Hong Kong's social welfare and services have undergone many changes. The concept of community services has evolved in the Hong Kong context. Community support is strengthening, and bottom-up services always tackle the grassroots communities and reflect the help required by the needy. In recent decades, more stakeholders, especially those in higher education industry, use service-learning as a pedagogy to develop youth capabilities, e.g. communication skills, caring disposition, leadership skills and interpersonal skills, and serve the community. With the support of the Li & Fung Foundation together with the Hong Kong Institute of Service Leadership and Management (HKI-SLAM), service leadership was introduced to eight UGC-funded universities in 2012 and they have been funded for 5 years to develop service leadership initiatives for the young people in Hong Kong. The joint partnership and continuing discussion of service leadership have inspired some stakeholders to develop a new model in both university education and post-industrial service economy. This will prepare Hong

Kong's young people to not only become effective leaders but also become a caring person to the disadvantaged in an ever-changing society.

This chapter discusses the development of social services and welfare in Hong Kong, the evolution of community service, how service-learning and service leadership were introduced in Hong Kong and the process by which leadership qualities can be trained through the service-learning and service leadership model.

DEVELOPMENT OF SOCIAL SERVICES AND WELFARE IN HONG KONG

The development of social services and welfare in Hong Kong starts from providing emergency relief to simple social assistance and then to the development of a social security system. In the early days of the settlement of Hong Kong, a large number of Chinese came to Hong Kong to make a living. Many of them were immigrants from southern China, and they left their parents, wives and children behind on the mainland. They did not have strong social support and network in those early days. There were no social services and welfare provided to the immigrants. They had to rely on mutual help and support within the community of immigrants. Some Chinese and religious groups (e.g. Clan associations) offered emergency relief to some of these communities in need. Two main charity organizations, Tung Wah Group of Hospitals (TWGH) and the Po Leung Kuk (PLK), were set up by Chinese merchants/elites in 1872 and 1878, respectively, to address migrants' needs in relation to medical, relief, education and funeral services. Some churches also built schools and hospitals for those belonging to the lower socio-economic class and those who lived in poor living conditions in the Hong Kong society. Following this, the Hong Kong College of Medicine (which later became the University of Hong Kong) was set up in 1887. In the early 1900s, more internationally affiliated non-governmental organizations (NGOs) with faith-based organizations, such as the Salvation Army, YMCA and YWCA, set up branches in Hong Kong.[1]

In the 1950s along with the demographic challenges, Chinese organizations (e.g. Kaifong Association that joined hands with TWGH and PLK), overseas relief organizations (Red Cross and Salvation Army) and government departments (like the Social Welfare Department) became the main providers of social assistance. With the support from charities and the government, social services were driven by motivations for acts of compassion and mercy in the Hong Kong society.

---

[1] Ng, G. T. (2013). "The Context of Social Welfare in Hong Kong: History, Economics, and Politics". Blog post: Singapore Association of Social Workers, http://www.social-dimension.com/2013/08/the-context-of-social-welfare-in-hong-kong-historyeconomics-and-politics.

Community Services, Service-Learning and Service Leadership in Hong Kong   225

In the 1970s, more directed social services and welfare were provided for the people in Hong Kong, especially after several socially disruptive strikes and riots in 1960s. In order to stabilize the society, the Hong Kong government paid more attention to the social welfare, housing and education policies and addressed the needs of the people in Hong Kong. The government took over the role of managing charity organizations and provision of basic welfare services. Gradually, it provided funding to charity organizations to support the needy in the community, and more community services funded by the government were developed. Also, the government took up the responsibility to provide social security and eventually developed a social security system for the Hong Kong people.

It took about 20 years to develop the system, but social challenges (e.g. unemployment, poverty, economic downturn and high housing costs) continuing to be more serious in Hong Kong, examples of which are as follows: the Gini Coefficient in HK has been deteriorating, unemployment rate is high, the housing price in Hong Kong is the most expensive in the world, etc. With the increasing demand for the welfare, a central question for social welfare is whether Hong Kongers can turn to other means to maintain social stability in Hong Kong and cultivate a culture of mutual support and care through community services.

COMMUNITY SERVICES IN HONG KONG: VOLUNTEERISM

Volunteerism is a form of community services. It always plays a significant role in the welfare and progress of developed and developing countries.[2] It can not only cultivate the collective action and spirit to address the needs of the society but also connect different groups (youth, elderly, women, disabled people, families, etc.) to serve together for the betterment of the society. Volunteering promotes social harmony and develops close interpersonal relationships among people in its society. Hong Kong has more than 1.3 million volunteers registered and over 3,200 organizations participating to create various community service opportunities for volunteers to take up and serve the society as a whole. In 2018–2019, the estimated spending on social welfare in Hong Kong is around HK$84.2 billion, and the government has already doubled its spending in this area compared to a decade ago (Social Welfare Department, 2019). In order to build a more caring and

---

[2] Harrold, S. K. E. S. (2000). "Levels of Participation and Promotion of Volunteering Around the World. The Third Sector: Beyond Government and the Market". A seminar organized by the Central Policy Unit on 25th July, 2000, The Government of Hong Kong Special Administrative Region: The Hong Kong Convention and Exhibition Centre. Lee, E. W. Y. (2005). "The Politics of Welfare Developmentalism in Hong Kong". In H-j Kwon (ed.), *Transforming the Developmental Welfare State in East Asia*. New York: Palgrave Macmillan, pp. 118–139.

inclusive society, the Steering Committee on Promotion of Volunteer Service has been striving to promote volunteerism to all the sectors. The four subcommittees under the steering committee focus on the following:

1. promotion of student and youth volunteering,
2. promotion of corporate volunteering,
3. promotion and publicity of volunteer service,
4. promotion of volunteering in community organizations.

These subcommittees work together with the 11 district co-ordinating committees, and the district social welfare officers are committed to promote volunteerism, create sustainable and innovative services and foster mutual support among the people in Hong Kong. According to Yip,[3] the Director of Social Welfare Department, the department will "continue to uphold the 'people-oriented' approach and strive to deliver services tailored for the public". People-oriented approach is always a strategy in engaging the community in Hong Kong.

PROMOTION OF COMMUNITY SERVICES AND SERVICE-LEARNING IN THE EDUCATION SECTOR

Other than the Social Welfare Department's efforts, the education sector in Hong Kong has been playing an active role to promote community services and service-learning. Many schools have been encouraging students to do community services as a kind of character-building education. In 2006, Lingnan University (LU) was the first university setting up an Office of Service-Learning (OSL) to formalize and integrate meaningful ideas and concepts related to social welfare services into the academic curriculum. With over 50 years of experience in providing "Education for services" in Hong Kong, Lingnan has been actively teaching students to contribute to the society. In 2014, Lingnan decided to make service-learning as a graduation requirement in order to instil the serving and caring qualities among Lingnan graduates. Other than Lingnan, currently more than 10 institutions in Hong Kong have set up similar offices or centres to promote service-learning. For example, Hong Kong Baptist University set up a Center for Innovative Service-learning in 2016. Hong Kong Polytechnic University set up an OSL in 2012 and immediately announced to the public that all the new students in 2012 have to undertake service-learning course as a graduation requirement. The University of

---

[3]Yip, C. (2018). *Volunteer Movement Yields Encouraging Results Over Past 20 Years*. Hong Kong: Social Welfare Department, https://www.info.gov.hk/gia/general/201812/02/P2018113000733.htm.

Hong Kong also set up an experiential learning centre in 2008.[4] Using service-learning as a pedagogy is popular not only among higher education institutions but also among primary and secondary schools. In 2012, the new senior secondary school curriculum in Hong Kong was launched. Community services under the category of Other Learning Experiences became one of the five essential learning experiences to nurture respect, care for others and a sense of civic responsibilities among students in Hong Kong. Some schools even use service-learning pedagogy in their liberal studies curriculum to address various community issues, including climate change, ageing population, low-income family and waste management. Irrespective of the type of service-learning or community services adopted in the higher education or secondary school setting, positive impacts on students' personal development, academic learning, service leadership and career aspiration[5–8] and community impacts and sustainability have been proven.[9]

Service-Learning and Service Leadership

Since 2012, other than promoting service-learning, there had been more discussions among higher education institutions on how to promote service leadership in Hong Kong. This was because of the generous donation made by the Victor and William Fung Foundation to all the government-funded universities to develop Service Leadership Initiatives (SLIs). The HKI-SLAM headed by Dr. Po Chung, who is the co-founder of DHL International, developed a service leadership model and helped

---

[4] Ma, H. K. C. (2018) "Service-Learning development in Higher Education in Hong Kong" in Hong Kong in 2017: Two Decades of Post-1997 Hong Kong Developments edited by T.W. Lim and T.Y. Kong. Singapore and New Jersey: WSPC.

[5] Ma, H. K. C. and Chan, C. M. A. (2013). "A Hong Kong University First: Establishing Service-Learning as an Academic Credit-Bearing Subject". *Gateways: International Journal of Community Research and Engagement*, 6, 178–198.

[6] Ma, H. K., Chad Chan Wing-fung and Alfred Chan Cheung-ming (2016). "The Long-Term Impact of Service-Learning on Graduates' Civic Engagement and Career Exploration in Hong Kong. Service-Learning and Community Engagement in Asian Higher Education". *USA: Journal of Higher Education Outreach and Engagement*, 37–56.

[7] Ma, H. K. C. and Dawn Fei Yin Lo (2016). "Service-Learning as an Independent Course: Merits, Challenges, and Ways Forward". *USA: International Journal of Research on Service-Learning and Community Engagement*, 4.

[8] Shek, D. T. L., Yu, L. and Ng, C. S. M. (2016). "Evaluation of a General Education Program in Hong Kong: Results Based on Multiple Evaluation Strategies." *International Journal of Child and Adolescent Health*, 9(2), 263–273.

[9] Wood, C., Banks, S., Galiardi, S., Koehn, J. and Schroeder, K. (2011). "Community Impacts of International Service-Learning and Study Abroad: An Analysis of Focus Groups with Program Leaders". *Partnerships: A Journal of Service-Learning and Civic Engagement*, 2(1).

the universities in Hong Kong to develop the related curriculum.[10] The SLI aims to not only promote a new model of Service Leadership and learning in the post-industrial Service Economy but also prepare students to become effective leaders in their careers and community, especially in the current ever-changing economic and social landscape. According to the HKI-SLAM framework, *Service leadership is about consistently providing high quality personal service to everyone that one comes into contact with, including one's self.*[11] HKI-SLAM tried to broaden the definition of leadership and further include self-leadership with a focus on ethics. It defined the concept in the following manner: *Leadership is a service aimed at ethically satisfying the needs of self, others, groups, communities, systems, and environments.*[12] Due to the concept of service leadership, HKI-SLAM also broadened the definition of service to include not only work done by one person or a group for the benefit of others but also self-reflective thinking and purposeful efforts one undertakes to improve one's ability to satisfy one's needs in order to serve others. Thus, "service" is defined as follows: *Service includes self-serving efforts aimed at ethically improving one's competences, abilities, and willingness to help satisfy the needs of others.*[13]

How HKI-SLAM defined service leadership is quite similar with service-learning as service-learning also emphasizes training an individual to understand the world from the perspective of self, others, community, country and the whole world. Though Ma *et al.*[14] stated that, "Service-Learning is a teaching method that combines academic knowledge and community service" (p. 3), it actually also cultivates empathy and a caring disposition. The hyphen between "service" and "learning" represents the importance of self-reflection when serving and learning from others. Service-learning can be the means to develop service leadership qualities. Some of the funded universities used service-learning as a vehicle to develop SLI. Each university has its own characteristics and features/focus when they launch the SLI; for more details, please refer to Table 1.

Each university has its own SLI developmental path and the instructors help to develop programmes and curriculum to echo with the concept of service leadership. The first 2 years of implementation were highly diversified and universities were examining their own ways/approaches in implementing the curriculum.

---

[10] Shek, D. T. L. and Lin, L. (2015). "Core Beliefs in the Service Leadership Model Proposed by the Hong Kong Institute of Service Leadership and Management". *International Journal of Disability and Human Development*, 14(3), 233–242.

[11] *Ibid.*, p. 238.

[12] *Ibid.*, p. 238.

[13] *Ibid.*, p. 238.

[14] Ma, H.K. Carol, Chan, C.M., Chan, Liu Cheng Alice, Mak Mui-fong Fanny (2018). *Service-Learning as a New Parodigm in the Higher Education of China.* Michigan: The Michigan State University Press.

Table 1. Service leadership initiatives among universities in Hong Kong.

Universities	Characteristics and highlights	References
City University of Hong Kong (CityU)	The Service Leadership Initiative (SLI) of City University of Hong Kong operates under an integrated framework of social innovation, entrepreneurship and student service leadership.	http://www.cityu.edu.hk/serviceleadership/about.aspx
Hong Kong Baptist University (HKBU)	"The Service Leadership Education (SLE) project aims to develop in students the capacity to deliver services with competence, character and care. GE courses incorporating the ideals of Service Leadership are purposefully designed and delivered/disseminated to build leadership competencies into our students. Ethical practices and the importance of positive social relationships are strongly emphasized to equip the students to be good service leaders. We hope that students can develop the valued characteristics of effective leaders, including empathy, openness in mind, being creative, socially responsible and reflective."	http://ge.hkbu.edu.hk/service-leadership/
Lingnan University (LingnanU)	The Service Leadership Initiative (SLI) of Lingnan University operates under a service-learning framework and the programme objectives are as follows: 1. to prepare students to become future community leaders by nurturing their service leadership skills, commitment to personal and social responsibility and insight into real-world challenges; 2. to provide a practical platform for students to demonstrate their potential for career advancement in a service-oriented economy; 3. to provide on-the-job coaching and mentoring for students, along with opportunities to diagnose and meet service needs through first-hand practical experiences; 4. to enable synergy between academic and local knowledge; 5. to foster service innovation for the benefit of the community.	https://www.ln.edu.hk/osl/ourproject_internship.php
The Chinese University of Hong Kong (CUHK)	"The Service Leadership Initiative at The Chinese University of Hong Kong involves an interdisciplinary General Education three credit 14-week course based on the premise that all students possess the potential to be service leaders. The course aims to promote service leadership through cultivating appropriate knowledge, skills, character and care. It introduces students to theories of leadership from the disciplines of management, political science, psychology and sociology with instructors from the appropriate faculties and departments teaching the classes."	https://entrepreneurship.bschool.cuhk.edu.hk/SLI

(*Continued*)

Table 1. (*Continued*)

Universities	Characteristics and highlights	References
The Hong Kong Institute of Education (HKIEd)	"Student leadership development model, under the operation of the Student Affairs Office (SAO) in the Hong Kong Institute of Education (HKIEd). The office consolidates and shares our unique experiences in service leadership development at HKIEd in the co-curricular context and examines how this approach could be further developed and enhanced to benefit other experiential learning programs in future."	
The University of Hong Kong (HKU)	"The SLI takes place in the summer, where student interns work as a team (groups of 3–5) at one of our community partners to initiate, develop and implement (a) service task(s). By making use of their social sciences and multi-disciplinary knowledge, student interns contribute as shared leaders to help the organisations generate innovative solutions to authentic problems. The Service Leadership Internship (SLI) has four major objectives: (1) to strengthen the students' sense of social responsibilities in leadership, (2) to help the students acquire the personal competencies in leadership, (3) to help the students acquire the social competencies in leadership, (4) to enable the students to hone their leadership skills in authentic service to the community."	http://www.socsc.hku.hk/sli/
The Hong Kong Polytechnic University (PolyU)	"Several credit-bearing subjects have been developed at The Hong Kong Polytechnic University (PolyU), including a 2-credit 'service leadership' subject, a 3-credit 'service leadership' subject in the Cluster Area Requirement, a free elective 3-credit 'service leadership' subject, and a 3-credit 'service leadership through serving children and families with special needs' subject. Non-credit-bearing service leadership programs including the Global Youth Leadership Program and Wofoo Leaders' Network have also been designed."	https://www.polyu.edu.hk/apss/subject/APSS1A21%20Service%20Leadership.pdf
The Hong Kong University of Science and Technology (HKUST)	"Service Leadership Initiative (SLI) focuses on the education and promotion of service leadership at the Hong Kong University of Science and Technology (HKUST), and provides future engineers with opportunities for service leadership development. Service leadership development is essential for their future careers since Hong Kong, a cosmopolitan metropolis, has over 90% of the GDP from the service sector and engineers are professionals who provide technical and expert services to clients."	http://e2i.ust.hk/err/projects/

Case Study of Lingnan University

Lingnan University (LU) is very clear on what it should do to promote service leadership as the university has a strong history of "Education for service". With the setting up of OSL in 2006, LU has integrated Service Leadership development opportunities into seven credit-bearing courses that have a co-curricular service-learning component: *Introduction to Business, Social Marketing, Corporate Social Responsibility, Leadership and Teamwork, Services Marketing, Strategic Management* and *Service Leadership Practicum*. The "Service Leadership Practicum" course was jointly developed by the OSL and the Faculty of Business because the SLI has inspired the team to further think about course integration with service-learning and service leadership in university education. It took almost 2 years to develop the course because LU (of which the author was a founding member) already had the experience of organizing non-credit-bearing service-learning internship to formalize the course materials. Initially, the associated curricula sought to foster 10 service leadership attributes, namely ability, insight, motivation, discipline and self-confidence, in order to achieve the following:

1. demonstrate attention to verbal and to non-verbal messages;
2. pinpoint problems and propose relevant solutions;
3. notice other people's needs and strive to address those needs;
4. express ideas clearly while offering original and constructive opinions to improve performance;
5. build positive social relationships that satisfy others and foster cohesiveness;
6. improve self-leadership and self-management competencies;
7. deliver what one has promised;
8. strive to make a difference to the organization and/or community;
9. exert positive influence on others' thinking and decision-making;
10. monitor and coordinate progress against deadlines, with appropriate time management practices.

After implementing the internship, LU teaching team (including the author) further developed the following 10 intended learning outcomes for the Service Leadership Practicum course:

1. *Actively listening to others*: Paying close attention to what other people are saying; showing them that you are paying attention.
2. *Anticipating and solving problems*: How you detected and defined problems; how you identified and proposed relevant solutions.
3. *Caring disposition*: How you discovered other people's needs and took positive action to address those needs.

4. *Showing originality in expressing opinions*: How you offered original and constructive opinions to improve performance.
5. *Contributing to cohesiveness and close relationships:* How you helped to foster the development of harmony, cohesiveness and close relationships with others.
6. *Committing to continuous improvement*: What you have been doing to improve your self-leadership and self-management competencies.
7. *Undertaking delegated responsibilities*: What you have been doing to ensure that you carry out what you have promised to others.
8. *Civic engagement*: How you have been striving to make a difference to the organization or community.
9. *Influencing others*: How you exerted a positive influence on others' thinking and decision-making.
10. *Project coordination skills:* how you monitored and coordinated progress, for example, through time management and checking progress against deadlines/ expectations.

These outcomes checklist became LU's (author was a founding member) guidelines for designing the practicum and understanding how students develop their service leadership qualities. Each enrolled student is required to join a team-based Service Leadership through Service-Learning Project, administered by LU's OSL, addressing these service leadership learning outcomes. Other than that, the OSL at LU arranges stand-alone Service Leadership Practicum courses carried out in NGOs and social enterprises. Each practicum addresses a unique "mini-mission" requiring students to practice service leadership learning outcomes. This curriculum bearing three-credits enables each student to practice service leadership through Service-Learning under supervision and work full-time in a host community organization such as a social enterprise or NGO over an 8-week period during the summer term.

LEARNING AND TEACHING METHODS

The practicum period was preceded by workshop and training (12 hours in duration) that introduced the key attributes, dispositions and organizing principles of service leadership, the principles of Service-Learning and the nature of community organizations. Under supervision, students undertook self-diagnostic exercises to identify developmental opportunities and priorities for focused learning during the practicum period. They were also guided on how to reflect critically on their own experiences as service leaders during the practicum period and how to draw out lessons from experience about service leadership practices and principles.

The practicum period lasted for 8 weeks, full-time. Students were placed individually or in small groups in organizations such as social enterprises or NGOs in Hong Kong that provide services to the community. With assistance from the OSL, each practicum slot was carefully and rigorously negotiated in advance with the respective host organizations to ensure that appropriate service leadership opportunities and challenges would be available; a partner organization representative from the host organization would be willing, able and available to serve as a co-educator throughout the practicum period; and employees of the host organization who worked alongside the practicum student will understand the purpose of the practicum. In addition, "mini-missions" were established for each student in consultation with partner organization representatives and the instructor. The mini-missions were also related to the overall mission of their respective host organization.

Throughout the practicum period, OSL provided orientation and regular training and reflection sessions to students. Students had to submit biweekly journals to the course instructor. They were required to make two individual presentations during the interim and concluding workshops. At the end, students also had to submit individual reflective essays to evaluate their own effectiveness in practicing service leadership to diagnose and meet the needs of the service recipients.

Here are some examples of the practicums and students' self-reflection:

Name of company	Position offered	Job description	Students' self-reflection
Non-governmental organization			
People Service Centre	Project Assistant	1. Assist with daily food recycle operation 2. Communicate with existing food recycle network 3. Assist with food recycle public education programme 4. Develop new food recycle network	"With the experience of working in this organization, I can have more opportunity to *help* more people in the poor situations. This is not only limited to distributing food and resources, but also helps people with their mental problems in daily life. This is really a great experience to get in touch with

(Continued)

234 Carol Ma

(*Continued*)

Name of company	Position offered	Job description	Students' self-reflection
		Mini-Mission: A student is required to conduct a background study of the service, assess the need of service users and develop an achievable and feasible individual mini-project under the 8-week placement framework with two to three major tasks with indicators (such as network building, food policy advocacy and public education programme).	different kinds of people, such as women and the homeless.... I think I have *made a difference* to the organization and the community because the bonding between the member themselves has been strengthened and they helped each other" — Student 1 who *served at People Service Center.*
Office of Service-Learning, Lingnan University	Project Trainee	1. Coordinate and assist the daily operation of Lingnan U Elder Academy 2. Support some administrative work of OSL **Mini-Mission:** Organize an Elder Academy overnight camp (held on 2–3 July) for 200 participants of elderly, primary and secondary school students.	"After this 8 weeks service practicum, I think I am *more prepared* and *capable to be a service leader.* With more opportunities to interact, discuss and cooperate with different people, I feel more confident of handling different inquiries from the elderly and other parties, more active to propose constructive plans and ideas to my supervisor, and more independent in facing pop up problems. In general, this practicum can *help me pursue great advance as to my leadership, communication and event management skills."* — *Student 2 who served at the Lingnan U Elder Academy, Office of Service Learning.*

Community Services, Service-Learning and Service Leadership in Hong Kong 235

(Continued)

Name of company	Position offered	Job description	Students' self-reflection
Social Enterprises			
Christian Action (Social Enterprise Division)	Program Assistant	1. Assist in the daily operation of the "Green Collection Program" 2. Co-ordinate with donors by e-mail and telephone 3. Input the donation data and generate a report 4. Prepare programme material/outdoor work for "Green Collection Program" activities **Mini-Mission:** Coordinate a charity book drive with corporates of the Hong Kong International Education Expo at HKCEC in July 2016.	"I became *more sensitive* to recycling in the hostel. Christian Action owns two collection banks in the campus. Normally, students donated many clothes to the collection banks near the check-out date of the hostel. Otherwise, the volumes of the collection banks are low. Therefore, it is possible to *encourage my classmate to donate their clothes within the campus rather than throwing away.* I think it is important to remind ourselves recycling is one of the methods to reuse the items we do not want or need. When I plan to give presents to my friends, I will try to make hand-made items instead of buying new items. After joining the programme, the *leadership attributes have never ended and I still have many opportunities to hold activities in the future and receive a new angle/perspective to recognize the concept of recycling."— Student 3 who served at Christian Action.*

(*Continued*)

Name of company	Position offered	Job description	Students' self-reflection
Yan Oi Tong Social Enterprise	Management Trainee	1. Develop or organize marketing campaign 2. Shop management 3. Administrative Work **Mini-Mission:** — In charge of Marketing campaign, such as Food Expo; — Service re-engineering, such as workflow review.	"After eight weeks practicum working experience in Yan Oi Tong Social Enterprise, I have learned a lot. I believe it is an ideal organization to *practice service leadership* because the culture and uniqueness of it gives a great support for student. The vision and value of Yan Oi Tong Social Enterprise are challenging for me. The idea of **helping deprived group and promoting environmental protection are meaningful** but it is hard to focus on cost effectiveness at the same time. However, it is the essence and mission of a social enterprise. So, in the practicum, I always needed to anticipate and *solve problem* when struggling on formulating marketing plans that incorporate economic sustainability, environmental sustainability and social sustainability. It trained *my skills in diversified thinking.*" — *Student 5 who served at the Yan Oi Tong Social Enterprise.*

(Continued)

Name of company	Position offered	Job description	Students' self-reflection
The Free Methodist Church of HK Social Service Division — Fantastic Kitchen	Student Intern	1. Assisting in the daily operation of Fantastic Kitchen 2. Conducting marketing research on social enterprise **Mini-Mission:** Marketing research on social enterprises, research on further development of social enterprises.	"In this summer, I grabbed a precious opportunity to have a *better understanding of service leadership* through joining service leadership practicum. It allowed me to *cultivate, train and demonstrate my service leadership skills* through an eight-week working experience in a social enterprise called Fantastic Kitchen. Not only did I improve my service leadership skills, but also made contribution to the social enterprise and the community. This practicum experience demonstrated that *improvement of service leader and service recipients can be derived from service leadership."* — *Student 6 who served at The Free Methodist Church of HK Social Service Division-Fantastic Kitchen.*

Students' self-reflection also helped the author and her colleagues to further strengthen their understanding of how students learn as a leader. Through trial and error, the author and her colleagues have also learnt how to enhance the Service Leadership developmental opportunities for students. The nature of the project also appears to be an important facilitating factor. The following four conceptual guidelines can be considered when developing partnership with the interested parties for the collaboration in developing future Service Leaders. The students should also be aware and be prepared to perform the different roles required for maximizing the effects of learning.

1. **Addressing the genuine needs/problems of partnership organization:** The partnership organizations/social enterprises have to sustain their businesses/services for achieving their social missions (e.g. helping the deprived/less privileged/disadvantaged groups in the society and environmental protection) in the long run.

    Thus, the following criteria may help identify the problems/genuine needs of a Social Enterprise:

    - They should be current and contemporary issues (to cope with the pressing needs of those in need managed by social enterprises with limited resources).
    - They can be achieved within a short time, e.g. a few months (to complement the study periods/semesters of students).
    - The outcomes can be anticipated/expected/implemented in terms of programme development, operational procedure improvements, etc.

    The direct impact to the development of social enterprise can be drawn. For example, the programmes will be used in real practical terms; operational efficiency has been achieved and is shaped by the recommendations of students; human resources development has been realized with the support of students' service and customer satisfaction has been achieved with the service delivery of students. Clear objectives and measurable outcomes best gauge and clarify the genuine resource needs of the Social Enterprise and facilitate project evaluation thereafter.

    When defining the problems/challenges or identifying the genuine needs of the social enterprises, the author advises that there is also a need to understand the following items:

    a. the products and services currently offered;
    b. the business problems/needs and expectations;
    c. the objections and concerns of partner organizations when using students as consultants;
    d. the risks they are willing to take with the consultancy service offered by students.

    Other than the above, we need to prepare the partner organizations with the following expectations (from 2 to 4):

2. **Acknowledging the consultancy roles of students:** Students, as external parties to the projects, can help review the real issues in an objective manner.

Students with business study backgrounds/trainings should be well-equipped with business knowledge and be trained in research mindset for addressing the needs of the social enterprises. Students should be ready to wear a consultant's hat and perform consultancy roles when the situation demands it. They should be prepared through briefing sessions and workshops to achieve these objectives.

For confirming the genuine needs/problems of a social enterprise/partner organization, the following conditions have to be considered:

- the opportunities to communicate with the social enterprises;
- continuous feedback/comments from the social enterprises for the students' projects;
- to carry out research if necessary for identifying the problem/needs of the social enterprises; the data collection process may include interviews with the parties concerned or questionnaire surveys.

Practicum arrangement: For practicum, the students will work full-time for a short duration. In fulfilling the consultancy role, the students can be guided with mini-missions through which they can help the social enterprises to fulfil the dual business and social missions more effectively.

To pull together wider expertise and knowledge of participating students, it would be advisable to organize a student group (consisting of a minimum of two students) to join the organization that is carrying out the service-learning project.

3. **Agreeing to provision of service leadership development opportunities for students:** For developing service leadership of students, the partner organizations should delegate projects to student management and not treat students as helpers or as an extra pair of hands. Students should be offered opportunities and free space for project development at their own discretion (i.e. involving decision-making opportunities). They should be provided with sufficient information for the development of these projects.

4. **Building up a service provider and service recipient relationship:** Acting as a consultant and service provider, the students should be treated at the same hierarchical level as the project administrators and other stakeholders and be empowered and trusted for their abilities to meet the needs of the service recipients (social enterprises/partner organizations). Therefore, the service provider–service recipient relationship should be developed together with the student–agency learning relationship.

The above-mentioned steps in the implementation process of project management/consultancy are very crucial in determining whether the students can actually help and address the needs of the service-learning organizations. The LU working teams treasured these experiences that inspired them to keep thinking on methods to improve the practicum and further investigate the effectiveness of the service leadership model. In their 2014 publication, Snell, Chan, Ma and Chan have also identified a roadmap for effective service leadership through service-learning projects (please see appendix).[15] This has become a milestone for strengthening the service leadership model at LU. Since then, the number of courses adopting service-learning as a pedagogy and setting service leadership as the developmental goal for students has increased.

CONCLUSION

As mentioned by Shek and Chung,[16] there are still unfinished tasks that service leadership educators can address. They are "evaluation, identification of success factors, role of service-learning, assessment, establishing the theoretical distinctiveness of the model, integration with Chinese cultural values, and the clarification of assumptions of leaders in the Service Leadership Model." Other than these qualities, the impacts of what the service leaders have achieved are also important for further investigations, especially since there is a lot of demand for services in social welfare within the Hong Kong society. Whether service leaders can help to fill in the community gap and mobilize more people to serve the needy is always a priority in this highly competitive and rapidly changing world.

Looking ahead, it is definitely vital to develop leadership qualities for youths in Hong Kong, especially in a new era of the competitive world. Using service-learning as a means to develop and nurture our youth to excel and commit to service leadership is particularly important. It will help them to overcome the social and socio-economic disruptions of contemporary lifestyles in a highly urbanized society and prepare them to become the future service leaders of Hong Kong.

---

[15] Snell, R. S., Chan, M. Y. L., Ma, C. H. L. and Chan, C. K. M. (2015). "The Service Leadership Initiative at Lingnan University". In Shek, D. T. L. and Chung, P. (eds.), *Promoting Service Leadership Qualities in University Students: The Case of Hong Kong*. Singapore: Springer, pp. 99–115; Snell, R. S., Chan, Y. L. M., Ma, H. K. C. and Chan. K. M. C. (2014). "A Road Map for Empowering Undergraduates to Practice Service Leadership through Service-Learning in Teams". *Journal of Management Education*, Online 14 August 2014. DOI: 10/1177/1052562914545631.

[16] Shek, D. T. L. and Chung, P. (eds.) (2015). "Service Leadership Education for University Students: Seven Unfinished Tasks". In *Promoting Service Leadership Qualities in University Students: The Case of Hong Kong*. Singapore: Springer, pp. 225–232.

APPENDIX: A ROAD MAP FOR EFFECTIVE SERVICE LEADERSHIP THROUGH SERVICE-LEARNING PROJECTS

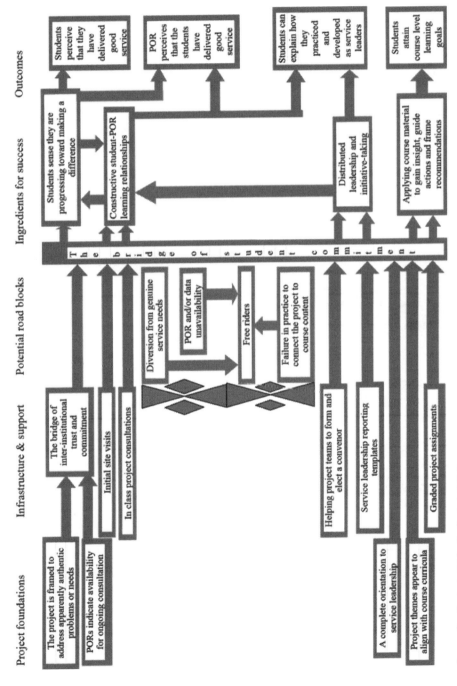

Source: See Footnote 15 for Snell *et al.* (2014).

Section C

LEADERSHIP IN ECONOMIC REGIONALISM

Chapter 18

INDIA IN SAARC: LEADER OR NOT?

S. Shahadave

Soka University of Japan, Tokyo, Japan

INTRODUCTION

The South Asian region is full of contradictions, and disparities. South Asia has experienced civil wars, war between nations, nuclear rivalries, insurgencies and terrorism, along with the other serious problems of poverty, environmental degradation, etc., in addition to significant problems associated with drugs and human trafficking. The region is home to 23% of the total world population as of 2017.[1] South Asian Association for Regional Cooperation (SAARC) is the largest regional organization in the world in terms of population.

SAARC showed potential, with growth averaging 6% for more than 20 years during the 1990s and 2000s,[2] and now holds top position as the world's fastest growing economic region, with growth expected to reach 7% in 2019.[3] Moreover, SAARC member states are rich with natural resources as well as human resources. While it offers huge potential for growth, the capacity of South Asia

---

[1] World Bank (2018). "South Asia Data". [online] https://data.worldbank.org/region/south-asia. Accessed 14 April 2019.

[2] Peiris, D. (2014). "South Asia Regional Brief". [online] *World Bank*, http://www.worldbank.org/en/news/feature/2014/03/24/south-asia-regional-brief. Accessed 26 May 2019.

[3] World Bank (2019). "South Asia Needs More Exports to Maintain Growth". [online] https://www.worldbank.org/en/news/press-release/2019/04/07/south-asia-needs-more-exports-to-maintain-growth. Accessed 26 June 2019.

is underutilized and economically disjointed. It accounts for around 4% of the total world economic output.[4]

Regional cooperation is a concept that took a foothold during 1960s in Western Europe. After the European Common Market was created, other developing countries established regional groups.[5] This trend of regionalism stayed strong even in the wake of globalization in the 1990s. SAARC is one of those initiatives which took form in the 1980s. Though regional cooperation (groupings) such as Association of Southeast Asian Nations (ASEAN) has been arguably fruitful in economic integration, SAARC is lagging behind.

Among all its member states, India's position within SAARC is very unique in many different aspects. India shares borders with all other South Asian nations. In terms of the size of its population, territory and GDP, it qualifies and both carries the image of an emerging economic power in the world. Therefore, India's role and responsibility in the region is, without doubt, very important for the region and perhaps the world.

In addition, given its central geographical location with common borders and geopolitical/economic size, India is the only country in South Asia which has unsolved (territorial and/or political) issues with all the other member states. Whether in the form of a war with Pakistan, border skirmishes with Bangladesh, unstable relations with Nepal or military intervention in Sri Lanka, India and its neighbours have a contentious relationship. Though it might be said that there are unjustified perceptions about India among its neighbours and while India does respect the sovereignty of all its neighbours, unsolved issues make neighbours apprehensive about India. However, there is no doubt about the role India can and should play for the integration of South Asia. India needs to assume additional responsibility for ensuing regional development. Statements from Heads of State at the inaugural summit of SAARC, in 1985, reflected this feeling.[6]

INDIA'S ROLE AS A REGIONAL LEADER

Regional leadership of India in SAARC should be based on mutual recognition of interests as suggested by Lahneman.[7] Another way India can assert its leadership

---

[4] World Bank (2019). "Data-South Asia". [online] https://www.worldbank.org/en/region/sar. Accessed 16 April 2019.

[5] Bhalla, A. and Bhalla, P. (2016). *Regional Blocs: Building blocks or stumbling blocks?* London: Palgrave Macmillan Limited

[6] Mohanan, B. (1992). *The Politics of Regionalism in South Asia.* New Delhi: Atlantic Publishers & Distributors.

[7] Lahneman, W. (2003). "Changing Power Cycles and Foreign Policy Role-power Realignments: Asia, Europe, and North America". *International Political Science Review*, 24(1), 97–111.

is by the use of its overwhelming material capability and the political will to use that capability to influence other member states. However, this will create extra tensions in the region which already has contentious histories.

Right now, South Asia is somewhere in the middle ground when it comes to using its dominant regional power and its ideas about regional integration. India is starting to assert itself as a regional power or leader. However, when it comes to taking on additional responsibilities, especially for economic integration and development, India tends to show reluctance. India still is uninterested in opening its market to the neighbours. Though India expresses its ambition to be recognized as a confident economic power in the world, it has never expressed its willingness to integrate within the South Asian economic space. Instead, its approach had rather been hesitant in integrating the linking up with the other South Asian economics.

India's reluctance in updating the Indo-Nepal Treaty of 1950 and also the Indo-Bangladesh Treaty of 1972 is one such example. In addition, while India does emphasize on free trade, it has not taken any measures to deal with tariff barriers which are the real constraints to intra-regional trade. For example, despite a general tariff-free access for Bangladeshi products to India, several Indian states often impose taxes on products like jute and batteries.[8]

On the contrary, there are always suspicions of India's intentions in the region by its neighbours. Still, it is expected to take up a crucial leadership role in integrating the South Asian economic bloc. India was and is expected to create confidence in South Asia to kick start the regionalization process.[9]

The size and position of India give it a special role of leadership in South Asian and world affairs.[10] Thus, it is time for India to change its hesitant attitude about greater integration. In many critical areas such as water, energy, trade and mobility, the region requires a comprehensive, collaborative and cooperative action from the regional states as such resources are becoming scarce.

Therefore, the question arises as to what India can do for the economic integration of South Asian nations. There may be various actions that India can take in order to make economic regionalism possible.

Relations between the two major SAARC member countries, India and Pakistan, have been a major impediment in the economic integration of this

---

[8] *The Financial Express* (2019). "Bangladesh Urges India to Withdraw Anti-Dumping Duty". [online] https://thefinancialexpress.com.bd/economy/bangladesh/bangladesh-urges-india-to-withdraw-anti-dumping-duty-1557840342. Accessed 8 May 2019.

[9] Mohanan, B. (1992), *op cit.*

[10] Schyns, B. and Meindl, J. (2005). "An Overview of Implicit Leadership Theories and their Application in Organization Practice". In Schyns, B. and Meindl, J. (eds.), *Implicit Leadership Theories: Essays and Explorations.*. Greenwich CT: Information Age Publishing, pp. 15–36.

region. India and Pakistan have held progress hostage due to their bilateral security issues. Though the security issues are political in nature, their impacts are felt in all the other issues that are important for economic integration.

India has always mentioned that until Pakistan addresses the problem of terrorism, real integration will not be possible.[11] Nevertheless, India can now look beyond that. China claims Taiwan as its province and while they may be inimical towards each other, they have a close trade and investment relationship (although facing increasing difficulties, particularly due to an anti-Beijing Taiwanese Tsai administration and a hard-line strongman Xi Chinese regime). Therefore, it would not be impossible for India and Pakistan to have the same kind of cooperation (separating economics from politics), if they truly want it to happen. Moreover, India should take the same approach towards the other neighbours. In addition, the separation of economics from politics practiced in the ASEAN consensual-seeking regionalism, which is open and loose and focuses on economic rather than geopolitical issues, excessively is an example for South Asian giants. India as well as Pakistan can take the initiative to separate economic integration from political issues.

Another issue is that India has always been interested in bilateral talks and treaties, including diplomacy carried out under the current regime of Modi. However, regional integration requires more multilateral connections rather than bilateral negotiations. India has a fear that if it agrees to multilateral treaties, its neighbours will group together against its interests. Moreover, the fear of losing economically to its neighbours and unnecessary pride stops India from being the true leader that it can become.

The foreign policy of Prime Minster Narendra Modi's administration gave emphasis to "neighbourhood first" policy, which prioritizes consolidating India's relations with its neighbours. However, it has not borne any fruit so far. Rather, relations between India and its rival Pakistan and long-time friend Nepal have deteriorated in the last few years.

For a genuine integration of the South Asian region, SAARC and India can learn from the experiences of the other regional groups. One such group is ASEAN. One thing that SAARC can learn from ASEAN is having regular meetings. These regular meetings help in building trust between rivals and making multilateral relations stronger. ASEAN has 1000 meetings a year on many issues.[12] India can take the initiative to build trust and cooperation in South Asia. These

---

[11] *The Economic Times* (2018). "Talks Not Possible Unless Pakistan Stops Terrorism: Sushma Swaraj". [online] https://economictimes.indiatimes.com/news/defence/no-talks-not-to-participate-in-saarc-unless-pakistan-stops-terror-eam-sushma-swaraj/articleshow/66844485.cms. Accessed 3 June 2019.

[12] *Oxford Business Group* (2019). *The Report: Myanmar 2015*. Oxford Business Group.

meetings can include different issues such as poverty reduction, environment, health, and education. All these problems are common to all the member states of the SAARC. Besides common challenges, there can also be common objectives to achieve, e.g. sustainable development goals are common global goals to work towards. Building on these common areas, SAARC can look towards more meaningful economic integration which would not be paralyzed by rivalry and mistrust.

One out-of-the-box approach India can take is letting its smaller neighbours to lead SAARC. Taking a back seat and letting countries such as Nepal and Sri Lanka lead will create an environment of trust and dispel clear apprehensions that neighbours always have towards India. India can study the role Indonesia played in ASEAN.[13]

Once it shows leadership in tackling common issues and challenges, India can then move towards deeper economic integration. To achieve this, taking pragmatic action to bypass regional politics and concentrating on common economic issues of development will pave the way towards greater integration. India needs to show the magnanimity of a leader and friend while accommodating the wishes of smaller neighbours.

Another important role of India will be to present itself as a hub for connectivity. Low levels of regional connectivity and lack of proper border infrastructure for the uninterrupted flow of goods and people have hindered the formation of regional supply chain. As India is connected with all the other member states, India's initiatives on improving the connectivity will be of paramount importance. It can cooperate and also invest in such infrastructures which will be beneficial for the unhindered flow of regional trade. Improvement in regional trade could lead to the realization of a mechanism for economic integration. The SAARC region already has a mechanism for economic integration. There is the South Asian Free Trade Agreement (SAFTA), at least in theory. With improving regional trade, these regional free trade agreements (FTAs) can be building blocks for real economic integration if member states indeed are serious about it. As the former prime minister of India, Dr. Man Mohan Singh said: "We have created institutions for regional economic cooperation but we have not empowered them adequately to enable them to be more proactive" in 16th SAARC summit in 2010, only creating physical institutions in theory would not be enough.[14] So taking a lead in

---

[13] Haidar, S. (2018). "SAARC can learn from ASEAN": Kishore Mahbubani. [online] *The Hindu*, https://www.thehindu.com/news/national/saarc-can-learn-from-asean/article22499756.ece. Accessed 3 April 2019.

[14] Jayaram, N. (2016). "Failure of Institutionalised Cooperation in South Asia". [online] Mantraya. org., http://mantraya.org/failure-of-institutionalised-cooperation-in-south-asia/. Accessed 17 April 2019.

building both physical and institutional infrastructures, India can show its leadership to integrate South Asia.

Another sector which India can play an important role for the SAARC is encouraging intra-regional investments. For example, Indian investments in Bhutan's hydroelectric resources are a major source of Bhutan's income. Another member state, Nepal, also has huge water resources. At a time when energy is becoming more and more important for India, investing in Nepal which has untapped water resources that are underdeveloped due to capital unavailability could benefit from intra-regional foreign direct investment (FDI) flows to achieve rapid economic development. On the one hand, India's need for more energy will be complemented by hydropower projects in Nepal. On the other hand, it could be a major source of income for Nepal as well. There might be other resources in other neighbouring countries which require FDIs. India should be more inclined to invest in these untapped resources and exploit it on mutually beneficial terms.

Bhutan, Nepal, Sri Lanka and the Maldives have a huge potential in tourism and are eager to welcome FDIs in this sector. India can take this opportunity to invest in such infrastructures which can benefit mutual interests, including tourism choices for Indians. With its population size and rising consumption power, India is a major source of tourists to most of these countries.

Next, India can work towards growing intra-regional trade. It can be a catalyst for mutual understanding and improving mutual trust among the member states. Also, it will be beneficial for all the members as well because intra-regional trade accounts for 50% of the total trade in East Asia but only a little more than 5% of South Asia's total trade by comparison.[15]

This is not beneficial for India either because, according to World Bank,[16] potential trade in goods within South Asia is valued at around US$62 billion but, at the present time, actual regional trade is US$19 billion, which is about US$43 billion below its potential.

CHINA IN SOUTH ASIA

India enjoys regional influence across South Asia due to various reasons such as economic strength, size and historical and cultural connections in the region. In comparison, China's involvement in South Asia is limited. However, it is changing rapidly as China is becoming a significant partner to South Asian countries in the

---

[15] World Bank (2018). "Realizing the Promise of Regional Trade in South Asia". [online] https://www.worldbank.org/en/news/feature/2018/10/09/realizing-the-promise-of-regional-trade-in-south-asia. Accessed 28 April 2019.

[16] *Ibid.*

region. It has invested in forging strong ties with smaller countries, especially in the areas of trade, diplomacy, aid and investment.

As China progresses with its grand ambitious plan of "Belt and Road Initiative" (BRI, a modern-day Silk Road), South Asia has become a "priority zone" in the scheme of the matter. Given South Asia's strategic location at the intersection point of the overland component of China-proposed BRI, China surely wants to have a foothold in South Asia. It is very crucial for China to consolidate its strategic presence. Thus, China remains steadfast in making inroads into South Asia.[17]

With a military base being planned in Pakistan and controversial commercial ports under construction in Sri Lanka or planned in the Maldives and Bangladesh, China is surely making its moves towards South Asia. Smaller states in South Asia are also hedging between India and China. They are not breaking away from India, but they are receiving higher levels of economic and military assistance from China. This will force India to do the same. However, India is in no such position to compete with China in this arena.

China's reach in this region as a trading partner has grown exponentially. China is currently the largest trading partner of Pakistan and Bangladesh and the second largest partner of Sri Lanka and Nepal.[18] This has happened even after India's FTAs with Sri Lanka, Nepal and Bhutan. In addition, China is the largest trading partner for India as well.[19]

For the time being, Chinese FDIs in this region are lagging behind those of India. However, during the last few years, Chinese investments have grown rapidly in Pakistan, Bangladesh and Sri Lanka.

CONCLUSION

South Asia has not achieved comparative levels of economic integration and economic growth compared to other regions such as ASEAN or EU. Continuous endeavour to integrate South Asia on the economic front has not borne much fruit due to various reasons but mainly political issues. Contentious history in the region has overshadowed all the attempts towards greater integration. As a result, South Asia is one of the least integrated region in the world. India, being the

---

[17] Singh, A. G. (2019). "China's Vision for the Belt and Road in South Asia". [online] *The Diplomat*, https://thediplomat.com/2019/03/chinas-vision-for-the-belt-and-road-in-south-asia/. Accessed 23 May 2019.

[18] World Integrated Trade Solution (WITS) (2018). "Data on Export, Import, Tariff, NTM". [online] https://wits.worldbank.org/Default.aspx?lang=en#. Accessed 19 June 2019.

[19] *Ibid.*

biggest economy of the South Asian region, has always been expected to play the role of a leader in this integration effort. There are differences in opinions about India's role within the region, the shape of its responsibilities as well as willingness in this matter, but no one denies the fact that the importance of India in this regional integration comes from its unique geographical position and the size of its economy.

Increasing regionalization of world trade and increased trade within regional trade blocks are a reality in the era of free trade and also are bulwarks against growing anti-globalization forces in the world. However, that is not yet the case with South Asia as it has only 1% share of the world trade while having more than 24% of the world population. Atal Bihari Vajpayee had once famously said: "You can change your friends but not neighbors".[20] Whatever problems, political disputes and confrontation may persist, member states including India cannot change their neighbours. Also, it cannot separate itself from the problems of its neighbours.

So leaving the political/geopolitical hesitancy behind, India will have to take up the role of a regional leader. India has to try to minimize the misunderstandings between its neighbours, gain trust from other member states in leading the region of South Asia and integrate the South Asian economy. This is especially the case as China is making its moves to be close to other member states of this region, India has to be very careful, active and fast in taking up the responsibility of a leader in integrating South Asia. If India becomes successful in playing the role of a leader in the economic integration of South Asia, its credibility will increase in international arena as well which is required as a pre-condition to establish itself as a leading emerging economic powerhouse in the world.

---

[20] *The Economic Times* (2003). "You Can Change Friends, Not Neighbours". [online] https://economictimes.indiatimes.com/you-can-change-friends-not-neighbours/articleshow/45796501.cms. Accessed 28 February 2018.

Section D

CONCLUDING SECTION

Chapter 19

CONCLUSION

T. W. Lim

Singapore University of Social Sciences, Singapore
National Univeristy of Singapore, Singapore

The major takeaway from this volume indicates that there is great diversity in leadership styles, application and implementation of those qualities. The concept of leadership can also be conceptualized at the macro, meso or micro levels. At the macro level, geopolitical leadership can take on different tracks. Chapter 2 by T. W. Lim indicates that not all constructivist schemes need to occur at the Track I level. Track II diplomacy and people-to-people exchanges are just as important for societies to understand each other at a deeper level. The US has been attracting academically strong persons and/or children from well-endowed families to study in the US for decades. Some of the returnees bring important knowledge and skills back to East Asia and created the so-called "East Asian economic miracle". China's Belt and Road Initiative is attempting to strengthen physical connectivity between countries by building transportation infrastructure, high-speed rails, highways, etc. Greater contact between individuals can lead to greater understanding, confidence-building measures and less tensions in the region and close the trust deficit. It also has the benefits of building trust for the next generation of East Asians.

Moving from regional ecosystems to country-specific political leadership systems, Chapter 3 by T. W. Lim demonstrates the complexities of domestic political structures and leadership systems in each constituent actor that makes up the regional political system. The Chinese case study appears to indicate a growing trend towards centralization of power, including Politburo membership reduction, making presidential and vice presidential posts tenured for life, extending stronger control over special autonomous regions and strengthening a strongman regime.

These measures are put in place due to perceptions of threats from the external changing environment and the accent on maintaining internal political stability. The Chinese government has many transitions to manage. Its economy is switching gears from Chinese exports to meet external demand to internal consumption as an engine of growth. Hong Kong is transiting from a British colonial outpost to an autonomous region with a high degree of self-rule to re-integrating to become a part of China. The Chinese Communist Party is also trying to stay relevant as questions of its legitimacy, legacy and relevance are raised. China is also coping with rapid urbanization as its rural populations shrink below 50% and the rise of the middle class, which is vocal about its environmental expectations and lifestyle choices. The challenges that China has to surmount are enormous. The systemic changes in leadership are put in place to manage; only time can tell the level of success attainable.

In Chapter 4, T. W. Lim continues with the area studies approach but moves from single-country study to a regional focus. It is a comparative chapter to provide further examples of different political systems in East Asia, in addition to the Chinese case studies. The complexities found in individual political systems are now further complicated by multiple domestic political systems found in East Asia. It also demonstrates the difficulties in forging regionalism due to the same complexities. Pragmatic self-interest motivates attempts to forge regional links. For example, in the growing contestation between China and the US, Beijing is trying to reach out to all friends, competitors and partners alike for solidarity in maintaining free trade. Thailand and China are bound together in "comprehensive strategic cooperative partnership", although skilful Thai diplomacy is hedging against Beijing's growing regional power and influence by tapping into its traditional friendship with the US (especially through military exchanges, e.g. Exercise Cobra Gold). The Thai royalty have had both positive and challenging exchanges in the past with the Chinese, justifying the approach of engaging all major powers simultaneously. The Islamic Republic of Pakistan is an ironclad brother (*tiegermen*) for Beijing, while North Korea is propped up by Beijing's material help. Perhaps the most important aspect of Sino-Thai relations is the personal ties between the Thai royal family and the Chinese leadership since both established official ties in 1975.

In Chapter 5, F. Vivien then moves on to analyze political leadership in managing peripheral relationships. In this case, Central Asia's contact, interactions and overtures to China become a case study. Vivien examines the impact of the rise of a great power like China and its impact on peripheral diplomacy. In some cases, there are accommodations made when smaller states are faced with the challenges of large proximate states and the ability to stand up for core principles when there is a need. In addition, beyond the actions of security cooperation, the question of an increased Chinese military presence in the area is becoming more relevant. Between 2014 and 2015, recurring rumours emerged in the form of plans to establish a Chinese military base in southern Kyrgyzstan.

Having discussed geopolitical, regional and domestic political leadership systems, Chapter 6 zeroes in even further on institutional and systemic studies. It is a case study of political and bureaucratic leadership in institution-building. In this chapter, W. K. Lim demonstrated the depth and extent of effort the establishment, i.e. the Chinese political leadership and experts, invested in building the nascent organizational field as its *de facto* "laboratory" to experiment with and refine its ideas around emergency management practices — particularly ideas about risk and governance — as it designed its policies and organizations. In reconfiguring its ensemble of laws, regulations and organizational processes on disaster management, Lim noted curation at work: the emergence and evolution of an ensemble of components that were inscribed into the field. The institutional vocabularies, i.e. the ideational components, were most obvious in legislative and administrative landmarks, such as the regulations and laws that were approved and enacted, especially during the intensive institutionalized period of field formation.

Chapter 7's political biography of Toru Hashimoto by Y. Godo ends with an observation about voter's desires and behaviours, particularly in the context of a desire for change. Godo stated, given that Japanese society is beset by a sense of helplessness with recession ongoing since the early 1990s, a new political ideology is needed to have a breakthrough. In that sense, Japan's current situation is one in which politicians and citizens are passively waiting for a knight in a shining armour to rescue them. However, even a charismatic personality like Hashimoto failed to present a new political ideology. Therein lies the dichotomy between aspirations for ideal leadership and the pragmatic reality of realpolitik.

S. King concluded Chapter 8 with a brief survey of successive leaders in Taiwan. He argued that Chen Shui-bian couldn't read the political tea leaves in Washington and his legal troubles marred the opposition's prized first chance at governing. In his view, Ma opened Taiwan's economy to mainland China, and by extension to the world, but misread the public mood as to how far and how fast to open further, how close was too close. The story is far from written on incumbent Tsai Ing-wen. For King, Lee Teng-hui, among all others, stands out to as Taiwan's prime leadership example who oversaw Taiwan's transition to full democracy, was its first freely elected leader and shepherded his homeland through the almost calamitous Third Taiwan Strait Crisis. Finally, King argues that honourable mention goes to Chiang Ching-kuo, whatever his true motivations, for the brave decisions he took in his final years.

The second political personality discussed in this volume is the charismatic Han Kuo-Yu of Taiwan. After vigorous discussions on the political force embodied within one individual, K. Tseng in Chapter 9 postulates that among those who have, in whatever form, demonstrated their intentions to run for the 2020 presidential election, they must be able to respond to the multidimensional issues and fickle mindsets of the electorate. For Han Kuo-yu, potential challenges in his political campaign would be that Han would need to re-elaborate his positions on the 92 consensus, which is strongly interlinked with the "One Country, Two Systems" policy. This is deemed by most Taiwanese as a threat to status quo and a denial of *de facto* independence of Taiwan.

Like Chapter 9, Chapter 10 by H. Y. Li also tackles the issue of political leadership legitimacy and aspirations for democracy. Li argues that due to the lack of legitimacy, the Hong Kong government is facing more and more challenges nowadays from political parties, non-governmental organizations and political and environmental activists. The mainlandization in Hong Kong boosts further discontents among Hong Kong people. After the handover, there are increasing regular and frequent protests against the Hong Kong government for its incapability in preserving the rule of law and various freedoms in Hong Kong. The inclination of formulating policies towards Beijing priorities inevitably further damages the credibility and legitimacy of the top Hong Kong leader known as the Chief Executive (CE) as well as the whole Hong Kong leadership. It appears there are some common political leadership issues among the Greater China entities.

Section B moves on to another genre of leadership concepts — Community Leadership. This section is designed in the tradition of applied knowledge as well as anthropological observation studies in terms of contents. Kenneth Wong's Chapter 11 provides a rigorous discussion of community leadership literatures before zooming in on the Singapore case study. Wong seeks objective studies by highlighting the caveat that constant improvements are necessary due to the fact that all social welfare and social caring systems that are put in place are by no means perfect. Thus, there is always room for improvement. While the state may take the lead in strengthening and improving the social development and inclusion, nothing beats having the community taking ownership of these functions to make a difference to the community.

In Chapters 12 and 13, W. Elim studied Yokohama Chinatown's (largest Chinatown in Japan) rich tapestry of ethnicities, civil society groups, local and overseas visitors and its sheer scale and size. She studied how culture is preserved under local community leadership in two overseas Chinese schools, more than 250 Chinese restaurants and shops and the two Chinese temples — the Temple of Guandi and the Temple of Mazu. These heritage sites as tourist assets enable Yokohama Chinatown to be ranked among the top three most-visited sightseeing spots in Japan among domestic tourists for over 10 years. The chapter discussed the state of community leadership in Yokohama Chinatown. Wong argues that her chapter's protagonist Jin's leadership and organizational features demonstrated strong effectiveness in bringing together the pro-PRC and pro-ROC teams to work on a single community-wide project. In settling the use of an empty land, Jin is a visionary in detecting the future shortage of open space for the overseas Chinese school to expand. To him, overseas Chinese education is an important platform for Chinese language and cultural knowledge to be passed onto the young generation. He also had a consultative leadership style and did not make the decision by himself. Instead, he consulted his institution's board members (both pro-PRC and pro-ROC individuals) and the general members of the public. Moreover, Jin promotes the preservation of local culture to strengthen a sense of belonging to the Chinatown.

In Chapter 14, through an experiential and practitioner's perspective, Dean Tan argues that the role that leadership (in this chapter: Student Leadership) plays generates more value-addedness out of youth contributions and produces more effective leaders among the future generations. The influence for youth development does not just stem out from positivity being the sole driver for the youth development, the success and positivity felt by individuals and teams (in this case youth team) performing their best reinforces the initial force. In summary, Dean Tan argues that the ideal leadership allows for the cultivation and improvement in the positivity felt by individuals in the group, thereby bringing about more possibilities and potentials as one internalizes the positive emotions and broadens his or her view on a situation. As one acts upon the agenda and objective that is set, one can see the plenary impact from not only one individual but also the different individuals who experienced these influences and took action to translate these experiences into actualization.

In Chapter 15, the second review/case study chapter of this section, W. X. Lim discusses the many aspects of Tzu-Chi's identity and how it is closely linked to the spiritual leader, Master Cheng Yen, thus forming an intimate teacher–student relationship between the leader and her devotees. This relationship is constantly strengthened through the profound teachings of Master Cheng Yen where she has demonstrated great determination, wisdom and charisma in preaching the Dharma. Master Cheng Yen and her lifelong project/creation, the Tzu Chi Foundation, is thus a great example of what a faith-based organization can achieve through employing modern organizational and leadership strategies and methodologies in the 21st century.

While Chapter 15 examined the tireless efforts of a major religious organization in community, Chapter 16 by J. Xue highlighted state institutions like Community Development Councils (CDCs) and their interfaith programmes in promoting religious harmony within the Singaporean society. Explorations into Faith (EiF) is an interfaith programme under the South East CDCs, one of the five

CDCs in the five districts of Singapore. Formed in 2007, the programme aims to build greater religious understanding, respect, trust and tolerance among a diverse group of people from different faiths. EiF is entirely volunteer-run, although the government sponsors event venues and refreshments.

Chapter 17 incorporates all the elements (imparting of knowledge, social development and youth/student leadership, non-tangible rewards of volunteerism) in Section B's chapters. C. Ma highlighted the multitasking role of students in her conclusion. Ma noted that, acting as consultant and service provider, the students should be treated at the same hierarchical level as the project administrators and other stakeholders and be empowered and trusted for their abilities to meet the needs of the service recipients (social enterprises/partner organizations). Moreover, in her view therefore, the service provider–service recipient relationship should be developed together with the student–agency learning relationship.

S. Shahadave's Chapter 18 ends with the observation that India also plays such an exception role within the South Asian region. He makes the argument that India will have to take up the role of a regional leader. India has to try to minimize the misunderstandings between its neighbours, gain trust from other member states in leading the region of South Asia and integrate the South Asian economy. This is especially the case as China is making its moves to be close to other member states of this region, India has to be very careful, active and fast in taking up the responsibility of a leader in the integration of South Asia. If India becomes successful in playing the role of leader in the economic integration of South Asia, its credibility will increase in international arena as well which is required as a pre-condition to establish itself as a leading emerging economic powerhouse in the world.

QUIZZES AND ANSWER BANKS

Chapter 1

1. The Cold War (1947–1992) was a _____ world. Fill in the blank with the most appropriate answer.
A. unipolar
B. multipolar
C. nonpolar
D. bipolar
Answer: D

2. USSR is also known as the _____? Fill in the blank with the most appropriate answer.
A. Russian Federation
B. Tsarist Russia
C. Soviet Union
D. Commonwealth of Independent States
Answer: C

3. The CLMV countries comprise _____.
A. Cambodia, Langkawai, Myanmar and Vietnam
B. Cambodia, Laos, Myanmar and Vietnam
C. Cayman, Lancaster, Mongolia and Vietnam
D. Cambodia, Laos, Malaysia and Vietnam
Answer: B

262   *Quizzes and Answer Banks*

4. The Japanese word 'Wa' is the Kanji (Chinese origins) character that means
   _____.
A. harmony
B. surprise
C. universal
D. nirvana
Answer: A

5. Kaohsiung mayor candidate Han Kuo-yu sparked off a fandom movement
   among his supporters popularly known as the 'Han wave'.
A. True
B. False
Answer: B

Chapter 2

1. When was the world led by two bipolar blocs split into two ideological
   systems?
A. 1941–1945
B. 1947–1992
C. 2011–2015
D. None of the above
Answer: B

2. Contemporary China has seen the rise of a strongman regime since 2013.
   President Xi Jinping is officially known as a _____ leader. Fill in the blank.
A. paramount
B. charismatic
C. dear
D. core
Answer: D

3. The term "CLMV" within ASEAN stands for "Cambodia, Laos, Myanmar and
   Vietnam".
A. True
B. False
Answer: A

Quizzes and Answer Banks 263

4. In Northeast Asia, respect for veteran or elder politicians springs from the Confucianist tradition of respecting seniors and reverence for authority. In terms of political traditions, is this statement true to a certain extent or absolutely untrue?
A. True to a certain extent
B. Absolutely untrue
Answer: A

5. North Korean is the last Stalinist communist state on earth.
A. True
B. False
Answer: A

Chapter 3

1. The Chinese Constitution was most recently changed to remove the two terms limit on the Chinese presidency and vice presidency. Is this statement true or false?
A. True
B. False
Answer: A

2. National People's Congress is one of China's 'twin parliaments' or *lianghui*. Is this statement true or false?
A. True
B. False
Answer: A

3. The idea of the Chinese establishment's 'China Dream' refers to which of the following items? Choose the most appropriate answer out of the lot.
A. Achieving the status of a constitutional monarchy.
B. Making China a developed country and economy.
C. Forming an EU-style regional bloc with India.
D. Withdrawal from the United Nations.
Answer: B

264   *Quizzes and Answer Banks*

4. The Gang of Six consists of former internal security tzar Zhou Yongkang, former President Hu Jintao's right-hand man Ling Jihua, one of the leading generals Xu Caihou, Sun Zhengcai and his predecessor Bo Xilai, former vice chair of Central Military Commission Guo Boxiong. Is this true or false?
A. True
B. False
Answer: A

5. The Belt and Road Initiative (BRI) is formerly known as the One Belt One Road or OBOR. Is this true or false?
A. True
B. False
Answer: A

Chapter 4

1. Emperor Jimmu is officially designated as the progenitor of the current Japanese lineage of monarchs. True or False?
A. True
B. False
Answer: A

2. The leader of the Samurais is known as the _____.
A. Chieftain
B. Zen Leader
C. Shogun
D. High Priest
Answer: C

3. The retirement and stepping of an Emperor (which recently happened to the Heisei Emperor) to make way for a successor is a rare event that has not happened for about 200 years. True or false?
A. True
B. False
Answer: A

Quizzes and Answer Banks 265

4. The affairs of the Imperial family are governed by the _____. Fill in the blank.
A. Coronation Legislation
B. Constitution of Hokkaido
C. Imperial Household Law
D. Yamato covenant
Answer: C

5. The longstanding ruling party in Japanese politics is known as _____.
   Fill in the blank.
A. Communist Party of Japan
B. Socialist Party of Japan
C. Constitutional Party of Japan
D. Liberal Democratic Party
Answer: D

Chapter 7

1. When was Osaka called "Great Osaka" and what was its population ranking in
   the world then?
A. the 1880s and the 8th
B. the 1900s and the 9th
C. the 1920s and the 6th
D. the 1930s and 5th
Answer: C

2. How is Osaka's per-capita income level today (in comparison with the other 46
   prefectures and Tokyo Metropolis)?
A. top
B. second (next to Tokyo)
C. slightly higher than the national average
D. lower than the national average
Answer: D

3. What was Toru Hashimoto's family line?
A. discriminated class
B. educated class
C. military class
D. ruling class
Answer: A

4. What was Toru Hashimoto's Osaka Metropolis Plan?
A. consolidate Osaka Prefecture and its neighbouring prefectures into Osaka Metropolis
B. dissolve Osaka City and neighbouring cities into special wards
C. move Japan's capital from Tokyo to Osaka
D. none of the above
Answer: B

5. Who was a major opposition group against Toru Hashimoto's Osaka Metropolis Plan?
A. citizens in Tokyo
B. public servants in Osaka
C. members in the National Diet
D. environmentalists
Answer: B

Chapter 9

1. Could Hong Kong leadership be regarded as democratic and accountable to ordinary people in Hong Kong?

Suggested Answer: No, the Chief Executive (CE), the head of the Hong Kong Special Administrative Region is elected by the Election Committee instead of universal suffrage, and the 1,200 Election Committee members are selected from 38 different professional sectors and district organizations. Moreover, the CE as the head of the executive must not belong to any political party according to the Basic Law, Such institutional arrangement makes the CE less relevant to the ordinary people and political parties in Hong Kong.

2. What were the Beijing institutions in Hong Kong before the handover in 1997? What were their roles in shaping China's policy towards Hong Kong?

Suggested Answer: Beijing's institutions in Hong Kong can be traced back to the era before the handover. They were the Ministry of Foreign Affairs (MFA), Hong Kong and Macao Affairs Office (HKMAO) and Xinhua News Agency, which all assisted Beijing in the Hong Kong affairs. The latter two institutions played a more important role during the discussions of Hong Kong's transition. First, the HKMAO was responsible for investigating and reporting the situations in Hong Kong to Beijing as well as promoting patriotic propaganda among the Hong Kong people. The Hong Kong and Macao Work Committee (HKMWC) was the *de facto* Chinese Communist Party in Hong Kong under the cover of Xinhua News Agency.

The committee had various affiliated members such as the Bank of China, China Resources Corporation, the China Merchants Group and China Travel Service, which had certain network and influence in Hong Kong. The Hong Kong and Macao Office under the MFA was relatively inactive when compared with the other two institutions.

3. What are the major changes of the Chinese institutions in Hong Kong after the handover?

Suggested Answer: After the handover in 1997, Beijing has expanded and enhanced its institutions to manage Hong Kong affairs. At the state level, Beijing strengthened the Hong Kong and Macao Affairs Office and established the Institute of Hong Kong and Macao Affairs under the Development Research Center of the State Council in 2003 since a half of a million Hong Kong people took to the street for demonstration. At the local level, the Hong Kong Branch of Xinhua News Agency was renamed as The Liaison Office of Central People's Government of China in the HKSAR.

4. How could Beijing coordinate various institutions in Hong Kong after the handover?

Suggested Answer: The Chinese government then established the Central Coordination Group for Hong Kong and Macao Affairs (CCGHKMA) which is now being chaired by the national leader Han Zheng, who is a Politburo Standing Committee member and a Vice-Premier of the State Council. The CCGHKMA is indeed a supreme institution above other established institutions in guiding Beijing's policies on Hong Kong. Such an institution gives Beijing direct control over Hong Kong affairs. Besides, the Institute of Hong Kong and Macao Affairs (IHKMA) was set up under the Development Research Center of the State Council. The IHKMA was founded probably because of the inability of the HKMAO and LOCPG in evaluating/coping with the social problems in Hong Kong, which ultimately led to the mass demonstrations. Thus, the IHKMA examines various latest developments in Hong Kong in the fields of politics, economics, society, culture and even religion in Hong Kong and Macao.

5. How does Xi Jinping define "One Country, Two Systems" in Hong Kong and why should Hong Kong act according to Xi's expectation?

Suggested Answer: Chinese President Xi Jinping further clarified the role of Hong Kong in "one country, two systems" in the 20th anniversary of Hong Kong's handover that "one country" is more important than "two systems", and "one country" is just "like the roots of a tree". It is also the first time a top Chinese leader emphasized that Hong Kong must act according to the Chinese national interests. Xi said: "[a]ny attempt to endanger China's sovereignty and security, challenge the power of the Central Government and the authority of the Basic Law of the HKSAR or use Hong Kong to carry out infiltration and sabotage activities against the mainland is an act that crosses the red line, and is absolutely impermissible."

===

Chapter 11

1. The type of Community Leadership demonstrated in our society is largely dependent on the _____.
A. extent of social development and inclusion within the society
B. extent of diversity of people
C. extent of political influence by the government
D. extent of foreign intervention by the international community
Answer: A

2. Which are the most important building blocks of Nation Building for Singapore?
A. bilingualism
B. provision of public housings
C. multi-nationalism
D. multi-culturalism
Answer: D

3. Social unrest caused by racial tensions during the early 1950s resulted from _____.
A. lack of common spaces for people to interact
B. lack of racial tolerance
C. lack of community participation
D. lack of government intervention
Answer: B

4. The People's Association was set up in _____ to promote social inclusion through citizens' participation in community and integration activities for both new and existing citizens.
A. 1955
B. 1960
C. 1965
D. 1970
Answer: B

Quizzes and Answer Banks 269

5. Self-help groups were set up to render support and assistance to Singaporeans of different ethnic groups except _____.
A. Association of Muslim Professionals
B. Chinese Assistance Development Council
C. The Eurasian Association, Singapore
D. Singapore Indian Development Association
Answer: A

Chapter 19

1. Track II diplomacy is important because of which of the following reasons? Please choose the most appropriate answer.
A. It opens up an alternate universe of beings from another dimension.
B. It is an exchange between governments and state agencies.
C. People-to-people exchanges are just as important for societies to understand each other at a deeper level.
D. It is equivalent to a top leadership summit.
Answer: C

2. CBM stands for? Choose the most appropriate answer.
A. Canteen ban management
B. Confidence business management
C. Coalition building manpower
D. Confidence-building measures
Answer: D

3. The top Hong Kong leader is known as the _____? Fill in the blank.
A. Chief Economist
B. Chief Executive
C. Chief Elector
D. Chief Executor
Answer: B

4. The largest Chinatown in Japan is situated in _____.
A. Hokkaido
B. Kyushu
C. Yokohama
D. Okinawa
Answer: C

Quizzes and Answer Banks

5. The spiritual leader of Tzu Chi religious organization is _____.
A. Master Luke Skywalker
B. Master Yen Ching
C. Master Ching Yen
D. Master Cheng Yen
Answer: D